INTERNATIONAL PERSPECTIVES IN SOCIAL WORK

COUNTERING DISCRIMINATION IN
SOCIAL WORK

International Perspectives in Social Work

Countering Discrimination in Social Work

Edited by Bogdan Lešnik

Ashgate

ARENA

Aldershot • Brookfield USA • Singapore • Sydney

Published by
Ashgate Publishing Limited
Gower House
Croft Road
Aldershot
Hants GU11 3HR
England

Ashgate Publishing Company
Old Post Road
Brookfield
Vermont 05036
USA

British Library Cataloguing in Publication Data
Countering discrimination in social work. – (International
 perspectives in social work)
 1. Discrimination 2. Social service 3. Social service –
 Sociological aspects
 I. Lešnik, Bogdan
 361.3

Library of Congress Catalog Card Number: 98-70986

ISBN 1-85742-436-0

Typeset by Express Typesetters Ltd, Farnham, Surrey
Printed and bound in Great Britain by MPG Books Ltd, Bodmin, Cornwall

Contents

Editorial Board   vii

Notes on Contributors   ix

Introduction   xiii
Neil Thompson

1   Poverty and Deprivation   1
   Signe Dobelniece

2   Globalisation and Gender Relations in Social Work   15
   Lena Dominelli

3   Affirmative Action: A Counter to Racial Discrimination?   33
   Lena Dominelli

4   Social Work and Independent Living   49
   Bob Sapey

5   Facing our Futures: Discrimination in Later Life   67
   Mary Marshall and Cherry Rowlings

6   Lesbians and Gay Men: Social Work and Discrimination   89
   Helen Cosis Brown

7   Intellectual Disability, Oppression and Difference   111
   Tim Stainton

8   Strategies of Empowerment: Taking Account of Protests by People   133
    Robert Adams

9   Towards a Theory of Emancipatory Practice   165
    Neil Thompson

Editorial Board

International Perspectives in Social Work

Notes on Contributors

Signe Dobelniece
Signe Dobelniece gained her Bachelors degree from the University of Latvia in philosophy and her Masters degree in social work from the University of Gothenburg in Sweden. She has worked as a sociologist, mainly researching problems of education and youth. Currently she teaches sociology and social work and does research at the University of Latvia. She has written a number of works on poverty.

Lena Dominelli
Professor Lena Dominelli has worked as a community worker, social worker and probation officer. She currently teaches and does research at the University of Southampton in England where she is the Director of the Centre for International Social and Community Development. She is also President of the International Association of Schools of Social Work. She has written extensively about social work and social policy. Her recent key books include: *Anti-Racist Social Work* (1988), *Feminist Social Work* (1989 (with E. McLeod), *Women and Community Action* (1990), *Gender, Sex Offenders and Probation Practice* (1991), *Women Across Continents: Feminist Comparative Social Policy* (1991), *Anti-Racist Probation Practice* (1995) (with others) and *Sociology for Social Work* (1997).

Bob Sapey
Bob Sapey has worked as a social worker, training officer and care manager. He currently teaches and does research at the University of Central Lancashire in Preston, England. He has written about social work with disabled people and about the impact of technology on the practice of social workers in a range of academic journals. He has recently collaborated with

Michael Oliver to produce the second edition of *Social Work with Disabled People*, which will be published in 1999.

Mary Marshall

Mary Marshall, OBE, has worked as a child care officer, social worker, lecturer in Applied Social Studies, Liverpool University, and Director of Age Concern Scotland. She is at present Director of the Dementia Services Development Centre. She has edited and co-edited a number of books on ageing and dementia; she is the author of the classic *Social Work with Old People* (1983, second ed. 1990) and of *'I Can't Place this Place at all': Working with People with Dementia and their Carers* (1996).

Cherry Rowlings

Cherry Rowlings is a professor of social work at Stirling University in Scotland. She has extensive background in research, teaching and management. She is the author of *Social Work with Elderly People* (1981) and co-editor of *Past Trauma in Later Life: European Perspectives on Therapeutic Work with Older People* (1997).

Helen Cosis Brown

Helen Cosis Brown is Head of the Department of Health and Social Care at the University of Hertfordshire, England. She worked as a social worker and a manager for ten years in an inner London local authority social services department. She has a particular interest in fostering and adoption as well as social work with lesbians and gay men. She has recently published *Social Work and Sexuality: Working with Lesbians and Gay Men* (1998).

Tim Stainton

Dr Tim Stainton had worked as a social worker, policy analyst and consultant in the intellectual disability field for the past twenty years. He was formerly assistant professor at the McGill School of Social Work in Canada and is presently a lecturer and co-ordinator of community care programmes in the Department of Social Policy and Applied Social Studies at the University of Wales in Swansea. He has researched and published on a wide range of subjects concerned with social work, difference and intellectual disabilities, notably a theory of disability rights, *Autonomy and Social Policy* (Avebury, 1994). He is currently working on a major study of the historical and intellectual construction of intellectual disability in western modernity.

Robert Adams

Robert Adams is Professor of Human Services Development and Professorial Research Fellow at the Policy Studies Research Centre, University of Lincolnshire and Humberside, Hull, England. He has published widely on aspects of protest, empowerment and criminal justice. His most recent books include *Protests by Pupils: Empowerment, Schooling and the State* (1991), *Prison Riots in Britain and the USA* (1994), *Social Work and Empowerment* (1996), *The Personal Social Services: Clients, Consumers or Citizens* (1996), *The Abuses of Punishment* (1998) and *Quality Social Work* (1998).

Neil Thompson

Professor Neil Thompson teaches in the School of Health and Community Studies at North East Wales Institute and is a Principal Consultant with Ashley Maynard Associates. He is the author of a number of social work books, including *Anti-Discriminatory Practice* (2nd edn. 1997), *People Skills* (1996) and *Promoting Equality* (1998).

Introduction

Neil Thompson

There is no doubt that issues of discrimination and oppression have now established themselves explicitly as a major feature of social work theory and practice, partly in response to a growing recognition that traditional forms of practice have tended to neglect such matters and the structured inequalities on which they are based. This is not to say that traditional approaches to social work have paid no attention at all to discrimination and oppression (clearly, that would be an overstatement). However, the traditional approaches have not given such matters the consideration they merit in terms of the central role discrimination and oppression can be seen to play in the lives of so many of social work's service users: women subjected to patriarchal power relations that place them in a subordinate social position and cast them in the role of carer and homemaker; members of ethnic minorities exposed to racist acts, attitudes, assumptions and structures; older people written off as being of little or no social worth; disabled people seen as second-class citizens, peripheral to the social mainstream; and various other groups stigmatised, excluded or disadvantaged by powerful cultural and structural forces which serve to discredit individuals and groups who do not fit into narrowly defined notions of 'normality'.

Much has been written about issues of inequality, discrimination and oppression in terms of policy, theory and practice. What this book aims to do is to pull together a range of materials addressing various aspects of inequality to provide an overview of the current 'state of play' in the development of emancipatory forms of practice that seek to counter discrimination and oppression.

Various authors have come together to offer insights into understanding the complexities of promoting more egalitarian forms of practice and social relations, each bringing a distinctive perspective on his or her topic or theme. The aim is to provide a balance between breadth and depth, with the range of topics covered offering a degree of breadth, while their treatment in each of the chapters brings a degree of depth. Although there are clearly recurring themes, as one might expect, each chapter addresses its subject matter in its own way, with no attempt made to establish a uniformity of style, structure, focus or ideological slant. Indeed, the book represents the diversity so characteristic of the subject matter it covers.

There are nine substantive chapters in all. Signe Dobelniece provides, in Chapter 1, a clear and helpful account of poverty and deprivation in Latvia in the period of post-Soviet reconstruction. While much of her analysis addresses specific issues relating to the re-emergence of an independent republic following a major social transformation, there are also parallels that can be drawn with the detrimental and dehumanising effects of poverty and deprivation in other settings and contexts. Her insightful chapter provides us with a number of important themes and issues relevant to addressing poverty and deprivation as part of a strategy of emancipatory social work practice.

In Chapter 2, Lena Dominelli explores the theme of globalisation and examines its implications for the complex topic of gender relations in social work. She defines globalisation as 'a world system of capitalist domination' and argues that the development of the quasi-market, the purchaser-provider split and increased bureaucratisation and managerial control are all part of a process that involves the deprofessionalisation of social work and its construction as 'women's work'.

Lena Dominelli is also the author of Chapter 3, which has as its theme the role of affirmative action as a counter to racial discrimination. She explores a range of attempts that have been made to tackle and eradicate racism and concludes that it is necessary for anti-racists to rethink the ways in which they are conducting their struggles and develop new ways of moving forward.

In Chapter 4, Bob Sapey focuses on the notion of independent living as a helpful theme in understanding disablism. Basing his analysis on the social model of disability, he examines the potential for social workers to help disabled people to achieve the goal of independent living. He also explores the conflicts between the functional and civil rights interpretations of independence and considers the need for changes in social policy and social work practice.

Chapter 5 is concerned with the discrimination experienced by older people. Mary Marshall and Cherry Rowlings provide a lucid exposition of an important set of issues relating to ageism. By focusing on working with people with dementia, they are able to show how ignorance and negative assumptions have the effect of stultifying practice. They argue the case for challenging ageist attitudes and practices and for treating people with dementia as citizens.

Helen Cosis-Brown's exploration of discrimination against gay men and lesbians forms the basis of Chapter 6. The author provides an historical and international overview of lesbian and gay oppression, and follows this up with a discussion of lesbian and gay identity. The chapter also addresses social work with lesbians and gay men and social work education and training, and concludes with a consideration of a number of possible ways forward in tackling discrimination on the grounds of sexual identity and the oppression that arises from it.

The discrimination and oppression experienced by people with an intellectual disability are examined in Chapter 7. Timothy Stainton discusses the various ways in which people deemed to have 'learning difficulties' or 'learning disabilities' are subject to patterns of exclusion. As he puts it: 'The gap between the rhetoric of inclusion and people's actual lives remains enormous.' Parallel with Marshall and Rowlings in Chapter 5, he argues the case for a stronger emphasis on equal citizenship.

Chapter 8 takes a different approach from the earlier chapters. Rather than focus on a specific area of discrimination, Robert Adams takes a broader view by concentrating on the range of potential strategies that could be drawn upon as part of a process of countering discrimination and oppression through empowerment. Recognising that empowerment is a 'plastic' term that can be used in different ways to suit different political and ideological perspectives, he concentrates on the importance of protest as a basis for working towards empowerment. He is critical of the tendency to overstate the potential of social work practice to contribute to the empowerment of service users, but none the less helps to take practice forward by outlining strategies that can make a positive contribution.

Finally, Chapter 9 comprises my own contribution to the debate in the form of an essay on the potential of existentialist philosophy to act as a coherent and far-reaching theory base to underpin the development of emancipatory forms of practice. The chapter recognises that, while a great deal of time, effort and energy have been invested in promoting equality through policy, practice, education and training, the theory base underpinning it all has received relatively little attention, and certainly not enough to match the vitally important role of countering discrimination and oppression in social work. The theory base presented is not intended as a definitive statement or final word on the subject, but rather as a contribution to what should be a continuing open debate.

This book can be seen as part of a broader process of placing issues of discrimination and oppression firmly on the social work agenda, but not as part of a dogmatic agenda of 'political correctness' in which simple 'right answers' replace critical analysis and sound assessment based on skilled work. Rather, it should be seen as contributing towards a foundation for critically reflective practice in which social workers bring to bear their understanding of inequality, discrimination and oppression in working sensitively and constructively towards empowerment – assisting relatively powerless individuals and groups to gain greater control over their lives by tackling the personal, cultural and structural barriers that stand in their way.

1 Poverty and Deprivation

Signe Dobelniece

Abstract

Poverty and deprivation are significant aspects of the social fabric. This chapter explores the nature, extent and consequences of poverty in Latvia in the current period of post-Soviet social reconstruction. This provides an important case study of poverty and deprivation in one specific country but also offers potential insights for understanding issues of economic class and the allocation of financial resources more broadly.

Introduction

Poverty must be recognised as a complex phenomenon with varying causes and even more varying consequences. Common to all of them is the suffering people experience as a result of such poverty. However, this suffering may find expression in different ways. In some ways, it is difficult to speak about poverty and how people experience it in Latvia, as there is no official definition of what poverty is and no accepted criteria or methodology for its measurement within Latvian social policy. Alcock (1993) makes apt comment when he argues that there are:

> ... obviously quite different conceptions of poverty with quite different consequences for how poverty is identified and what policies might be developed to respond to it. To select one rather than another definition would thus lead to a very different approach to both the problem and the solution of poverty. (p.8)

As a consequence of a lack of a clear definition of poverty, there are no

1

precise data about people living in poverty, and no agreed framework for conceptualising the issues and developing appropriate policy responses. In some sources, up to 80 per cent of the population are mentioned in this context. That is why many of the processes operating in society may be looked upon as caused at least in part by poverty.

Discussion in this chapter revolves around some of the negative effects of poverty on demographic processes, consumption, health and education. Poverty involves both an economic and social aspect. The latter is discussed here in terms of the violation of human rights, human dignity, autonomy, life and happiness.

It will be argued that solutions can and should be sought in the stabilisation and development of micro- and macroeconomic processes, state social policy and in changes in people's attitudes. The question of attitudes or perceptions is particularly significant for, as Alcock (1993) argues:

> We all perceive poverty, like other social phenomena, through an ideological framework; and for each of us that framework and those perceptions of poverty are unique. However, although unique, they are not isolated. Our perceptions and attitudes are governed in large part by broader social influences, in particular the ideologies of powerful social figures and social forces, which receive publicity through the media, through politics, through education and through social interactions. The public images of poverty are central in determining private perceptions. (p.19)

Poverty in Latvia

Poverty would appear to be a relatively new phenomenon in Latvia. Prior to the dissolution of the Soviet Union, if poverty was at all present, it was latent. It was not a topic for discussion, largely due to the official Marxist-Leninist ideology. According to this ideology, there were no social problems to be found in a socialist society. People started to talk about poverty, survival and other such phenomena in the late 1980s and early 1990s, with the collapse of the USSR and the consequent processes of transformation. This was a time when a significant part of the population was faced with poverty and experienced its consequences. The deterioration of living standards is not always linked with poverty, but rather with deprivation, as the latter has brought different restrictions and, to be sure, detrimental consequences for people's lives.

Causes of poverty

The causes of poverty are various and complex. Only some of the more evident ones will be mentioned here. After regaining independence in 1991, Latvia began a transition from a totalitarian regime to democracy and from a command economy to relations regulated by the free market – that is, to totally different political and economic systems. The transition involved important structural changes in all spheres of life, with those in the economic and social protection spheres more noticeable for ordinary people. Economic reforms included many unpopular measures and created unexpectedly harsh results in production, wages, consumption, trade and inflation. The severity of decline in these spheres even surprised International Monetary Fund planners (Dreifelds 1996: 114), and caused considerable distress in the population.

Although now recording modest Gross Domestic Product (GDP) growth, within recent years, GDP had decreased to almost half its former level (from 1989 to 1995 by 46 per cent) (*Latvija Pārskats* 1996: 44). Production decreased even more (Oslands 1996: 22). Liberalisation of prices was closely related to hyper-inflation, with its maximum (958 per cent) occurring in 1992. In recent years the rate of inflation has decreased significantly (estimated to be at less than 10 per cent in 1997), but it is not compensated for by an increase in the rate of income. Usually poor living conditions are associated with being out of the labour market. The transition brought about a change in this: labour-related poverty. There are spheres, especially those financed by state budget – education, medicine, culture, social assistance and so on – where wages are relatively low. They are lower than average and frequently also lower than the subsistence or survival minimum. Even if there has been an increase, it does not match the rate of inflation. This results in a significant deterioration of purchasing power for the population and in the general level of economic well-being.

The restructuring of the economy brought along a new phenomenon for Latvia – unemployment – which did not exist officially in the USSR. In 1996 the official unemployment rate was 7.1 per cent (*Diena*, 2 October 1996), with a trend towards gradual increase. According to survey data provided by the Central Statistical Bureau (CSB) of Latvia, it is significantly higher. At the end of 1995 18.9 per cent of the economically active population was looking for work (*Ziņojums* 1996: 9). Special attention must be paid to increasing long-term unemployment (42.6 per cent of all unemployed in 1995), as this indicates the severity of the problem. Unemployment is not evenly distributed throughout the country. There are regions, especially in eastern Latvia, where the unemployment rate is almost three times higher than the average and almost ten times higher than in the capital, Riga. That high level of unemployment can be dangerous, not only for the economic survival of the population, but also for their psychological well-being. It can be closely related to a range of negative phenomena, such as moral degradation, depression, looking for escape in alcohol, suicide, and so on.

Another trend, characteristic of the period of transition, is a rapid change in social structure caused by social differentiation within the population according to their material well-being. And this also was new. People were used to thinking in terms of equality. At the very least an idea about citizens being equal members of a socialist society was created and sustained. Therefore, the distribution of household income that has become more unequal during the transition is even more painful. Researchers speak about a hyper-differentiation that has taken place in most post-communist countries. To characterise this process, a Gini coefficient can be used. It shows how equally or otherwise an income is distributed among the population. In the late 1980s the Gini coefficient was about 0.2–0.3; in 1993 0.40; in 1994 0.42. For comparison, this index is higher in Latvia than in any of the G-7 countries, where it fluctuated between 0.28 and 0.32 (*Latvija Pārskats* 1996: 25–6), and it shows that income is distributed more and more unequally in Latvia, that the rich get richer and the stratum of those living in poverty is increasing. In 1996 the bottom decile received only 3.3 per cent of all resources while the richest 10 per cent had about 25 per cent at their disposal (*Diena*, 8 April 1997).

The poverty line

There are no accurate data available about the proportion of the population living in poverty in Latvia. Several reasons can be mentioned to explain this situation, one of which is that there is no agreement as to an official definition specifying what poverty is, or what criteria and methodology should be used for its measurement.

To protect the population in a rapid decline of living conditions, as an equivalent to a poverty line, a subsistence minimum (minimal consumption basket) was introduced in 1991. The government was not able to provide the population with an income equal to the subsistence minimum, therefore a crisis subsistence minimum was introduced in 1992. The crisis minimum is oriented mainly towards providing for basic physical existence. This also was not an adequate solution to the problem, as there was still a significant gap between real income and the costs of a crisis minimum consumption basket. According to household budget survey data, 56 per cent of the population had a lower income than this. The average household income per capita corresponds to 92 per cent of the crisis subsistence minimum; average pension to 71 per cent, and minimal salary to 75 per cent. Unemployment benefit is even less. To reduce the number of people eligible for social assistance, the government in 1993 issued regulations which stated that the people who receive social assistance are mainly those whose income within the last three months has not exceeded 75 per cent of the crisis subsistence minimum, and who do not have relatives able to assist (see Dobelniece 1997: 209).

Here we can see three different 'poverty lines', which could be used to estimate the proportion of the population in poverty. Lately CSB of Latvia has used quite a different approach to the calculation of who is included in the category of 'poor' – the poverty line is associated with a proportion of average wages. According to this approach, low income is equal to 45 per cent of average wages, and the income of living in poverty to 60 per cent of the low income. According to this methodology, 60 per cent of the population are on low incomes and 24 per cent are poor (*Diena*, 17 October 1996).

As we see, all calculations of poverty lines or estimates of the number of people in poverty can be totally arbitrary and relative. If the poverty line is changed from a subsistence minimum to 75 per cent of the crisis subsistence minimum, we get a significantly lower proportion of people defined as poor. Does this mean that their condition changes, that their well-being improves and they are able to meet ends if they are not defined as being poor? Of course, it is hardly the case that they will manage any better simply as a result in a change in the definition or conceptualisation of poverty.

To a large extent, it is not important which definition of poverty is applied – absolute or relative – or even where the poverty line is set, as this can only have the effect of changing the relative proportions of poor and non-poor. What is perhaps the most important factor is the need to recognise that people can and do experience extreme suffering as a result of poverty, regardless of definitions and the fact that:

> ... poverty is a problem the effects of which are felt in a myriad of different ways: in hunger and early death, in poor health, despair and depression, in the corrosion of people's well-being and social relationships, and in frustration and anger. (Novak 1996: 85)

Poverty diminishes the quality of a person's life in many ways, and most of the consequences of living in poverty are in direct conflict with human rights.

The consequences of poverty

Poor people get less of everything that is considered important and necessary for a decent life, that is, less money, food, clothing, shelter. The deprivation experienced by poor people is pervasive. Children brought up in poverty are more likely to fail in school, to drop out of school. They are more likely to develop mental health problems, are more susceptible to chronic illnesses, and are less likely to be covered by health insurance. They are more likely to lose jobs and to drop out of the labour force. They are more likely to experience hostility and distrust. They are less likely to participate in meaningful groups and associations. As the ultimate deprivation, they are likely to die at a younger age (Lauer 1989: 244).

Let us try to examine some of the negative consequences of living in poverty in Latvia. They find their expression in various ways and in different areas. The deterioration in living standards is closely linked with social and demographic processes in society, and has a direct or indirect impact on them. Since 1991 there has been a decrease in population (−17.3 thousand in 1995) (Statistical Yearbook 1996: 48), which is a result of an extremely low and decreasing birth rate and a high death rate. There were almost half as many children born in 1995 as in 1987, or 8.6 per 1,000 inhabitants, while there were 15.5 deaths per thousand. The average number of children born to a woman has also decreased from 2.016 in 1990 to 1.252 in 1995 (Oslands 1996: 37). This number is significantly lower than is necessary, even for maintaining the status quo. At the same time, the Baltic countries, and especially Latvia, have one of the highest number of abortions: 25.9 thousand or 120 induced abortions per 100 live births (Statistical Yearbook 1996: 155). It is difficult to argue that these trends are directly caused by poverty, although there can be a causal relationship. According to research data, people would like to have two or three children (average 2.1), but they cannot afford to have them. To explain the relatively low number of children they do have, respondents mention as main reasons: economic crisis; unemployment; poor living conditions, and an inability to provide for and take care of children properly (*Zvidriņš* 1996: 4–5). This is closely related to the increasing number of abandoned children due to the poor economic conditions for families: there were 56 cases in 1990 and 188 in 1993 (Statistical Yearbook 1996). These processes can be looked upon as an example of discrimination against one sector of the population on the basis of their material status and a deprivation in terms of the ability to choose freely the number of children. Finally, it can be considered as a set of restrictions that violate human rights of reproduction.

The result of the ongoing demographic processes affects both individuals and society in many ways. One of them in particular is the ageing population, a trend that means that the level of demographic burden (population under and over working age per 1,000 population of working age) is increasing. In the case of Latvia, with low levels of pensions and salaries, this indicator has a significant negative impact on living standards.

The deterioration in living conditions has influenced life expectancy, which has decreased from 66.3 years in 1988 to 60.8 years in 1995 for males and, for females, from 75.1 to 73.1, respectively (Statistical Yearbook 1996: 69).

Demography is closely linked with the economy, as well as with social policy. Researchers have agreed that existing demographic processes are caused mainly by economic crisis. Other influencing factors to be identified are the emergence of a new pattern of reproduction (women tend to have children later) and inadequate family policy (Tulva 1997: 36–38).

Another area where declining economic possibilities overtly find their expression is that of consumption. With the decrease in real income, there has been a significant drop in the purchasing power of the population. This has in turn influenced consumption patterns. According to household budget survey data, about 60 per cent of households hardly manage to balance their budget, and 15 per cent are in debt. These figures are probably not sufficiently informative, as there can be different needs and wants of households, and it is possible that most people cannot afford what they want. It does not mean that they should necessarily be defined as poor. More informative is the following data: 61 per cent of households do not have enough resources for food; 10 per cent suffer from serious shortages in this respect (*Ziņojums* 1996: 47). It means that a large proportion of the population does in fact live below the poverty line, with all of the attendant consequences: decreased food consumption, which has nutritional consequences, unpaid rent and utility bills and so on. The result is that many people do not enjoy a fully-fledged physical existence, to say nothing of any satisfaction of their social or psychological needs.

From 1989 to 1994, the average per capita consumption among the residents of Latvia declined by 12 per cent to 2,293 kilocalories (*Latvija. Pārskats* 1996: 25). According to expert calculations, the minimum daily nutritional requirement is 2,683 kilocalories (*Bērni un ģimenes Latvijā* 1995: 95), which means that people are actually receiving only 85 per cent of what they need.

Poor families and children living within them are affected more severely, in so far as they consume even less. According to CSB data, there is a correlation between the per capita income and the number of children in a household: the more children, the lower the level of resources and, consequently, fewer consumption possibilities. About 70 per cent of all children live in households with a low income, and around a third of them in poor families (*Diena*, 14 September 1996). Even if people tend to choose relatively cheaper products and cut down on more expensive items, they cannot obtain as much as nutritional specialists suggest. Malnutrition and a nutritionally inadequate diet are not only a problem for today, but also of the future. Inadequate nutrition affects people's health and is especially dangerous for children, in so far as it threatens their normal course of development.

Table 1.1   Consumption of food
(per capita annually, kg)

Product	1992	1993	1995	Poor families to average (%, 1993)
Meat and meat products	61.59	47.38	52	71
Milk and diary products	381.34	323.54	348	82
Fish and fish products	10.86	5.77	10.8	64
Eggs	216	175	209	76
Bread and cereal products	90.65	74.93	89	82
Potatoes	100.99	97.90	105	99.7
Vegetables	67.64	56.30	61	73
Fruit and berries	33.56	28.79	37	69
Sugar (incl. sweets)	21.99	18.35	23	73
Margarine and other fats	2.32	1.05	2.7	62
Vegetable oil	2.25	1.59	6.9	62

Source: Statistical Yearbook 1996: 104;
  Bērni un ģimenes Latvijā 1994, 1995: 93.

In most cases the eating pattern is not determined by choice, preference or historically developed traditions, but rather by price and disposable resources. The same can be said about the structure of household consumption expenditure. Probably, it can be said that there are significant external factors regulating people's behaviour in these areas. This is a question of the locus of control. External regulating factors in most cases are perceived as restrictions that cannot be influenced – they cause dissatisfaction, frustration and feelings of helplessness.

The proportion of income spent on food is one of the accepted indicators that characterise standards of living: the data show how low the level of economic well-being of the population is, as people must spend more than half of their income. Expenditure for food in the two lowest deciles is even higher and constitutes up to 70 per cent. In comparison, only 15 per cent of the household budget is spent on food in Sweden (*Sweden* 1992: 18). In some countries a household is considered poor if more than 50 per cent is spent on fixed costs (food, rent, transport, insurance and so on) (Stropnic 1993: 13). It is interesting to note that the average Latvian household has a lower standard of living than British families living on state benefits. In Britain, food accounts for, on average, around 30 per cent of income (excluding housing costs), but the British average household has not spent as much as

Table 1.2   **Household consumption expenditure**
(per cent)

Expenditure	1990	1995	1996
Food	37.7	44.2	53.4
Alcohol and tobacco	4.8	5.6	—
Clothing and footwear	19.2	8.1	5.5
Gross rent, fuel, power	4.0	14.1	14.3
Furniture, furnishings and household equipment and operation	6.9	2.9	2.5
Health care	2.1	3.3	3.9
Transport and communication	7.5	7.8	6.7
Recreation, entertainment, education, cultural services	8.8	6.3	6.7
Miscellaneous goods and services	9.0	7.7	4.5

Source: Statistical Yearbook 1996: 87.

30 per cent on food since 1970 (Bradshaw and Holmes 1989: 133–4).

It is difficult to compare the situation in Latvia with developed Western countries, but it gives significant information about the extent of deprivation of the residents of Latvia. It creates an impression that life there is more like mere survival than actually living. In effect, for a significant proportion of households, everyday life is a struggle for survival. There is a great deal of research data to confirm this. In addition to inadequate diet, a significant proportion of households have difficulties in paying all of their rent and utility bills; only 56 per cent report that they are able to do so (*Diena*, 17 October 1996). Families with low or average incomes (and they are in the majority) cannot meet their needs for clothing and footwear, health care, recreation and so on. People cut down on most of their expenses, and spend most of their leisure time at home or choose to engage in activities that cost nothing. But it is more and more difficult to find such activities available in the situation of a market economy, when it is declared that one should pay the price for everything, and everything has a price. This can be confirmed by data about the declining number of attendances at theatres, museums and cinemas. From 1990 to 1995 the overall number of attendances declined by 2.9 times to museums, 2.3 times to theatres, 19.4 times to the cinema (*Latvija. Galvenie* 1996: 17).

Of course, a lack of resources limits people's activities in other spheres of life as well. One of the most important, with far-reaching consequences, is education. Actually, there has been no illiteracy in Latvia for decades; the country has been known for a high level of education of its population.

Under the Soviet regime, there was compulsory secondary education. Now there is a growing number of children who do not attend school, many of them not starting school at all. Astonishingly, there is no accurate data on these matters available. According to different sources, the number of children not attending school is somewhere between 2,500 and 25,000. Twenty-three per cent of those at the age of 15 did not have primary education in 1995 (*Ziņojums* 1996: 44). Recent data from the Ministry of Education show 15,879 people between the ages of seven and 15 years not attending school (*Diena*, 20 August 1997). This situation arises for various reasons, but it is assumed that the main reason is the poor material conditions of the families. The consequences are that these children in most cases are out of any control, in the street, under 'bad influences'. In later years, it is likely that they will add to the unemployment figures, as people without knowledge and professional skills are not valued in the labour market and are therefore not able to compete. In addition, they are not considered as equal and sound members of society. Perhaps worst of all, they will drift into the criminal world. In most cases this is not due to direct choice, but because they are not able to envisage an alternative, since schooling costs money, even if it is stated that, in principle, primary education is free of charge. Parents are not able to buy clothing and footwear, to say nothing about other items of equipment or resources necessary for school.

It is well known that lack of resources has an influence on health (see, for example, the Black Report on health in the UK in Townsend et al. 1988). This finds expression in different ways and affects both physiological and mental processes. Health is an important prerequisite for successful participation in all spheres of life, and this is also the indicator which shows the potential resources of a nation. And, of course, this depends to a great extent on the prevalent standard of living in the country concerned.

Latvia's health care system is in the process of transformation. The main objectives of the programme of change are the introduction of a health insurance system, and a change in individuals' attitudes towards their health, who must learn that no one but themselves are responsible for their health. Up till now, in many cases there has been no tradition of valuing good health and therefore of health promotion. This is quite probably a part of the legacy of the Soviet regime where ill people could frequently enjoy different privileges; in this respect, it was often quite profitable to have poor health. It seems that this attitude still prevails, despite the fact that the external circumstances have changed quite considerably.

The NORBALT survey data give a picture of a self-evaluation of individuals' health condition (see Oslands 1996). Only 3 per cent of respondents evaluated their health as very good; 22 per cent, good; 49 per cent, average; but a quarter of respondents considered their health as poor (19 per cent) or very poor (6 per cent). The data show also a connection between economic conditions and health. Individuals who had economic difficulties within the last year report worse health than others not so affected by adverse economic circumstances. People with poor health are more frequently excluded from the labour market. These processes are interrelated: poor health can be both a cause and a consequence of poverty.

In general, some unfavourable processes have occurred in health care in Latvia after the restoration of independence: increasing morbidity, especially of socially determined diseases such as tuberculosis (active form), sexually transmitted diseases, alcoholism and drug addiction. Alcoholism is closely related to the rate of suicide and is considered to be one of the main reasons of that. In 1995, there were committed 1024 suicides or 40.7 per 100,000 inhabitants. The suicide rate is much higher in rural than urban areas, 52.0 and 35.7 per 100,000, respectively (*Statistical Yearbook* 1996: 66). These figures show a close correlation between well-being and suicide. Often people who are not able to adjust to the new demands of the market economy, who cannot find a place in the labour market, who cannot cope with everyday difficulties, and are not able to arrange normal family life, choose this kind of solution to all problems. These causes of suicide are more noticeable among socially less-protected group members, for instance, pensioners, disabled people and so on. It is not surprising, then, that 44 per cent of men and 59 per cent of women who committed suicide were aged 50 or over (*Pielikums* 1996).

Not all of those living in poverty choose such an extreme solution. Many people suffer from apathy, depression, morbidity and other kinds of psychological disorders. To a great extent, this is a result of the everyday pressures people must cope with. The struggle for survival can generate levels of stress that lead to psychosomatic illnesses.

Though the situation with regard to the population's health is far from desirable, in comparison with other countries, Latvia has one of the lowest levels of financing for its health care system. Increasingly, the burden of cost for health care is put on the shoulders of the population. Those who have resources can be 'conscientious', take responsibility and look after their health. However, there is a choice between buying bread or visiting a doctor, in most cases a decision will be made in favour of the former. The situation in the health care system and its availability to residents also quite clearly demonstrates violation of human rights, especially those of people living in poverty.

The social dimensions of poverty

Poverty can be looked upon and discussed in a number of ways. There is the economic dimension – in most cases measured by income and explained by the unequal distribution of material resources – but this does not give the full picture. One can agree with the statement that poverty cannot be understood, and is not experienced in terms of income alone. Poverty is a relationship: it is a relationship ultimately to wealth, but it is mediated through people's experiences of the labour market, of state bureaucracies, of the family and patriarchy, or racism. It involves complex patterns of power and powerlessness, multiple facets of deprivation, and issues of humiliation and self-respect. Such experiences cannot be measured, cannot be understood, solely in terms of income (Novak 1996: 87). Consequently, poverty must be looked upon also from the point of view of social and political perspectives.

In the transformation from a centralised economy to free-market capitalism, the part poverty plays in society can be seen to be significant. As Novak (1988) argues in relation to the British social security system:

> Throughout its history its primary role has been to uphold the operation of a capitalist labour market, with its social and sexual divisions of labour, and to control and contain the inequalities and poverty that result. In the course of its history the state has had to respond flexibly to the political challenges created by poverty. But the social security system has never been intended to abolish poverty, nor has it been capable of doing so. The centrality of poverty to capitalism, and the importance of social security as a means of maintaining poverty and of 'moralising' and regulating the poor, has and will set the limits of its operation. (p.200)

Whether and to what extent these patterns will apply in Latvia's new and developing regime remains to be seen. However, the importance of poverty as a factor within the social fabric as a whole cannot be denied.

Whilst recognising that every individual has the right to human dignity, the right to be treated as an adult equal member of society, it also has to be recognised that these rights are violated in relation to people in poverty. At best, it can be argued, poor people tend to be treated paternalistically. At worst, they tend to be subjected to contempt and rejection (Lauer 1989: 246). Poor people are looked upon as lacking not only economic resources, and are therefore often treated as if they were deficient. The victims are blamed, and forced to blame themselves, for their condition. This is not that obvious in Latvia, where a great part of the population has experienced a deterioration in living conditions and is faced with poverty; most of the population can be defined as poor according to one or other definition of poverty. In this situation poor people are perceived as victims. They feel deprived. Most of them cannot enjoy the standard of living they had, they must cut their expenses, they cannot afford things they used to have, and so on. For example, people who worked for 30–40 years now get pensions that are equal to approximately to 75 per cent of the crisis subsistence minimum and to a half of the costs of the minimal consumption basket. This is perceived rather as a violation of respect to human dignity and finds its expression in anger, frustration and other kinds of negative feelings.

People living in poverty cannot freely exercise the right to autonomy and control over their lives. They have few if any opportunities compared to people at the upper end. Poverty presents an ongoing series of dilemmas.

The position of poor people contradicts a value of the right to life and the pursuit of happiness. The inadequacy of financial resources deprives poor people of freedom to pursue a full and happy life. Poverty brings more despair than happiness and more fear than fullness of life (Lauer 1989: 244–5).

According to CBS survey data on public opinion about economic changes in the country and family living conditions, among others, an indicator of confidence was measured. (For more details of the methodology, see *Pielikums* 1996). The indicator has been negative since 1993, when the survey began. It means that people are quite pessimistic in the assessment of their current situation and they also do not look to the future positively. About 60 per cent of respondents report a deterioration in economic conditions of their household. About one-third of respondents see a negative future. Only 7 per cent believe in the likelihood of improvement. Closely linked to these are data about the economic situation of the country.

The data show people's dissatisfaction with their living conditions; they express uncertainty and fear about today as well as the future. The residents of Latvia are less satisfied with their life than people in most parts of other countries, including the developing countries. Researchers from the US and the Netherlands, independently using different methodology, found that people in the former communist countries are least satisfied with their life – the Baltic countries, Bulgaria, Belarus, Russia. Their findings show that even the populations of India, China, Nigeria are happier (*Zvidriņš* 1996: 4–5). This can probably be interpreted in terms of psychological response associated with loss. Within the last years there has been a significant deterioration in the economic situation of a major proportion of the population. It is difficult to give up what one used to have and to accept a decline in economic and social well-being, to adjust to new conditions. In most cases a natural reaction is dissatisfaction and a feeling of injustice.

Great hopes were associated with independence, but the reality that has emerged is totally different from what was expected. Independence did not bring immediate improvement in all spheres of life – quite the opposite in fact. There are serious problems, serious deterioration in many areas, and the social sphere has suffered a great deal, as have others. There is, of course, no panacea. None the less, something can be done, if not to abolish poverty, then at least to diminish the proportion of people living in poverty and lessen people's sufferings from the effects of poverty. Experts see the stabilisation and development of macro- and micro-economic processes as one of the most important ways of moving forward positively. It is also necessary to develop social policy and to pay more attention to the social sphere. At the same time, we must not neglect efforts to bring about changes in people's attitudes. It is also important to get rid of the 'learned helplessness' that can so easily arise as a consequence of extended periods of living in poverty.

References

Alcock, P. (1993) *Understanding Poverty*. London: Macmillan.
Bērni un ģimenes Latvijā 1994 (1995) Rīga: UNICEF.
Bradshaw, J. and Holmes, H. (1989) *Living on the Edge. A study of the Living Standards of Families on Benefit in Tyne & Wear*. London: Tyneside Child Poverty Action Group.
Diena (1996, 1997) (A daily newspaper).
Dobelniece, S. (1997) 'Poverty in Latvia during the period of transformation', *Humanities and Social Sciences. Latvia. Social Changes in Latvia*, No. 4 (13) 96 / 1 (14) 97, University of Latvia, Riga.
Dreifelds, J. (1996) *Latvia in Transition*. Cambridge: Cambridge University Press.
Latvija. Galvenie statistikas rādītāji 1996 (1996) LR Valsts statistikas komiteja, Riga.
Latvija. Pārskats par tautas attīstību 1996. (1996). Riga: UNDP.
Lauer, R.H. (1989) *Social Problems and the Quality of Life* (4th edn). Dubuque, Iowa: W.C. Brown Publishers.
Novak, T. (1988) *Poverty and the State: An Historical Sociology*. Milton Keynes: Open University Press.
Novak, T. (1996) 'Empowerment and the Politics of Poverty'. In Humphries, B. (ed.) *Critical Perspectives on Empowerment*. Birmingham: Venture Press.
Oslands, O. (ed.) (1996) *Dzīves apstākļi Latvijā*. Riga: LR Valsts Statistikas komiteja.
Pielikums Latvijas statistikas ikmēneša biļetenam, 8 (1996). Riga: LR Valsts Statistikas komiteja.
Statistical Yearbook of Latvia (1996). Riga: Central Statistical Bureau of Latvia.
Stropnic, N. (1993) 'The relativity of poverty lines', paper presented at the 3rd European IUCSD Conference. Farfa, Italy, 9–11 September.
Sweden (1992) Stockholm: The Swedish Institute.
Townsend, P., Davidson, N. and Whithead, P. (1988) *Inequalities in Health: The Black Report and the Health Divide*. Harmondsworth: Penguin.
Tulva, T. (1997) 'Current Changes and Social Problems in Estonia'. In Tulva, T. (ed.) *Some aspects of Estonian Social Work and Social Policy*. Tallin: TPU, Department of Social Work.
Zinojums par Latvijas tautsaimniecības attīstību (1996) Riga: L.R. Ekonomikas ministrija.
Zvidriņš, P. (1996) 'Tautas dzīvotspēja mazinās', *Skola un Ģimene*, Nr. 10.

2 Globalisation and Gender Relations in Social Work

Lena Dominelli

Abstract

The forces of globalisation have had a profound impact on social work. They have altered its raison d'être *and changed its methods of working. This chapter explores the ways in which globalisation has affected gender relations in social work and argues that their major role has been to deprofessionalise and refeminise the profession. This has been done by imposing the quasi-market of the purchaser-provider split on reluctant professionals, increasing managerial control over front-line workers, undermining professional autonomy, bureaucratising the interaction between workers and 'clients' and excluding 'clients' from having either a real choice about the services they receive or having a real say in how these are designed and delivered.*

Social workers, involved as they are in a locality-based profession which is deeply implicated in the structures of the nation-state, have tended to ignore the impact of globalisation on their practice. This is an unfortunate position to adopt because as I hope to demonstrate in this chapter, its effects on the profession have been profound. The gendered nature of the relations that globalisation has set in train are also very important, particularly in social work which as a profession carries a historical legacy of being considered a woman-dominated low-status entity preoccupied with carrying out 'women's work'.

The main concern of this chapter is to examine globalisation and the ways in which its dynamics have shaped the restructuring of social work in terms of its gendered working relations, service delivery, and education and training. I will focus primarily on the experience of the United Kingdom in laying out my arguments. But the macrolevel analysis I present resonates in other parts of the world (Kelsey 1997). This should not come as a surprise given that I am looking at globalisation, which implies in this case a world system of capitalist domination.

Globalisation

The term globalisation became a fashionable term in the 1980s to indicate a new direction in the processes of capitalist accumulation (Sklair 1991). It has been defined as the deepening and widening of market driven relations of production on a global scale. And, it is becoming evident that it has three principle interactive characteristics which differentiate it from previous modes of international capitalism. These are the establishment of a global market principle, the deregulation and liberalisation of financial markets and flexible accumulation. In academic circles, this set of relationships is said to comprise post-fordist relations of production (Boyer 1988; Jessop 1990). Cox (1981) added the dimension of the 'internationalisation of the state' by which he meant that the nation-state takes responsibility for transforming domestic economic relations into those consistent with the imperatives of the global market. The implementation of this task ensures that nation-states become allies of financial capitalists who operate within the processes of global capital accumulation and lay the foundations for altering the relationship between the nation-state and its 'citizenry'.[1]

The nation-state's role of promoting global capitalist relations have placed social work in the firing line of those global economic forces that have substantially altered its own remit. The methods whereby this objective was achieved was the transformation of relations of reproduction into a commodity relation popularly known as the purchaser-provider split. The state ceases to function as a provider of services, leaving the responsibility for their actual delivery to the independent sector made up of commercial and voluntary enterprises. Instead, the state concentrates on being a purchaser which distributes financial resources necessary for ensuring services are delivered to those needing them through tightly defined contractual relations. Whilst such moves have fragmented service delivery from the one-stop shop envisaged by the Seebohm (1968) reorganisation of local authorities, these have centralised financial power and decision making in the hands of the state. These dynamics have also increased the role that men play in social work's financial and managerial ranks. Indeed, they have increased the number of non-social work managers who make policy to be implemented by primarily women staff on the front line.

The three key features of globalisation mentioned above refer primarily to the production side of capital accumulation. But, the 'internationalisation of the state' the reproduction side of social relations, also brings into the discussion. This includes both the daily and intergenerational reproduction of people. The dynamics of reproduction are those directly involved in how people live their daily routines and are those aspects of social relations in which social workers as practitioners are embedded. These are also the ones that are most crucial to their encounters with others, particularly their 'clients', work colleagues and employers. However, I would add that social work as a professionalised state activity also plays a role in the production part of the equation if that is understood to involve capital accumulation.

Thus, within the welfare state, women experience the impact of the dynamics of globalisation in their roles as 'clients', waged professionals and paid carers. Outside of their direct influence, women are implicated in these dynamics as unpaid carers who are asked to pick up the tab in the gap between state-funded initiatives including those in the commercial and voluntary sectors which receive state subsidies and individual needs. But before focusing on gender relations, I want to lay out the way in which the state, including the welfare state, is deeply implicated in sustaining globalisation within its jurisdictional boundaries.

Contract government and the Taylorisation of professional labour

In countries which have had a strong welfare state and a large public sector encompassing the provision of both industrial goods and services, the nation-state has been the custodian of substantial capital resources. In Britain, for example, the state encompasses about 40 per cent of gross domestic product (GDP) within its clutches. Concentrated under the aegis of government, these resources constituted an entity which could be released to private capital for accumulation under the appropriate conditions. The government, run by politicians subscribing to monetarist doctrines, passed policies and created the infrastructure which would make such an eventuality possible. This included setting up 'think tanks' and involving businesspeople to proclaim on the virtues of the private market over the welfare state in providing welfare services. Published in 1988, the Griffiths Report for the care of older people, for example, was the outcome of one such initiative which set about to inculcate business ethics into the service ethos.

However, in implementing this political project, there were practical ideological questions which the government had to address. These included the popularity of the welfare state, particularly those dimensions which were concerned with health and education. These had maintained public support despite various critiques of the inadequacy of the services which were being delivered that had been elaborated by white women, black people[2] and disabled people amongst others. What claimants, including white women and black people, were demanding in particular were provisions which responded to their needs and were relevant to their assuming control over their lives (Brooke and Davis 1985; Hanmer and Statham 1987; Dominelli and McLeod 1989; Dominelli 1988; Ahmad, 1990; Morris, 1991).

Globalisation was expressed in the ideological arena through monetarist doctrines which became associated with the 'New Right'. Right-wing adherents of monetarist doctrines such as Thatcher in Britain, Mulroney in Canada, Muldoon in New Zealand and Reagan in the US were able to both articulate its precepts and to implement them in their respective countries. This was initially achieved through their control of government and subsequently through their restructuring of the entire state apparatus in accordance with the principles of a monetarist-oriented free market. These protagonists were extremely successful in their endeavours and over a period of years, were able to profoundly alter the welfare state and its organisation of service delivery, people's expectations about publicly funded provisions aimed at ensuring their well-being individually and collectively, and the organisational culture operating within workplaces in the public sector.

In Britain, this change was wrought through the use of economic instruments and legislation rather than through the launch of an ideological attack on the fundamentals of the welfare state (Dominelli and Hoogvelt 1996). The net effect of this ingenious methodology was that the welfare state was restructured in ways that were antithetical to the discharge of collective responsibility for the well-being of others. This shift was achieved without a debate on what kind of welfare state the British people including those excluded from active citizenship wanted. In other words, democratic process was ignored as the basis of decision making in a critical area of controversy like the type of welfare state the populace required or wanted. Additionally, the bonds of solidarity between individuals represented through the creation of publicly funded welfare provisions were ruptured as each person became responsible for his or her own welfare needs. Margaret Thatcher put it most vividly when she acclaimed that there was 'no such thing as society, only individuals'. She was later to add, 'and families' when it became clear that certain individuals, particularly those with a certain degree of in-built dependency such as children and older people would not be able to survive without the support of others. Furthermore, this addition was essential to the desire of New Right ideologues to assert the authority of the traditional two-parent heterosexual family and the values it endorsed which they felt were in dangerous decline (Levitas 1986). The decline of the 'traditional' family was laid at the door of the welfare state which encouraged women's dependency by paying them to stay at home without a man in tow (Gilder 1984; Murray 1984, 1990, 1994); cuckolded men by making redundant their role as provider and demanded that children living in poverty and excluded from mainstream society become the responsibility of their parents on penalty of loss of benefits, imprisonment or both (Gilder, 1984).

The economic instruments used to foster the development of a market-oriented welfare state in Britain were the Financial Management Initiative (FMI) of 1982, the New Steps Initiative (NSI) combined with the introduction of compulsory competitive tendering (CCT) in 1988, the Private Finance Initiative (PFI) of the early 1990s and the 'Best Value' initiatives of 1997 which replaced CCT. The FMI began to introduce the idea of professionals being systematically held accountable for how they used the resources which the state had placed at their disposal. This move began to individualise professional accountability, and coupled with legal attacks on trade union activity, sought to shrink the potential for the display of interpersonal solidarities amongst the workforce. At this point, the state was seeking to reduce the power of professionals by changing their value base while at the same time retaining service provision within the ambit of the welfare state.

The NSI brought in the structures of 'contract government' as the means whereby the state could ensure that those enterprises that had been entrusted with public resources were working in ways that were consistent with its aims and objectives as the principal who had funded the activities of those working as the sub-contractors or agencies charged with delivering the provisions it authorised (Greer 1994). NSI also ensured that quality management procedures were instituted into the public sector so as to facilitate the processes of flexible accumulation and production. These included procedures covered by quality assurance protocols such as BS5750, total quality management and performance-related pay. The NSI initiative thereby enabled services formerly provided by the welfare state to go into the private commercial or voluntary sectors without ceding full control to the providers who held its contracts.

Contract government introduced the 'contract' culture for service provision, a range of service providers in certain areas and reduced the extent to which professionals could exercise autonomous decision-making capacities in the course of their work. In this way, the professional power base, whether in the academic or practitioner arena, was undermined as these individuals fulfilled the contracts which they had so eagerly sought. The PFI was introduced to provide funding for capital projects that the state has either refused to support or claimed to have insufficient resourcing for.

These financial initiatives were accompanied by reports which sought to turn the welfare state into a business enterprise like any other. For example, the Griffiths Report castigated the lack of managerial control over those workers engaged in providing welfare services to those in residential establishments. The National Health and Community Care Act of 1990 which demanded the introduction of what became known as the 'purchaser-provider' split in the personal social services was posited as the solution to this problem. This also demanded greater collaboration between competing agencies involved in providing the necessary services. The fact that even the professionals concerned agreed that there was a need for more user-friendly changes meant that there was less systematic examination of what provisions were evolving through the proposed restructuring. Thus, they missed the threat that it posed to both the existence of easily accessible publicly funded provisions and professional power.

These moves required legislative and managerial initiatives which sought to deny the welfare state the role of provider of services by separating the 'purchaser' function from the 'provider' one and redirecting the latter function towards the so-called 'independent' sector comprising of the commercial sector and the voluntary one. These changes also sought to impose stronger managerial control over the workforce and labour process. Through the method of 'contract' government, it was expected that professional autonomy and professional power would be reduced. The restructuring which these initiatives set in train was also intended to deliver greater choice for consumers (Greer 1994).

The labour process was subjected to the imperatives of 'contract' government and resulted in the fragmentation of their work. In the arena of professional practice, this was achieved through the introduction of 'competence-based social work' which operated on the basis of reducing the complex tasks formerly undertaken by social workers into their basic constituent parts or discrete elements (Mainframe, 1994). This process of fragmenting the labour process mimicked fordist methods of production and enabled the farming out of tasks formerly undertaken by qualified professionals to be done by lower paid and less well-qualified workers, most of whom were women training through National Vocational Qualifications (NVQ) arrangements. This assisted in a reduction in the labour costs born by social welfare agencies, but also ensured the formation of a more flexible and therefore more easily deployable' workforce. Dominelli and Hoogvelt (1996) call this the 'Taylorisation' – the introduction of factory processes of production – of professional labour. This process also promoted managerial control over practitioners through the allocation of work according to procedures specified by management, the assessment of workers' performance through outcome measures and the regular surveillance of their work through bureaucratic instruments of assessment.

Additional legislation has been initiated to curb the power of the unions, including those in the public sector. Over a period of time, these initiatives limited the rights of workers to undertake secondary picketing and thereby support the struggles of other workers (Joyce et al. 1987). This legislation also endorsed changes in the relationship between the leadership, its activists and lay members. Furthermore, unions were required to hold ballots before taking strike or other forms of industrial action and subjected to liability claims against their assets for losses employers incurred during specific forms of action taken against them. Additionally, the government excluded union leaders from discussions about the direction in which the national economy should head (Joyce et al. 1987). This package of anti-union measures successfully curtailed a potential source of opposition to the monetarist path being adopted by government. Indeed, as a result of the constraints imposed on trade union activism, the popular display of support for the miners who resisted the restructuring of their industry through the Miner's Strike of 1984–5 failed to block the monetarist advance and resulted in the destruction of a mining industry in the public sector. Additionally, women were to bear the brunt of the failure of trade unionism to defend their members' interests: during the Thatcher era, women became the largest group of employees in the paid workforce of the welfare state to be affected by its restructuring. As a result of the cost-cutting basis of these changes, women's wages dropped and job security decreased once private employers took over the service delivery function from the state. Cutting costs and making profits out of people's needs became the priorities guiding such developments. It remains to be seen whether Harriet Harman's promise that this will not happen under the Labour administration will be upheld. I am somewhat pessimistic about this being adhered to, given that the process is being driven by monetarist responses to globalisation – a Tory priority the current Labour government is committed to upholding, at least in the short term.

Since the mid-1980s, social work has become an increasingly technicist activity rather than a professional activity, as managerialism has extended its tentacles into daily work routines. As we shall see later, the spread of competence-based approaches to social work and the promotion of workplace-based training under the aegis of the National Vocational Qualifications (NVQs) have been critical in endorsing this approach.

Gendered relations in social work

The Seebohm (1968) reorganisation of social work during the 1970s changed the gender balance of the profession. The creation of large bureaucratic empires which replaced the smaller agencies delivering the personal social services was a major force behind this change. Seebohm's wish to have community-based services in which 'clients' needed to attend only one office to access whatever services they needed resulted in a dispersed array of service providers giving way to the social services department. In this shake-up, women lost ground at management level: whereas women had tended to manage the smaller units, men were now appointed to manage these large bureaucracies (Walton 1975). Men were also drawn more fully into training and joined the practitioner's ranks in greater numbers as a result of the better conditions of service and rates of pay which were becoming available as social work became more professionalised and unionised. Even then, men in social work followed different career paths from women, rising through the ranks and into more prestigious jobs, especially those in the child welfare arena (Walton 1975; Howe 1986; Dominelli 1997).

During the late 1980s, declining rates of pay and the increasing unattractiveness of a social work that became subjected to the dictates of 'contract' government, an intensified managerialist ethos and deprofessionalisation, discouraged male applicants in both the educational and practitioner spheres. As a result, the numbers of men entering the profession dropped considerably. This pattern has been exacerbated by the intensification of these processes during the 1990s. As a consequence of exercising other more attractive options, fewer men are joining the main-grade practitioner's ranks. This is encouraging both the refeminisation and deprofessionalisation of social work (Dominelli 1996, 1997).

Thus, women social workers have experienced the impact of globalisation to a greater extent than men. To begin with, women continue to comprise the largest group of employees in social work who have been subjected to the dictats of managerialism and the changing nature of the profession as a result of competence-based social work. Moreover, women have been bound within a profession that has traditionally been assigned a low status (Flexner 1915; Heraud 1979), received poor rates of pay and held more limited direct control over their work than has been the case in the male-dominated professions of law and medicine. Additionally, what women did in paid employment mirrored their experience of unpaid caring work performed for the benefit of others in the home. However, the processes of globalisation exacerbated the marginalism of their profession and locked them more firmly into a tight definition of their professional roles.

This occurred as a result of the Taylorisation of the labour process in which they were engaged whether they wished to be or not. The implications of Taylorisation for women social workers was to further reduce the influence they could exert over a profession which had not been subject to their control, but which had always been dependent on either men or the state for its existence and resourcing. Following the purchaser-provider split, women became increasingly required to work within bureaucratic parameters which curtailed their capacity to work with the whole person or respond to a range of needs and problems which 'clients' bring with them.

Social workers were called to greater accountability, but not in ways which improved the delivery of services to 'clients' which were needs-led rather than budget-led assessments to be honoured. Accountability has been expressed largely in terms of how social workers spend the resources which had been placed at their disposal rather than how many of the actual needs identified they meet. This approach has made it easier to blame the individual worker when things have gone wrong and have enabled the popular press to demonise social workers whatever they do, particularly when it comes to addressing problems encountered within the child protection arena. Yet, although the bulk of child abuse scandals have been perpetrated by men social workers, women social workers are usually the ones who have born the brunt of the changes that follow. Women often find themselves castigated for not addressing the issues whilst in post, thereby ensuring that women, not men are held responsible for failing to protect vulnerable children and avoiding discussions about resources and support available to social workers who undertake one of the toughest forms of interpersonal work existing today.

By pathologising the social workers, resource shortages and the problems of co-ordinating increasingly fragmented services have escaped notice except in the footnotes of public curiosity. Yet these issues combined with those of inadequate training for practitioners lay at the root of many of social workers' failures to deliver appropriate services. Matters have developed in accordance with the assumption that women can stretch resources in the paid workplace with the same skill as they do at home to cover any demands that are placed upon them.

Ironically, gender has also featured as a matter of concern in other ways. During the 1980s, several high-profile cases in which social workers abusing children in their care have come to the fore, for example, the 'pindown' regime in Staffordshire and sexual abuse in Leicestershire. The perpetrators were men, yet the implications of these dynamics have not been systematically explored to date. Yet, in Cleveland, when two women were involved in calling attention to child sexual abuse being perpetrated on children primarily by men that they knew, the popular press had no compunction in highlighting the gender implications. By blaming the women practitioners involved in this case, the woman doctor and a woman social worker conducting the investigations were pilloried for peddling feminist dogma and for being feminists who were deliberately picking on innocent men to promote their ideological bias against men (Bell 1985). That 91 of the 127 allegations of sexual abuse were to be subsequently proven true and that both the doctor and social worker in question had lost their jobs and been gagged from telling their side of the story in the process did not concern the popular media (Channel Four 1997). The Butler-Schloss Enquiry sought to make sense of the affair and highlight how Marietta Higgs and Sue Richardson had tried to do their job and protect abused children within an unforgivable scarcity of resources, an impossible situation which failed to adequately surface in the press discussion about their interventions (Butler-Schloss 1988).

Despite the Taylorisation of social work through the competence-based approach to its activities, men continue to dominate the top managerial ranks of the profession (Grimwood and Popplestone 1993). Approximately, 12 per cent of directors of social services are white women. No black woman has yet attained these heights. However, in recent years, more women, black and white, and some black men have been drawn into the middle-management ranks. Those occupying these posts are sitting between a rock and a hard place. Most of their time is consumed with implementing policy directives which have been formulated by others, particularly men who have not had front-line experience and do not necessarily meet the needs of 'clients'. Talented women who do not wish to be subjected to such processes have refused to enter managerial ranks (Durrant 1989). Those that have thought they might be able to make a difference by introducing more user-oriented and anti-oppressive systems of working and service delivery leave within short periods of time because they feel thwarted by unresponsive mechanisms, procedures and colleagues (Durrant 1989; Dominelli 1997).

Women engaged in unpaid caring work are also experiencing the impact of globalisation and monetarist doctrines which demand the reassertion of traditional family relations and values. These have women and children in a dependent position *vis-à-vis* men and insist that women provide as much unpaid caring services as are required by the extended family which can legitimately call upon their labour. Such injunctions fly in the face of women's position in the waged workforce and the enormous contribution they make to their families' financial survival. Family poverty would quadruple without the contribution that comes from women's waged labour (Family Policy Studies Centre 1984). This aspect of women's lives is particularly acute for black and white working-class women who often assume the role of main breadwinner because their male partner is either unable to get work or in a job that is insufficiently remunerated to enable the family unit to survive on his pay packet alone. For such a woman, the two-earner family is essential for maintaining a decent standard of living.

Familialist assumptions ignore the fact that the low-waged part of the labour market is also inhabited primarily by women (Armstrong 1984). These women do not earn enough to buy high-quality child care for their children. The requirement that they work in such jobs if they wish to draw benefits is an unjust one which conveys the clear message that the right to family life can only be enjoyed by those who have enough money to pay for it on their own. Such injunctions also ignore the rights of children to live in a reasonable degree of comfort and security whether or not their parents work in highly paid posts. Such rights can only be assured if people accept collective responsibility for children – a matter which is anathema to right-wing ideologues who deplore people who have children whose well-being they cannot afford to pay for.

Globalisation has also impacted on social work education and training through the promulgation of the competence-based approach to it. Competence-based social work has endorsed the creation of lower-level qualifications known as National Vocational Qualifications (NVQ, now called VQ) system which awards certificates to women who have undergone limited social work training within the context of the workplace. Such training is useful in recognising work women have done for some time, but which has been previously unacknowledged as requiring skills. However, this approach carries with it certain dangers. It legitimates lower-level qualifications for women in a profession which is seeking to raise its qualifications and status, and locks women into a low-paid ghetto as N/VQs are not linked to higher qualifications and academic awards which enable women to access higher paid posts and to transfer their skills between occupational categories as well as within a given professional occupation. In the case of the UK, these NVQ qualifications are not recognised internationally, not even within Europe. Thus, women are further limited in terms of their potential mobility and the better remunerated jobs which can be accessed through the recognition of their awards.

Women's resistance

Women have not been inactive as the processes of globalisation have unfolded in their workplaces. During the 1980s, women were busy forming their own support groups in their places of employment to ensure that they could address issues of sexual oppression and sexism within social work. Feminists took a key role in such developments by creating feminist groups, networks and campaigns to caucus for social change and for women to support each other. For example, women managers formed Women in Management groups to facilitate their challenge of sexist relations within management ranks. Main-grade practitioners formed women in social work groups (Donnelly 1986).

Front-line women practitioners, black and white, have used their trade union connections to develop women's sections and caucuses within these bodies to challenge sexist policies and practices. These have ranged from those concerning women's reproductive rights to those dealing with promotion to the higher echelons of the profession. Equal opportunities policies, flexible working arrangements such as job sharing, sexual harassment policies and better services for older, lesbian, disabled and black women, owe much to feminist action and scholarship on these fronts.[4]

Many of women's gains were achieved in spite of resistance to their proposals across all levels of the labour hierarchy and from both genders (Whitlock 1987). Some activities, for example, those which were promoted through the efforts of women in Women's Units and funded by local authorities, lost their funding in the mid-1980s when politicians began to ridicule the expenditure of resources to fight racism and sexism (Whitlock 1987) as 'special interests' which bore little relevance to the lives led by the majority of women. Ultimately, local authorities like the Greater London Council were abolished because Margaret Thatcher considered their support of anti-racist and feminist initiatives unacceptable in the British context as she defined it (Livingstone 1987).

The lack of central state support for feminist activities within mainstream service provisions has been a major reason for the failure of feminist initiatives to make as substantial an impact as might have been expected given that their concerns have relevance for half the population of this country. But women's demands for social change are threatening to the status quo. Hence, negative reactions to them can be anticipated.

In the academy, feminist scholars began to question the empiricist basis of knowledge, challenge its claim to universality despite its failure to acknowledge women's experiences (Adamson et al. 1988) and seek to create new paradigms for practice as teachers, researchers and practitioners. Key elements in their projects were feminist principles which had been formulated largely within the activities fostered by the women's movement. These included notions such as:

● The personal is political
● Women's experience must be made visible
● Women must speak for themselves in their own voices
● Theory and practice are integral to each other

- The creation of women-centered services which are designed, and run by women
- The importance of self-criticism and responding to critiques made by other women
- The validity of experiential knowledge.

Despite these aspirations, feminists, as part of the socially divided societies in which they live have not succeeded in implementing these principles to their own satisfaction, let alone that of the critics within their own ranks. For example, lesbian women (Hanscombe and Forster 1982), black women (Lorde 1984; hooks 1981, 1984, 1989, 1993), disabled women (Morris 1991) have written extensively of the failure of mainstream feminism, particularly that advocated by white middle-class women (Barrett and McIntosh 1982) to address their interests and needs on par with their own. Others whose lives have traversed several social divisions have complained that neither of their concerns have been adequately addressed (Begum 1994). Claiming that oppression should not be ranked according to a hierarchy prioritising one form over the others, these critics have argued persuasively that oppression from all sources impacts on them simultaneously (Collins 1991; Lorde 1984). They therefore characterise many of the responses which have been made by white women as tokenistic rather than those endorsing full equality.

Part of feminists' failure to respond appropriately to the voices of other women is that women can be both oppressed and oppressing. For example, white women can be oppressed along the gender dimension but can also be oppressing black women along that of 'race'; heterosexual women can oppress lesbian women. Additionally, there are different types of feminism, each of which has its own focus and definition of equality and how to achieve it. Equality has been differentiated into equality of rights, equality of opportunity and equality of outcome. Each aspect is important in taking on board individual instances of discrimination, but except for the last aspect – equality of outcome – they do little to redress matters which are embedded within an individual's experience of collective oppression. This refers to that form of oppression which an individual woman endures because she is a member of a particular social category and is treated in accordance with the stereotypes of inferiority associated with that group.

Gendered sexual politics between men and women have become inter-twined with the politics of identity amongst women to reflect the actual experience of women's lives. Through this process, the already fragmented nature of feminist politics is in danger of becoming even more so. Individualisation is important in a feminist context which seeks to locate the individual woman within her social situation or circumstances; however, in a period of rapid globalisation, such moves run the risk of destroying any basis for collective action between and among different groups of women. Realising this and doing something about it becomes important in establishing the bases for resistance to the forces of globalisation. For although individual resistance is a crucial dimension in the project of securing one's own liberation, resistance based on collective solidarities is more likely to lead to social change which will impact on many women's lives. Yet, this solidarity must be worked for. That is, it has to be created, not assumed. This requires women to examine the sources of difference between them, understand where these come from, how they can be valued and how to find the common ground on which solidarities can be created. Differences between women need to be respected and validated before women can begin to work with one another across and within them. Responding to this agenda, therefore, is a critical challenge facing women in today's world. In doing so, women engage as active agents creating their own histories and realities. Social workers must respond to these agendas if they wish to redefine their professionalism and work with women 'clients' in more egalitarian and less disempowering ways.

Conclusion

Globalisation and the privatisation of the welfare state has increased woman's insecurity in the paid labour market and forced her to reconsider her relationship with other women, members of her neighbourhood and extended family and children. Her roles within both the private and public spheres are again under scrutiny. Her capacity to act independently of the constraints imposed upon her by policymakers and the obligations stemming from a commitment to community and family networks, is limited to the spaces within which she creates her connection with others and sets her own individual agenda. At the same time, the exploitation of different groups of women is more closely aligned with their contribution to the exploitation of each other through the global labour market in both direct and indirect ways. So, the woman who loses her job in the West to the lower paid labour of her counterpart in the East is both exploited and exploiting, albeit in relations which she is scarcely aware of. Social workers have a responsibility to work through and with these contradictions to enable women who are living out these stories to tell them to the wider world and to seek ways in which women can be supported to rise beyond the constraints which bind their lives in oppressive ways. Women's liberation remains the goal of feminism. Social workers can contribute towards that by supporting women to gain control of their lives in a self-directed manner.

Notes

1   I have placed the term 'citizen' in quotes to acknowledge the fact that not all those who live in any particular country are formally acknowledged as people who enjoy or even have the right to enjoy the political, social and economic entitlements bequeathed by a nation-state to those it recognises as 'citizens' to the full. Citizenship is in many ways an exclusionary category which leaves out black and white women and black men as equal participants in society's decision-making bodies and resource-allocation processes or in accessing social goods.

2   I use the phrase 'black people' to denote those who are at the receiving end of racist attitudes and practices. This does not mean that these groups are homogeneous nor that their experiences of racism are exactly the same. In short, it is a heterogeneous category. But I utilise it to indicate that these groups are being subjected to racist dynamics. In Britain, the term has often been used with respect of people of African, Afro-Caribbean and Asian descent. Racism, however, impacts on a wider range of people, not all of whom have dark skin-colour (Dominelli 1988; D'Souza 1995).

3   I have placed 'client' in quotes to indicate the problematic nature of this term. However, I prefer it to consumer or user on the grounds that it is more broadly understood to mean the people that social workers work with.

4   The term 'feminism' is also problematic. Many people feel it is exclusionary in that it refers only to the activities of white middle-class women who are challenging existing social relations. Thus, many black feminists call themselves 'womanist' to differentiate themselves from white feminism. I do not feel that the term feminism should be restricted in these ways. White working-class women, black working women, older women black and white, black and white disabled women and others not listed, have engaged in feminist activities. Thus, I wish to retain the word and use it in its inclusive sense. If differentiating between groups of women is relevant to the point I am making, I will draw attention to this difference by saying, for example, black women. My using the term in its inclusive sense in this chapter does not mean that I do not support autonomous spaces for different categories of women when they feel they wish to work along different dimensions of their identities.

References

Adamson, N., Briskin, L. and McPhail, M. (1988) *Organising for Change: The Contemporary Women's Movement in Canada*. Oxford: Oxford University Press.

Ahmad, B. (1990) *Black Perspectives in Social Work*. Birmingham: Venture Press.

Armstrong, P. (1984) *Labour Pains: Women's Work in Crisis*. Toronto: Women's Press.

Barrett, M. and McIntosh, M. (1982) *The Anti-Social Family*. London: Verso.

Begum, N. (1994) *Disability and Ethic Minorities*. London: CCETSW.

Bell, S. (1987) *When Salem Came to the Boro'*. Harmondsworth: Penguin.

Brook, E. and Davis, A. (1985) *Women, the Family and Social Work*. London: Tavistock.

Butler-Schloss, E. (1988) *Report of the Enquiry into Child Abuse in Cleveland, 1987*. London: HMSO.

Channel Four (1997) Programme on the 'Cleveland Child Abuse Scandal', *Black Bag*, Sept.

Cheyne, Christine, O'Brien, Mike and Belgrave, Michael (1997) *Social Policy in Aotearoa New Zealand: A Critical Introduction*. Auckland: Oxford University Press.

Collins, P. H. (1991) *Black Feminist Thought: Knowledge, Consciousness and the Politics of Empowerment*. London: Routledge.

Cox, R.W. (1981) 'Social Forces, States and World Orders: Beyond International Relations Theory', *Millennium*, **10**(2): 139–53.

Culpitt, I. (1992) *Welfare and Citizenship: Beyond the Crisis of the Welfare State*. London: Sage.

Dominelli, L. (1988) *Anti-Racist Social Work*. London: Macmillan. 2nd Edition in 1997.

Dominelli, L. (1996) 'Deprofessionalising Social Work: Equal Opportunities, Competences and Postmodernism', *British Journal of Social Work*, **26**: 153–75.

Dominelli, L. (1997) *Sociology for Social Work*. London: Macmillan.

Dominelli, L and Hoogvelt, L. (1996) 'Globalisation and the Technocratisation of Social work', *Critical Social Policy*, Spring.

Dominelli, L. and McLeod, E. (1989) *Feminist Social Work*. London: Macmillan.

Donnelly, A. (1986) *Feminist Social Work with a Women's Group*. Norwich: University of East Anglia Monographs.

D'Souza, D. (1995) *The End of Racism: Principles for a Multiracial Society*. New York: Free Press.

Durrant, J. (1989) 'Continuous Agitation', *Community Care*, 13 July: 23–5.

Family Policy Studies Centre (1984) *An Ageing Population*. London: FPSC.

Flexner, A. (1915) 'Is Social Work a Profession?, *Studies in Social Work*, 4. New York: New York School of Philanthropy.

Gilder, G. (1984) *Wealth and Poverty*. New York: Basic Books.

Greer, P. (1994) *Transforming Central Government: The New Steps Initiative*. London: Open University Press.

Griffiths, R. (1988) *The Griffiths Report*. London: DHSS.

Grimwood, C. and Popplestone, R. (1993) *Women in Management*. London: Macmillan.

Hanmer, J. and Statham, D. (1987) *Women and Social Work: Towards Woman Centered Practice*. London: BASW/Macmillan.

Hanscombe, G. and Forster, J. (1982) *Rocking the Cradle: Lesbian Mothers*. London: Sheba Feminist Publishers.

hooks, b. (1981) *Ain't I a Woman? Black Women and Feminism*. London: Pluto Press.

hooks, b. (1984) *Feminist Theory: From Margins to Centre*. Boston, Ma: Southend Press.

hooks, b. (1989) *Yearning: Race, Gender and Cultural Politics*. Boston, Ma: Southend Press.

hooks, b. (1992) *Black Looks: Race and Representation*. London: Turnaround.

hooks, b. (1993) *Sisters of the Yam: Black Women and Self-Recovery*. Toronto: Between the Lines.

Howe, D. (1986) 'The Segregation of Women and their Work in the Personal Social Services', *Critical Social Policy*, 15: 21–36.

Jessop, B. (1990) 'Regulation Theories in Retrospect and Prospect', *Economy and Society*, **10**(2): 153–216.

Joyce, P., Corrigan, P. and Hayes, M. (1987) *Striking Out: Trade Unionism in Social Work*. London: Macmillan.

Kelsey, Jane. (1997) *Rolling Back the State: Privatisation of Power in Aotearoa/New Zealand*. Wellington: Bridget Williams Books Limited.

Levitas, R. (ed.) (1986) *The Ideology of the New Right.* Cambridge: Polity Press.
Livingstone, K. (1987) *If Voting Changed Anything, They'd Abolish It.* London: Collins.
Lorde, A. (1984) *Sister Outsider.* New York: The Crossing Press.
Mainframe (1994) *Review of the Diploma in Social Work: A Functional Outline.* Communication to External Assessors. July, August. London: CCETSW.
Morris, J. (1991) *Pride Against Prejudice: Transforming Attitudes to Disability.* London: The Women's Press.
Murray, C. (1984) *Losing Ground: American Social Policy, 1950-1980.* New York: Basic Books.
Murray, C. (1990) *The Emerging British Underclass.* London: Institute of Economic Affairs.
Murray, C. (1994) *Underclass: The Crisis Deepens.* London: Institute of Economic Affairs.
Olsson, Suzzan (ed.) (1992) *The Gender Factor: Women in New Zealand Organisations.* Napier, NZ: The Dunmore Press.
Seebohm, L. (1968) *Report of the Committee on Local Authority and the Personal Social Services.* London: HMSO.
Sklair, L. (1991) *Sociology of the Global System.* London: Harvester Wheatsheaf.
Spoonley, Paul (1988) *Racism and Ethnicity.* Auckland: Oxford University Press.
Walton, R. (1975) *Women in Social Work.* London: Routledge and Kegan Paul.
Whitlock, M.J. (1987) 'Five More Years of Desolation', *Spare Rib*, 180, July, p. 15.

3 Affirmative Action: A Counter to Racial Discrimination?

Lena Dominelli

Abstract

Racism has dogged Western countries for centuries. It has proved extremely adaptable in meeting new circumstances and being incorporated into attempts aimed at dismantling it. Thus, legislative changes, anti-racism awareness training, affirmative action programmes, have all failed to eradicate it. Indeed, in the current controversies, affirmative action programmes have become the centrepiece of a backlash against anti-racist initiatives and been accused of promoting 'reverse discrimination' which penalises white men. This article explores some of the issues involved in the debates over affirmative action and concludes that more needs to be done if the collective grievances of people who have been wronged historically are to be fully addressed.

Countering racial discrimination in Europe has been on the agenda for some time. In recent periods, a number of different policy initiatives have been instigated to deal with the problem. These have ranged from societal-level measures such as specific forms of legislation aimed at making certain types of behaviours unlawful, to individual programmes aimed at increasing personal awareness. In addition, both black and white anti-racists have launched various social movements which have sought to eliminate it, for example, Rock Against Racism, *SOS-Racisme*.[1] On a continental level, the European Union named 1997 as European Year Against Racism in an effort aimed at raising a broader political commitment to racial equality. Yet, despite efforts to oppose it, widespread racial discrimination persists throughout Europe (Cheles et al. 1991; Bjorgo and Witte 1993).

Though racism has been evident in Europe for centuries, the forms it takes have constantly adapted to changing circumstances and acquired new dimensions. The more recent racist discourses have been directed against approximately 18 million legal inhabitants of Europe without European Union (EU) nationality and an unknown number of others who have not entered the continent through legal means. Most of this target group has Third World origins. Even if legally domiciled, these people have few, if any, social, economic and political rights in most European countries. They are usually found at the lower rungs of the labour hierarchy, undertaking jobs that white European nationals do not want at low rates of pay. These people form part of a large socially invisible group of people who are marginalised and excluded from having access to society's resources and its decision-making structures.

They are at the receiving end of racism, particularly the virulent forms articulated by Far Right organisations. By racism, I refer to a set of racialised power relations which are based on the belief in the inherent superiority of one 'race' over (an)other(s) and thereby its right to dominate (Lorde 1984: 115). Not all people who are currently targeted by racists in Europe have black skin colour. Some are white, for example, people of Germanic ethnicity who hail from the former Eastern Europe in Germany, Irish people in Britain, Southern Italians or *meridionale* as they are disparagingly called, in Italy (Bossi 1992), Algerian nationals in France and those who originate in the former Yugoslavia. Some, like the first three categories are also EU nationals and are additional to the numbers cited above. Some others have had Arabic ancestors, as in the case of people from North Africa in France and Italy and those from the Middle East in France. Others hail from Turkey, and reside mainly in Germany (Walraff 1991) and the Netherlands. These last three groups are linked together by their Islamic faith, more than their ethnicity, a factor they share with white Muslims from the former Yugoslavia. Islamophobia has become the latest expression of cultural racism in Europe and targets those following Koranic lifestyles.

Thus, contemporary racist discourse focuses on cultural attributes which differentiate the targeted groups more than the biological features which formed the crux of earlier forms of racist discourse (Barker 1981), particularly that which became known as 'scientific racism' (Adas 1989). Although currently associated with discussions around people of African descent (Hernstein and Murray 1996), 'scientific racism' was initially aimed more against people of the 'Caucasian race' which it subdivided into Nordic, Alpine and Mediterranean, than it was those of African origins (D'Souza 1995). It thereby created a racialised hierarchy of skin colour amongst the 'white race' that cast as inferior those who had darker skin tones. 'Race' and racism are, therefore, social constructs aimed at creating, re-creating, enforcing and re-enforcing relations of domination which racialise the personal and collective identities of people. That is, they make explicit those dimensions of life which matter for the purposes of asserting the racial superiority of the dominant ethnic group.

Despite their shared plight, the diversity contained within these racialised groups makes it difficult to plan a common policy or set of policies which will address their need to be fully accepted as an integral part of the body politic with as much a right to be admitted into civil society and call on social resources as any one else living in Europe.

Moreover, their exclusion from civil society has been punctuated with overt acts of hostility and physical violence carried out against them. Since the 1980s, violence against those who are racially discriminated against has increased dramatically (La Rose 1991; Bjorgo and Witte 1993). These have varied from the horrific murders of Turkish families carried out by neo-Nazi right-wing extremists in Germany to the *'Terroni a casa'* epithets telling Southern Italians to leave Northern Italy or else!

These attacks have been paralleled by the increasing electoral popularity of extremist right-wing parties and the mainstreaming of many of their ideas, particularly with regards to immigration controls, throughout Europe. The immigration debate provides the respectable face of racist ideologies on the continent today. This discourse has been conducted primarily in terms which seek to belittle and dehumanise those seeking entry so that their unacceptability can be expressed as a need to reduce their numbers for the purposes of retaining 'harmonious race relations'. This line of reasoning has the advantage of shifting the debate on to those seeking entry, be they (im)migrants, asylum seekers, refugees, rather than upon the necessity of the receiving country to tackle manifestations of racism within its own borders. This treatment has also encompassed people of similar ethnic origins or characteristics who are already resident in Europe and turned them into objects for attack. So, for example, British blacks born and raised in England complain that they are subjected to unwarranted police harassment despite being part of the law-abiding segment of the population (Gordon 1984). As long as this mentality persists, the issue of how to develop truly multicultural societies cannot be properly addressed. Yet, finding a way of resolving these tensions in anti-racist directions is a crucial matter for European nation-states to address as they prepare to leave the twentieth century behind. The importance of effectively countering racism becomes even more urgent given the globalising tendencies of the current phase of capitalism and its capacity to homogenise diverse cultures by incorporating them into its ambit despite wishes to the contrary expressed by those adhering to lifestyles organised along different lines.

Racism is a problem that impacts on social work as well as the broader society in which the profession is located. In this chapter I examine some of the issues that racism poses for a social work profession that is developing within the context of globalisation. In the course of doing so, I focus on the policy of 'affirmative action' as a way of dealing with the problems engendered by the various aspects of racial discrimination.

Anti-racist initiatives and social work

(Im)migration is the main issue around which European discourses about black people are being conducted through an approach that is primarily assimilationist in its orientation. Moreover, this agenda and the multiculturalist one are the key ones endorsed by most people in Europe. Anti-racist initiatives have been developed in reaction to the failure of assimilationist and multicultural approaches to integrate black people into predominantly white societies on an egalitarian basis. However, these have 'caught on' to any appreciable extent in only a few places, for example, the UK. In Britain, anti-racist social work began to gain ground in the mid-1980s when a number of social forces favoured its development. One of these was that black organisations had been challenging the paucity of services being delivered to them by mainstream agencies for some time and had developed more ethnically sensitive alternative forms of social work practice under their control. Agencies had begun to substantially extend their activities in the arena of equal opportunities, partly in response to the pressures exerted upon by black people. And, academic critics had highlighted the extensive inadequacies of earlier approaches such as assimilationism and multi-culturalism in combating racism.

Unlike other approaches which took as given the appropriateness of the society's basic structures for all those living within its borders, anti-racist social work questioned the very basis on which social relations were predicated and found them wanting: they were premised on the accept-ability of racial inequalities between people. Within the social work arena, a crucial assumption which helped to maintain an inegalitarian framework in place was that which took for granted that all people were the same. From this it followed that their needs were the same. It was presumed, therefore, that any mainstream service which had been developed to meet a particular requirement of the dominant group would be appropriate for any group of people who had that need. The main exception to this view of the matter with regards to black people was the fact of their migration to Europe.

The majority of those who came were expected to remain for only a short time. For those who stayed, the issue of their settling in was couched in assimilationist terms. Leaving their lands of origin was expected to create temporary problems of adjustment which social workers were expected to address (Cheetham 1972). Thus, black people might need additional assistance in the initial stages of living in their new homeland in order to adapt to the status quo or society as they found it. But once they did this, they would be fine. In short, it was anticipated that black people would follow the path of other waves of migrants and be swallowed into the broader society. There was no expectation that once in their new society black people would become part of that society and thereby engage in shaping its future development alongside those who were already there. In short, the passivity of black people was prescribed at the expense of their agency as actors in their own right. People, however, do not create history in this manner. They shape it according to their own needs, as subsequent events have demonstrated.

The assimilationist approach to social work has also been termed the 'universal' or 'colourblind' approach (Dominelli 1988). It is rooted in assimilationist ideologies in which it is assumed that the 'foreigner' would adjust and shortly become indistinguishable from the country's nationals although their skin colour might be different. In the cultural domain, the country is expected to maintain its allegedly homogeneous character. Whilst the intentions behind wanting to treat everyone the same might have been 'noble', the universalist position was doomed to failure. For it believed that the equality that it had to achieve in the social sphere was already in place. Moreover, in casting its definitions of reality on this universalistic basis, this approach has failed to acknowledge power differentials in the way in which society has been organised. Particularly important in this regard have been the racialised hierarchies which have been most evident in the employment field and education. The colourblind approach has impacted on social work as a locus of employment and a provider of educational opportunities. Additionally, in endorsing white supremacy, assimilationism has pathologised black cultures and ways of doing things. Furthermore, it has lacked a theory and a practice which is capable of adopting fundamental social change as the cornerstone of its methodology.

Predicated on the importance of securing social change, anti-racist social work sought to undermine racist dynamics by understanding and addressing their complexity. Part of its analysis has entailed dividing racism into several interconnected forms: personal racism which draws on the attitudes and behaviours of individuals who have rejected equality between different racialised groupings; institutional racism which focused on the daily routines and legislation which structured practice, and cultural racism which reflected the values and mores of the dominant ethnic group in society and applying the insights this garnered (to the activities of the social work profession (Dominelli 1988). Moreover, anti-racists such as Dominelli (1988) have argued that the interdependence of these three dimensions of racism has meant that a change in one of these would be accompanied by change in the other two. Thus, a dialectical process of concurrent action, reaction and interaction have to be successfully negotiated if attempts to secure social change are to be realised. This requirement has made countering racism a difficult project and a number of different strategies have had to be utilised in dealing with it.

One of these strategies entails creating legislative changes which make the public demonstration of racist acts illegal. In Britain, for example, the Race Relations Act of 1976 sought to reduce overt expressions of racism in public arenas. Prior to this, their display had been commonplace particularly in the fields of housing and employment. Initially, this move was thought important in eliminating personal forms of racism since this was seen as a primary cause of racism in society. Whilst eradicating personal racism is an important strategy to pursue, it is not enough. A further problem of the legislative approach is that it dwells on the individual and on this basis cannot deal adequately with injustices which have a group orientation. Yet, injustice aimed at individuals because they are members of a particular group is a key feature of racism and the discrimination it engenders. Hoisting erroneous assumptions about a group upon an individual is also a characteristic of racialised stereotyping which leads to discriminatory behaviour.

Public sector welfare agencies were later to incorporate specific strategies into their workplace, including the belief that racism was limited to personal racism and could be tackled by focusing largely on the individual's actions. As a result, racism awareness training became a key feature of the anti-racist struggle in social work. Its emphasis on individuals, their responsibility in countering racism and undertaking action that ensured that nothing illegal was done, was a major advance in getting a particular person to do something about his or her own racism. This enabled the individuals involved to concentrate on the specific personal contribution each of them had made and continued to make in maintaining the edifice of racism. Its major disadvantage was that it could miss the tripartite basis of racist dynamics and the interdependent interaction between them. Thus, a solution which focused only on the individual could not adequately address structural racism in either its institutional or cultural variant.

As a consequence of the failure of such strategies to deal successfully with racism, the idea of positive discrimination in favour of oppressed groups began to take root. This drew on the notion that each group in the population should be represented in key economic activities according to its proportionality in the population (Cahn 1995). Using positive action to reduce racial discrimination, affirmative action was initially formalised in the US during the mid-1960s as part of the 'Great Society' programmes which were aimed at tackling poverty primarily amongst African American black people. Positive discrimination quickly became 'affirmative action'. In its early days, the key arenas in which it operated were the employment field and education. In the beginning, 'affirmative action' was intended to convey the idea that if all other things were equal, for example, their qualifications were the same, a person from either an ethnic minority group or a woman would be given the job or place in college (D'Souza 1995).

Whilst this version of positive action was adhered to in a number of places, others quickly diluted its principles in their 'pure' form. Part of the reason for this change of tact was the failure of employers and educational establishments to recruit sufficient numbers of suitably qualified black people and white women to make a major impact on their lack of representation in key areas of public life. Eventually, the system of 'quotas' for different ethnic groupings and women was created to fill this gap. Under its procedures, the principle of proportionality was to be maintained by ensuring that each major ethnic group would be represented according to its presence in the population. The introduction of 'quotas' and 'contract compliance' as the mechanisms through which positive discrimination was enacted provided the driving force which led to the rapid expansion of positive action schemes. Following through on the requirements these imposed has also enabled firms and universities to access the additional funding that have been made available through affirmative action programmes for those who met the appropriate quotas.

It did not take long for the standards required of applicants for either jobs or places in universities to be lowered to fill set quotas (D'Souza 1995). Such developments set the scene for those opposing affirmative action to undermine its objectives and exaggerate its limited achievements (Cahn 1995). Conservative writers and the media also began orchestrating hostility towards affirmative action policies and practices and fanned feelings of frustration experienced by white men (Wilson 1995). Moreover, as far as the popular white consciousness was concerned, the black people benefiting from affirmative action initiatives began to be deemed incapable of competing fully with their qualified white peers. The belief that black people got jobs or places in universities which they did not merit, gained ground. Soon, white men started to openly express their frustration with this mechanism and commenced a strong protest movement which insisted that they were now the ones who were being discriminated against (Cose 1993). They coined the term 'reverse discrimination' to name their plight. During the 1990s, their voices grew louder and they organised attempts to rescind what they labelled unwarranted gains made by women and ethnic minority groups (Ayres 1995; Barrett and Zachary 1995; Johnson 1995). Proposition 209 passed by the electors of California in the US in late 1996 was one piece of legislation designed to achieve this purpose.

Though potent, the view espoused by these white men – that white men have become the underdogs – is largely misplaced. They do not reflect the dominant picture evident in the social structure of American society. White middle-class men still dominate the higher echelons of the American economy and political scene where the most important social decision making bodies are located. Women and black people in the US have made gains only in a few areas of employment and are largely segregated into particular job categories and rise only up to a certain level (Swoboda 1995). Thus, a gendered and racialised division of labour persists. The shortage of blue-collar jobs for white working-class men is attributable to the decline of manufacturing industries as the outcome of the processes of globalisation which has transfered 400,000 manufacturing jobs from the West to Third World countries with lower production costs and less well-unionised workforces (Dominelli and Hoogvelt 1996).

Alongside those white men who have expressed dissatisfaction with the affirmative action system because they feel that it has treated them unfairly, others have questioned the principles on which this policy has been based (Duke 1991). Some of these critics, for example (Galeano 1992), have questioned the legitimacy of asking a particular individual to personally bear the cost of putting right past injustices committed by one group against another. These people have argued that affirmative action runs the risk of unfairly penalising an individual who may have played no specific role in discriminating against either black people or white women. They do not think that the issue of one individual enjoying taken-for-granted privileges which have been founded on the capacity of people who share membership of a particular group to exploit those of another group at an earlier point in their history, is relevant.

Another point that has been raised by the opposition to affirmative action is that it undermines the principle of meritocracy by giving preferential treatment to people who do not have the requisite qualifications to meet the job specifications or course admissions requirements (Brooks 1996). The failure to uphold the merit system has been interpreted as an unjustified lowering of the standards for a particular occupation or course. This position has also been used to reinforce prejudiced views that women or black people are unable to perform to the standards that white men are expected to reach. Furthermore, this conclusion has been generalised to encompass all people from a particular category whether they have gained their posts as a result of affirmative action or through their own merit. Thus, the stereotyping of white women and black people has assumed a new form. Some African Americans have also bewailed this development and rejected the idea that 'the system' has been responsible for the inability of black people to make it in economic terms over the decades during which the gains of the civil rights movement have been in place (Steele 1990). Personal responsibility for one's own position whether at the top or the bottom of the scale have been called in to fill the void this failure has created.

The controversies over affirmative action have encouraged the abandonment of the idea of securing justice for groups of people who have been wronged historically, whether on gender or 'race' grounds. However, even those whose opinions endorse the rejection of this policy suggest that compensation can be an appropriate method of discharging this historical debt. But recently, even this view is falling into disrepute as some of its supporters have begun to feel that 'affirmative action' has become a problematic way of achieving a compensatory outcome. That some individuals who might have been privileged under the old system now lose out can be accepted by some as an inevitable by-product of a response which is not intended to last forever. Yet, despite the thirty years that affirmative action has been practised, the end does not seem to be in sight. None the less, compensation remains the best system for addressing the issue of righting past wrongs that has been devised in the current circumstances.

Other people accept the principle of compensation, but have argued that this should have been addressed at the time that the offences were committed so that the guilty party and the one to whom the reparation was due could be more easily determined and paid directly rather than being put into effect many years later when the evidence for assessing individual damage and apportioning personal culpability were no longer readily available. One reasoning behind this position on the 'race' front is that it is now difficult to decide the level of compensation owed to each person because it is impossible to ascertain how much harm has been done to each individual as a result of a system of slavery which ended some while ago, let alone how to determine what each of them might have achieved had slavery not impeded their progress (Cahn 1995). Proponents of this view have also maintained that as the issue of compensation is too hard to sort out fairly, it is reasonable to conclude that nothing should be done about it. Thus, those adhering to this position have felt that not providing compensation under these conditions is a morally acceptable option (Hacker 1992). This stance is problematic because it penalises those who have suffered injustice without dealing with the advantages that have accrued to those who benefited from an unjust system.

Another group has focused on the impracticality of allocating culpability through the method of aribitrarily assigning individual responsibility to each person for the purposes of calculating the amounts of compensation to be paid by them individually because doing otherwise would be difficult given the absence of historical data on which to base this computation. In relation to 'race', this opinion has been rationalised on two different grounds. One is that identifying particular acts of exclusion is not the same as proving who has committed them and working out what the compensation due is as a result of this (Hacker 1992). The other is that only those white people who have benefited directly from specific instances of racial oppression are liable. The rub is in proving or agreeing who composes this group – all white people, rich white people, white middle-class men, white working-class men, white men? In the US, this latter view is also complicated by virtue of the racism experienced by white groups not directly involved in institutionalising slavery. These include more recent immigrants, particularly those from Asia and Latin America, people of Jewish or Irish descent and others who have also been discriminated against by white Anglo-Saxon Americans because of their racial or ethnic backgrounds.

In Britain, affirmative action in the sense of preferring one racial group over another or establishing quotas for particular ethnic groups, is illegal, although aiming for a more equitable system of representation by setting loose targets to be reached is not. Additionally, it is possible to obtain an exemption from the Race Relations Act (RRA) 1976 for what is called a 'genuine occupational qualification' (GOQ). This part of the legislation restricts applicants to a particular post to those specified and must be argued for on a case-by-case basis, for example, advertising for someone of Arabic origins for the post of mullah (Islamic priest) in a mosque. Successfully petitioning for GOQ status means that an employer will not be sued for restricting jobs to particular categories of people. However, the use of GOQ exemptions has not proved fashionable. There are few situations in which it genuinely applies. Moreover, people have felt uncomfortable arguing for exceptions of this nature. Hence, the use of GOQ has not been invoked frequently in the British context.

None the less, British social services departments have used such exemptions to attract social workers from specified ethnic minority groups to work with members of the public who share their ethnicity. Whilst indicating a commitment to increasing the representation of ethnic minority social workers and obtaining a broader cross-section of the population in the practitioners' ranks, this practice has carried the risk of locking ethnic minority practitioners into work aimed exclusively at ethnic minority groups or short-term employment which has not allowed these social workers to develop a career in mainstream grades. Consequently, many social workers from ethnic minority groups have been restricted to inhabiting a professional ghetto in which low pay and job insecurity are a normal part of their working conditions.

The British situation also differed from the American one in that slavery was not systematically practised on the British mainland. Thus, the slave trade which has nourished cities like Liverpool has been less directly visible to the bulk of their inhabitants than it has been in the American Deep South where the master-slave relationships characteristic of plantation society flourished openly. Hence, the experiences of black Britons are not strictly analogous to those endured by African Americans. The rejection of black British people as an integral part of the country's social makeup and their exploitation as low-paid waged labour, however, has made racialised class relations an important aspect of racial conflict in the UK. Furthermore, the role that black British people have played in advocating for the world-wide abolition of slavery and getting this action accepted by the general British populace has affected interracial relations by emphasising black people's abilities to take control of their own lives and shape history. These actions have emphasised their strengths and resilience and challenged white people's stereotypes of them as passive victims of white people's dictats. For these reasons, it is important that the experiences of racism which have impacted upon black Britons are theorised and understood in their own specific terms. Without this, it would be difficult to develop effective services that are appropriate to their particular needs.

The rejection of US-style affirmative action in Britain has meant that initiatives aimed at remedying racial injustices have been based on having a twin-track approach. One avenue has been that of passing enabling legislation which has made possible the creation of specific services for ethnic minority groups under their own control. Such developments have brought with them the attendant problems of the marginalisation and co-option of black activists (Mullard 1973; Gilroy 1987). The other has been to look for ways of encouraging black people to apply for mainstream jobs in greater numbers and providing access courses to prepare students for entry to the same college classrooms that have housed white students. This latter path has led to a plethora of activities in which black and white professionals have sought to spread information about employment and educational opportunities to people living in black communities, for example, by advertising in the black press, leaving information leaflets in black community centres and linking up with voluntary organisations which have attracted a black clientele.

These measures have been useful in getting informative materials through to people who have normally been excluded by the traditional methods of advertising in the predominantly white media. However, these have presumed that the problem has been one of poor communication between the 'races' and lack of opportunities for the education of black people. Proceeding on this basis has individualised the issues and focused on what can be done on the personal level. Consequently, these ways of tackling the issue have been unable to challenge the system of racial discrimination which has curtailed black people's access to jobs and educational opportunities. And, the collective basis on which racial discrimination has been predicated and perpetuated has been ignored. These approaches have also placed the onus for doing something about their situation on the individuals who have been at the receiving end of racial discrimination without doing likewise for the perpetrators. Additionally, these approaches sustain the principles associated with meritocracy, although the application of criteria based on merit have unfair outcomes for those subjected to racial injustice.

Racism has impacted differentially on the diverse groups who come under the umbrella of the term 'black Britons'. Moreover, their experiences have varied according to their ethnicity and gender. For example, black women of African-Caribbean origins have been more successful than their male counterparts in both the education and employment stakes. More recent studies (Modood et al. 1996) have revealed that some Asians from the Indian sub-continent have progressed up the income hierarchy more rapidly and effectively than other Asian ethnic groups, like those from Bangladesh and Pakistan. Despite these gains, the overall size of the black British middle class remains small. Racial discrimination continues to flourish. Black people as a group are, on the whole, employed in low-paying jobs in Britain. They also receive fewer welfare services than white people, but are disproportionately represented in custodial settings. They share these latter two characteristics with their American cousins, despite their different histories. In continental Europe, black people tend also to occupy the lowest echelons of the labour hierarchy. But they usually have fewer social and political rights than British blacks who have recently migrated from 'New Commonwealth countries'. In Britain, these groups can vote in local and national elections after a residential period of one year. People of Irish origins and those from the 'Old Commonwealth' can do likewise.

Although the attempts to address issues of racial discrimination have been limited and their impact on bringing about its demise even more so, white people have often exaggerated the effects of their efforts in tackling it. In relation to social work, black people have been brought into the profession in ways that continue to marginalise their contribution and input (Rooney 1987; Dominelli 1988). So, despite a decade of initiatives on the anti-racist front in British social work, no black person has been appointed chief probation officer. A handful of black men have at some point reached the rank of director of social services. No black woman has reached this level to date. As of the middle of 1997, no black person had achieved the status of professor of social work either. Moreover, those black people currently in social work posts are expected to respond to the 'race' agenda in addition to carrying the same workload as their white colleagues. Whether black people are front-line workers or managers, the racist dynamics inherent in this treatment subjects them to a heavier burden of work (Rooney 1987; Ahmad 1990, 1992; Dominelli 1997). At the same time, service provision continues failing to meet black people's needs (Ahmad 1990).

Meanwhile, white people remain fearful of challenging black people even when the circumstances in a given situation make it imperative that they do so, because they want to avoid being labelled racist. This fear paralyses them into inaction through which bad practice and poor service delivery can be perpetrated (Ahmed 1982). In instances like cases of child abuse, such incapacity on the part of white workers can cost black 'clients' their lives, and has happened for some black children (see Blom-Cooper 1986). These weaknesses show the failure of anti-racist social work to become a method of working that white practitioners understand fully and feel confident in using effectively. But despite this problem, the opinion formers leading the white backlash against the stated objectives of anti-racist social work have been forcefully arguing its redundancy by exaggerating the beneficial impact of a colourblind approach to black people's well-being.

In Britain, the backlash was particularly virulent during the summer of 1993 when the popular press attacked anti-racist social work practitioners and educators for being 'politically correct' instead of engaging in sensitive practices which did not offend white sensibilities (see Appleyard 1993; Pinker 1993; Phillips 1993). Rather than demonstrating their case with factual evidence, the campaign was carried out on the basis of rhetoric and innuendo masquerading under a cloak of concern about the damage that anti-racist social workers were wreaking on vulnerable black clients. Their perspective was clearly one of endorsing the colourblind activities of white supporters of the status quo and the abolition of anti-racist social work. What they did not do was to consider the position of black people and their critique of the inadequacies of the system from which they expected to receive services suitable to their needs. Neither did these self-appointed critics of anti-racist social work mention the plight of black academics who had earlier been compelled to leave their places of employment for criticising the racist nature of the courses on which they had taught.

The attack these opponents mounted was aimed at trivialising anti-racist social work on the grounds that anti-racist initiatives had become an unnecessary response to a problem anti-racists had blown out of proportion because racism in British society had been virtually eliminated. Those who spearheaded the backlash had also attempted to define anti-racist projects as ways of doing a disservice to the interests of black people by distorting their experiences and views of the world. Those against anti-racist social work also sought to impugn the characters of those involved in anti-racist struggles instead of addressing the issues they posed.

Other limitations on the promise of anti-racist social work came through more indirect means. One of these was prompted by the Central Council for Education and Training in Social Work (CCETSW) promoting a competence-based social work paradigm which had been developed through a reliance on a functional analysis of practitioners' tasks. Additionally, CCETSW cut back on funding for practice teaching, thereby leading to the abolition of practice learning centres and impeding the creation of alternative forms of practice. Neither of these approaches were conducive to anti-oppressive practice of which anti-racism formed a part. Hence, black professionals rejected the competence-based model for being unable to address the needs of black people and condemned CCETSW's determination to proceed with competence-based methods of working in the face of opposition to it (Black Assessors 1994; Dominelli 1996). The discarding of CCETSW's Black Perspectives Committee was taken as a further sign of the low priority placed on anti-racist matters.

Conclusion

Racism continues to be a problem in the social fabric of countries throughout Europe. In this context, it is unfortunate that leading politicians have taken anti-immigrant views which feed on racialised stereotypes which portray different people as the 'Other' who is also inferior. The white power-holders' hostile reaction to anti-racist social work is therefore, extremely unhelpful: their opposition detracts resources from flowing into the development of anti-racist services. Thus, the limited starting base that anti-racist social work has had in the field will end up being curtailed even more at a point in time when it needs to expand.

At the same time, affirmative action has only a limited role to play in eradicating racism and promoting more egalitarian racial relations. It is not the way forward for those whose key concern is that of establishing a level playing-field in their attempts aimed at ensuring racial equality. Affirmative action presupposes the equality which needs to be created and it undermines the efforts of black people who are seeking recognition for the skills and talents which they already possess. It is time, therefore, that in the context of a globalisation in which the forms that racism takes have altered, that anti-racist practitioners and educators rethink the ways in which they are conducting their struggles against racial injustice and come up with new ways of moving forward if discrimination is to be effectively countered and eliminated.

Note

1   Identity is a complex social phenomenon and needs to be understood in its complexity. In this article, I use the term 'black' in its political sense to indicate groups of people who have been at the receiving end of racism. The term should not be taken to imply that this group or any other racialised group, including white people, are a homogeneous category.

References

Adas, M. (1989) *Machines as the Measure of Men: Science, Technology and the Ideologies of Western Dominance*. Ithaca: Cornell University Press.

Ahmad, B. (1990) *Black Perspectives in Social Work*. Birmingham: Venture Press.

Ahmad, B. (1992) *A Dictionary of Black Managers in White Organisations*. London: National Institute for Social Work.

Ahmed, S. (1982) 'Social Work with Minority Children and Families', Unit 16 in *Ethnic Minorities and Community Relations*, Course No. E354. Milton Keynes: Open University.

Appleyard, B. (1993) 'Why Paint so Black a Picture?', *The Independent*, 4 August.

Ayres, D. (1995) 'Conservatives Forge New Strategy to Challenge Affirmative Action' in *New York Times*, February 16, p. A–22.

Barker, M. (1981) *The New Racism: Conservatives and the Ideology of the Tribe*. London: Junction Books.

Barrett, P. and Zachary, G.P. (1995) 'Race, Sex Preferences could become a Target in Voter Shift to Right', *Wall Street Journal*, January 11, p. A–11.

Bjorgo, T. and Witte, B. (1993) *Racist Violence in Europe*. London: Macmillan.

Black Assessors (1994) 'DipSW Consultation a Sham' in *Community Care*, 13–18 October.

Blom-Cooper, L. (1986) *A Child in Trust: The Report of the Panel of Inquiry into the Circumstances Surrounding in the Death of Jasmine Beckford*. London Borough of Brent: Kingswood Press.

Bossi, U. (1992) *Vento Dal Nord. La Mia Lega*. Milan: Sperlieg Kupfer Editori.

Brooks, D. (ed.) (1996) *Backward and Upward: The New Conservative Writing*. New York: Vintage Books.

Cahn, S.M. (ed.) (1995) *The Affirmative Action Debate*. New York: Routledge.

Chambers, I. and Curti, L. (eds) (1996) *The Post-Colonial Question: Common Skies, Divided Horizons*. London: Routledge.

Cheetham, J. (1972) *Social Work with Immigrants*. London: Routledge.

Cheles, L., Ferguson, R. and Vaughan, M. (1991) *Neo-Fascism in Europe*. Harlow: Longman.

Cose, E. (1993) *The Rage of a Privileged Class*. New York: Harper Collins.

Dominelli, L. (1988) *Anti-Racist Social Work*. 2nd edition published in 1997. London: BASW/Macmillan.

Dominelli, L. (1996) 'Deprofessionalising Social Work: Anti-Oppressive Practice, Competences and Postmodernism', *British Journal of Social Work*, Spring.

Dominelli, L. (1997) *Sociology for Social Work*. London: Macmillan.

Dominelli, L. and Hoogvelt, A. (1996) 'Globalisation and the Technocratisation of Social Work', *Critical Social Policy*, Spring.

D'Souza, D. (1995) *The End of Racism: Principles for a Multi-Racial Society*. New York: Free Books.

Duke, L. (1991) 'Cultural Shifts Bring Anxiety for White Men', *Washington Post*, January 1, p. A–14.

Galeano, E. (1992) *We Say No: Chronicles 1963–1991*. New York: W.W. Norton.

Gilroy, P. (1987) *Their Ain't No Black in the Union Jack*. London: Hutchinson.

Gordon, P. (1984) *White Law: Racism in the Police, Courts and Prisons*. London: Pluto.

Hacker, A. (1992) *Two Nations: Black and White, Separate, Hostile, Unequal*. New York: Ballantine Books.

Hernstein, R.J. and Murray, C. (1994) *The Bell Curve: Intelligence and Class Structure in American Life*. New York: Free Press.

hooks, b. (1992) *killing rage; ending racism*. Harmondsworth: Penguin.

Johnson, T. (ed.) (1995) *The New Conservatives*. New York: Free Press.

La Rose, T. (1991) *Neo-Fascist Violence in Europe*. London: Runnymede Press.

Lorde, A. (1984) *Sister Outsider*. New York: Falling Wall Press.

Madood, T., Werbner, P., Beishon, S. and Virdee, S. (1997) *Ethnic Disadvantage in Britain: The Fourth National Survey of Ethnic Minorities in Britain – the PSI Report*. London: PSI.

Mullard, C. (1973) *Black Britain*. London: Allen and Unwin.

Phillips, M. (1993) 'An Oppressive Urge to End Oppression', *The Observer*, 1 August.

Pinker, R. (1993) 'A Lethal Kind of Looniness', *The Times Higher Educational Supplement*, 10 September.

Rooney, B. (1987) *Resistance to Change*. Liverpool: Liverpool University.

Steele, S. (1990) *The Content of our Character*. New York: St Martin's Press.

Swoboda, L. (1995) *Job Discrimination in the United States*. New York: Random House.

Walraff, G. (1991) *Faccia da Turcco*. Salerno: Tullio Pivonte Editore.

Wilson, J.K. (1995) *The Myth of Political Correctness: The Conservative Attack on Higher Education*. London: Duke University Press.

4 Social Work and Independent Living

Bob Sapey

Abstract

This chapter examines the potential for anti-discriminatory practice with disabled people. The key to this is whether social workers are able to help disabled people to achieve the goal of independent living. The conflicts between the functional and civil rights interpretations of independence are explored and related to models of disability, social policy developments and changes in social work practice.

The paper asserts that acceptance and understanding of the social model of disability is a pre-requisite for anti-discriminatory practice. It also argues that despite the clear influence of the individual model of disability in the formulation of social policy, the Community Care (Direct Payments) Act 1996 offers the best opportunity for independent living since 1948 and that social workers are potentially influential in its implementation. However, it will be necessary for them to make some changes in practice if they are to assist in the removal of disabling barriers, including their own history of oppression.

Introduction

Independent living has been and remains one of the main aims of the disabled people's movement. It is dependent on a number of other issues such as education, employment, housing and personal assistance. Social workers play a key role in the provision of some of these services, particularly personal assistance and housing. This paper seeks to review the current practice of social work with disabled people in the United Kingdom and consider whether it has the potential to contribute towards independent living and if so, how. While an examination of past and current social work practice might reveal something of the answer to this question, it would be largely meaningless in the absence of a clear understanding of what is meant by independent living and of the structures within which social workers operate. To understand the meaning of independent living, it is necessary to explore the conflicting models of disability employed by welfare professionals and disabled people, while the structural context requires an examination of the legal constraints and opportunities that exist within contemporary social policy.

What is 'independent living'?

There are two competing views of what independent living means. The first of these which has been dominant within welfare professions is essentially a functional analysis of what people are able to do for themselves. This approach is concerned with the deficits of individuals which are measured in relation to a concept of normality from which people with physical impairments are deemed to deviate. As such it aspires to correct faults or at least to make up in some way for the difficulties they experience through the provision of aids, adaptations and rehabilitation. At its core however is its focus on the individual and this leads to what Brisenden has termed an 'ideology of independence'. He suggests that disabled people become victims of this ideology as:

> It teaches us that unless we can do everything for ourselves we cannot take our place in society. We must be able to cook, wash, dress ourselves, make the bed, write, speak and so forth, before we can become proper people, before we are 'independent'. (Brisenden, cited in Morris 1993: 8)

The alternative view of independence comes from the disabled people's movement and is concerned less with the ability of individuals to undertake tasks themselves than with their right to determine how, where and when these are done. The focus therefore shifts from the inadequacies of the individual to the barriers that confront people with impairments, both in the physical sense and in terms of constraints on autonomy. However this is much more than an alternative functional analysis of those barriers as the assumptions on which its philosophy is based indicates:

- that all human life is of value;
- that anyone, whatever their impairment, is capable of exerting choices;
- that people who are disabled by society's reaction to physical, intellectual and sensory impairment and to emotional distress have the right to assert control over their lives;

– that disabled people have the right to fully participate in society. (Morris 1993: 7)

While the functional model of independence draws on medical, psychological and sociological concepts of normality, this competing model argues its case on the basis of human rights within a recognition and valuing of the range of human diversity. As such it rejects the concept of a normal human being and instead argues that people are disabled by a societal reaction to any deviation from a socially constructed perception of normality. This is the basis of the social model of disability.

Finkelstein (1980) argues that an individual model of disability is the product of a failure to see disability as a social relationship. He suggests that the normative understanding of disability arises from the helper–helped relationship that places the focus on the disabled person as the one requiring help and therefore the one with the problem. This relationship, that has been constructed by non-disabled people but has become the hegemony for both disabled and non-disabled people, is one that fails to see disabled people other than as dependent. In rejecting the individual model he argues that the term disability should instead be seen as a process of oppression and exclusion of people with impairments by a society which takes no account of their individual or collective needs.

Oliver (1983) developed this social model in an examination of the role of social work with disabled people in which he argued that the individual model of disability, which had been the primary influence in the development of social work practice, was incoherent for two reasons. First it is essentially deterministic, that is to say, it holds that impairment necessarily leads to a range of predictable outcomes for the individual; secondly, it fails to accord with the experiences of disabled people. Social work, he argues, has developed the theoretical basis for its practice within a paradigm of thinking that enables social workers to impose their definition of reality on their clients. The social model on the other hand represents a paradigm shift which would challenge the assumptions of knowledge that have been made. He explains:

> This social model of disability, like all paradigms, fundamentally affects society's world-view and, within that, the way particular problems are seen. If the problem of housing for disabled people is taken as an example, the individual model focuses on the problems that disabled people encounter in terms of getting in and out, bathing, access to the kitchen, the bedroom, and so on. In short the approach focuses on the functional limitations of individuals in attempting to use their own environment. The social model, however, sees disability as being created by the way housing is unsuited to the needs of particular individuals. Thus we have 'housing disability'. (Oliver 1983: 24–5)

The challenge for social work was to develop ways of practising that would be consistent with theorising of disability as a form of oppression caused by social reactions to impairment rather than pathologising the individual. Finkelstein (1991) however has argued that social work is also part of the problem because of its position within the structure of welfare. By placing disability policy within the arena of welfare we reinforce the notion that the problem lies within the disabled person. The individual model of disability treats the needs of disabled people as special and therefore requiring a welfare response; this reinforces rather than removes the barriers to the right of individuals to participate fully within society. This point is also made by Barnes (1997) who argues that the creation of welfare is part of the historical process by which capitalist societies have oppressed disabled people.

While Finkelstein (1991) maintained that the experience social workers have in working with people who are vulnerable or have been oppressed would be beneficial in helping disabled people to assert their rights, he has also suggested that it would necessitate the removal of 'services for disabled people' from the arena of welfare (Finkelstein and Stuart 1996). An overriding message of the social model of disability for social workers therefore is that they must not make the false assumption that it is the presence of an impairment that results in the need for social work intervention. The assumption of such a causal relationship is a fundamental problem of the individual model in that it ignores social relationships in the process of disablement.

At a practical level the conflict between these two models of disability and definitions of independence have been most pronounced in relation to the provision of segregated institutional care. The experience of segregation, which has not been limited to nursing and residential homes but is also integral to much home care (Feidler 1988; Morris 1993), has been instrumental in the foundation of the disability movement. In Britain, the current political organisation of disabled people began in the 1960s with the actions of people such as Paul Hunt who 'was one of the first disabled people to confront segregation and institutionalisation as a form of oppression' (Campbell and Oliver 1996: 18). In a parallel development in the United States, Ed Roberts, a student at the University of California at Berkeley, began to challenge the assumptions that had been made about the position of disabled people in society:

> In the beginning Roberts himself wasn't sure a 'crippled' man belonged on a college campus like Berkeley. Limited opportunities 'did not seem like discrimination,' he says, only something to be expected. 'We had such strong feelings of inadequacy.'

On the Berkeley campus, however, Roberts watched as black students and women students challenged similar assumptions about their assumed inferiority. 'When women talked about being objects, I understood,' he recalls. When blacks and women talked about the power of language, 'underneath I got more and more angry at the way people perceived me as a vegetable with no future.' Adds Roberts, 'We were all talking about the same issues'. (Shapiro 1994: 1)

In Berkeley, Roberts and other students started the Physically Disabled Students Program with the help of a small federal grant and later in 1972, when many of them had left the university campus, they formed the first Center for Independent Living (CIL) so that disabled people could help each other to find jobs, housing and personal support. In the US the CILs were able to bid for federal and state funds and to take over the provision of services for disabled people. By doing this on the basis of disabled people being in control of the way services were provided, the CILs were able to reject the institutional solutions that had been provided in the past (Shearer 1984). Their campaigning eventually led to a more radical outcome than the restructuring of welfare with the passing of comprehensive anti-discrimination legislation in the Americans with Disabilities Act 1990 (Oliver 1996). However, despite this success, welfare policy in the US still ensures that 80 per cent of the Medicaid budget for support to disabled people is spent on nursing homes.

In the UK, the 1948 National Assistance Act which was one of the foundations of the modern welfare state, placed the responsibility and funds for providing personal care services with local authorities. While they were permitted and did fund the provision of care in registered homes run by voluntary organisations, it was illegal for them to make payments to individuals for personal care, and their institutional practices meant that the only contracting of services undertaken was with established charities. In effect this prevented groups of disabled people from taking over in the way that the CILs had in the US. The alternative approach here led to the formation of the Disablement Income Group (DIG) which aimed to pressurise the government into providing a national disability income to all disabled people as of right, but this campaign was vulnerable to co-option and soon became a bandwagon for the large disability charities, that were controlled by non-disabled people and which did not address the concerns of those people who were struggling to escape from residential care (Oliver 1996). As a result, the Union of Physically Impaired Against Segregation (UPIAS) was formed and in its statement of Fundamental Principles of Disability it declared:

Of course the Union supports and struggles for increased help for physically impaired people, there can be no doubt about our impoverishment and the need for urgent change. However, our Union's Aims seek the 'necessary financial ... and other help required from the State to enable us to gain the maximum possible independence in daily living activities, to achieve mobility, undertake productive work and to live where and how we choose with full control over our lives. (Cited in Oliver 1996: 24)

As in the US, disabled people in Britain are rejecting the institutional solutions of the welfare system within which social workers are prominent – they are involved in the admission of disabled people into institutions, they often help to staff them and their administration of community services is commonly experienced as segregating. What is being sought are structural changes that would permit disabled people to be free of the constraints of a social relationship that results in their oppression and segregation and as such, a major aim of the disabled people's movement has been the passing of effective anti-discrimination legislation (Barnes 1991). Although the Disability Discrimination Act 1995 has now reached the statute book, this has been criticised for both making discrimination legitimate in certain circumstances and for the government's failure to provide the structural support to ensure its implementation (Gooding 1996). Currently, therefore, it is through a range of welfare enactments that the lives of disabled people and their hopes for independent living are controlled.

Social policy and disability

Between 1948 and 1990, the National Assistance Act has been amended and supplemented by three pieces of legislation that directly affect disabled people. The first of these, the 1970 Chronically Sick and Disabled Person's Act, gave local authorities the duty to provide a range of community-based services. However this Act was never properly funded and because of its original status as a private member's Bill, there have been continual legal arguments over whether it placed a duty on local authorities, or simply empowered them, to provide these services. Later in 1986, another private member's Bill succeeded to become the Disabled Persons (Services, Consultation and Representation) Act. While this attempted to close some of the loopholes that local authorities had used to avoid the provision of services, it was quickly superseded by the National Health Service and Community Care Act 1990 which transferred the responsibility for much of the funding of services from the Department of Social Security (DSS) to local authorities. In addition it introduced certain free-market principles to curtail the cost of these services and promoted a change in the practice of social work to achieve this, known as a 'needs-led' service.

The White Paper 'Caring for People' (Department of Health 1989) that preceded the 1990 Act and the subsequent policy and practice guidance (Social Services Inspectorate 1991a and 1991b) were all critical of the way in which social work agencies had solely concerned themselves with whether people needed the services they already offered and proposed the 'needs-led' approach as the solution. Taken in isolation of other policy developments at that time, this appears to be a viable response to what was clearly an unacceptable situation. Much of the available provisions were institution-based and needs for services were judged not in terms of the goals of individuals but on the basis of their ability to become more functionally independent as a result of receiving them i.e. they were based on the individual model.

Furthermore, even those services which were geared towards helping people to live independently at home were often run to the convenience of the provider, rather than the recipient. Macfarlane (1996: 7) comments on the way disabled people have experienced the rota system of home care services as 'being put into a "queue" which means there is a "waiting time" for most people which quickly becomes "wasting time" for the majority in the queue.' However, the 'needs-led' solution was part of a package of reforms that also involved the removal of community care payments from the Department of Social Security (DSS) and the Independent Living Fund (ILF). Although DSS payments had been restricted to residential and nursing homes, these were paid as part of the Income Support system and therefore as of right to anyone entering a home who had insufficient funds to meet the costs. There is no reason why the extension of this system to community care could not have been considered as an alternative other than the desire of government to place the funding in an area of welfare where rights could be budget-limited. The ILF made regular and occasional payments which covered the costs of care that local authorities either could not or would not provide, but when this was transferred to local authorities, the budgetary imperative reduced the maximum payments to a level equivalent to the top up payments for nursing homes. The total picture tends to suggest that the policy has more to do with gate-keeping and budget control than meeting the aspirations of disabled people.

The scepticism over the intent of the community care policy finds support both within the disabled people's movement and within social work. Sapey (1993) argued that it represented a continuation of the ideology of the Poor Law in that it is assumed that local authorities that are considered to be best placed to know the needs of an individual. Morris (1993) questioned the meaning behind the rhetoric of the Act and the subsequent statements from local authorities:

> The aim of independent living is held back by an ideology at the heart of community care policies, which does not recognise the civil rights of disabled people but instead considers them to be dependent people in need of care. (Morris 1993: 38)

Thompson (1993) also had doubts about the model of disability that lay behind the policies:

> The current emphasis on 'care management' as a key part of the development of community care also retains the influence of the medical model, for example in the assumption that the professional experts know best what the needs of disabled people are. (Thompson 1993: 114)

In addition to criticising the 1990 Act for reinforcing the role of local authorities as the arbiters of need, the disabled people's movement continued to argue its case for greater control by disabled people of their own personal assistance (Oliver and Zarb 1992; Morris 1993; Zarb and Nadash 1994). One of the results of these studies and the case they argued was the Community Care (Direct Payments) Act 1996 which amends the 1990 Act and fundamentally changes the structure of welfare as laid down in the National Assistance Act 1948, by allowing money to be given directly to disabled people. The case for this re-structuring was both ideological and economic:

> ... developing independent living options like Personal Assistance Schemes is not just morally desirable and professionally appropriate, but also offers the possibility of providing more cost effective and efficient services through switching from the overproduction of services that people don't want or need and the underproduction of those that they do, to a situation where the services that are produced and purchased by statutory providers are precisely the services that users want and need. (Oliver and Zarb 1992: 13)

This market approach was of course central to the 1990 community care reforms but what the implementation of the 1996 Act indicated was the government's intention to shift the purchasing of services from care managers to some disabled people. Their aim in doing this was to 'increase users' independence by giving them more control over the way the community care services they receive are delivered' (Department of Health 1996: Para. 3); the centrality of this Act in the future of welfare was apparent in the recent white paper *Social Services – Achievement and Challenge* (Department of Health 1997). However as with earlier legislation there is a gap between the rhetoric and reality. The guidance issued to local authorities on the 1996 Act makes it clearer than in any previous legislation that the decision to implement direct payments rests with them, not their service users:

> The Act gives local authority social services departments a power to make direct payments. It does not give them a duty to do so. Each local authority may decide for itself whether to use direct payments to meet the needs of its local population and, in each case, for which service or services to offer direct payments. (Department of Health 1996: Para. 6)

While the opportunity for disabled people to gain autonomy over their lives through the control of their own personal assistance now exists within the structures of welfare legislation, its implementation depends on the policies of each of the local authorities with responsibility for social services. Given their history in relation to the many attempts to avoid responsibilities under the 1970 Act and their failure so far to understand the implications of the social model of disability, it is likely to take a considerable campaign by disabled people and their supporters before direct payments becomes a widespread reality. Whether social work can be seen as an ally to such a campaign will depend to a great extent on whether its practice has changed sufficiently to make it part of the solution rather than part of the problem.

Social work practice with disabled people

In the early years of the disabled people's movement, social work practice was drawing upon ideas such as those from Miller and Gwynne (1972) who investigated the role of institutional care in response to the protests of their residents. Miller and Gwynne acknowledged that society's response to impairment through the provision of residential and nursing homes amounted to a process of social death, but because of the prevailing attitudes they brought with them and their prior ignorance of disability issues (Finkelstein 1991), they failed to see the potential for changing this. Rather they promoted what they termed a 'horticultural model' to replace the 'warehousing model' of care that they found to exist. This involved a shift from focusing on longevity to quality of life, a move from the care of the body to the care of the person. This in turn may have encouraged the growth of social care to replace nursing care, but it still maintained that such care would necessarily take place in the residential and nursing homes that were being rejected by disabled people themselves, and did not envisage the possibility of independent living.

In the 1980s social workers were made aware of the problems of the individual model approach with the publication of Oliver's (1983) book,

Social Work with Disabled People, and although it continues to dominate this area of the social work curriculum, there is less evidence that it has achieved the paradigm shift in practice that it called for. The Central Council for Education and Training in Social Work (CCETSW) made clear their support for the social model of disability both in relation to the recruitment of disabled people to social work courses and in terms of practice with disabled clients (Stevens 1991), but this continues to be in conflict with their assertion that anti-discriminatory practice can be undertaken by social workers employed within the disabling institutions that have been the focus of action by the disabled people's movement (CCETSW 1995). On one level this could be taken to simply reflect their 'realism' about the context of social work in Britain and their desire to raise standards and bring about changes in practice. John Thompson, chair of CCETSW England, argues for example that the council has a fine record as an advocate of quality and professional standards and that it continues to be needed as a champion within social work. On the other hand Jane Campbell, Co-Director of the National Centre for Independent Living, is more sceptical about their motivations and criticises CCETSW for continuing to support social work training that does not include working in partnership with disabled people and questions whether the organisation should not be 'razed to the ground' (PSW 1997). It would appear that social work as a profession finds it easy to accept the social model as an alternative to a medical model, but they show little evidence of having distinguished it from Miller and Gwynne's horticultural concept of care.

The problems that CCETSW have in promoting anti-discriminatory practice are compounded by political opposition from government to the stance they took on racism (Humphries 1993; Jones 1993) and by scepticism within the education field that their involvement in the development of competence-based education in alliance with the National Council for Vocational Qualifications is appropriate for an activity that requires communicative, not instrumental skills. Froggett and Sapey have argued in relation to anti-discriminatory practice that the competence approach has left social work:

> ... foundering in the mechanistic application of a political correctness which represents an ill-digested, prescriptive and rule-bound approach to which students must submit or rebel, but which they have little scope to interrogate and own, and the original point of which may well elude them. (Froggett and Sapey 1997: 50)

What is sought is a deeper understanding of the nature of oppression and the development of skills that reflect the complexity of practising social work within a state-sponsored welfare system. One of the key areas in this respect is that of assessing need and an examination of the more recent literature on social work and independent living reveals that some writers have begun to apply the principles of the social model of disability to this process.

Assessment of need has a long history in social work. The nineteenth-century Charity Organisation Society (COS), one of the first employers of social workers, followed the welfare principles of J.S. Mill in making use of skilled assessments to determine if the impact of providing help to each individual was likely to be a 'remedy' rather than a 'sedative' (Green 1992); an approach not dissimilar to that advocated by the current Labour government. A major purpose of assessment was the determination of who was 'deserving' or 'undeserving' of assistance and this continues to influence social work practice, as a recent comment of the ex-chief inspector for social services Sir William Utting demonstrates:

> ... the ways in which some workers discouraged 'dependency' should impress the most fervent advocate of Victorian values, and shows that the spirit of the Poor Law is alive and kicking nearly 50 years after its official internment. (Ellis 1993: 3)

Utting himself is an advocate of the 'needs-led' approach but that too has resulted in criticism from disabled people who experience its effects. Macfarlane (1996) argues that within a welfare system dominated by the individual model, budgetary and professional boundaries have not only led to a large number of assessors becoming involved with each individual, but it has also resulted in the failure to provide such basic services as the assistance to take a shower or a bath, because those involved cannot resolve their arguments over whether the need is medical or social. The solution to this failure of the expert model of assessment is, she argues, a combination of consultation and legal rights for disabled people. However, while involving users of services in the processes of assessment is undoubtedly part of the answer and receives much support (Morris 1994, 1995; Begum and Fletcher 1995), it must be based on a concept of need that is compatible with the social model of disability.

A normative concept of needs, on which the professional expert approach to assessment that dominates social work has been based, has been criticised as 'colonialist' by Doyal and Gough (1991). They seek instead to put forward the case for an objective and universal theory of human need that would allow the focus of debate to move away from what those needs are, to the extent to which any particular society is prepared to meet them. This has a number of clear advantages in that it moves us beyond the problems associated with 'deserving' and 'undeserving', and the influence of budgetary restrictions on the assessment of need, to the real debate which is concerned with our willingness as a society to accept a collective responsibility to meet the rights of all individuals to participate in social life without risk.

By establishing agreed ground-rules for what is needed, it also becomes possible to move away from the position in which it is the expert knowledge of social workers and others that determines need, to one where it is transparent, making it feasible for any informed individual to partake in the assessment. This then permits disabled people to undertake a self-assessment of need within a framework in which it is legitimised rather than belittled as merely their 'wants'. It has been argued within social work (Sapey and Hewitt 1991; Stevens 1991) that this makes use of the expertise of the people who know best what their own needs are and constitutes progress in terms of the role of social workers who would then act in a supportive capacity to self-assessment.

Middleton (1997) however warns that self-assessment can result in an avoidance of responsibility if it is adopted at the level of simplistic rhetoric and suggests that assessment is more than the identification of a list of needs:

> If assessment is to be a purposeful activity, it has to be more than that. Assessment is the art of managing competing demands, and negotiating the most reasonable outcome. It means steering between the clashing rocks of organisational demand; legislative dictates; limited resources; political and personal agendas. It includes having to keep one's feet in an inter-agency setting when the ground beneath them is constantly shifting. It is about making sense of the situation as a whole, and working out the best way to achieve change. (Middleton 1997: 3–4)

This argument recognises the political dimension of assessment, that is whether it is conducted within a social or individual model, but it also acknowledges the institutional and cultural setting within which it occurs. Furthermore, as assessment is a complex issue, it promotes the use of the experience that social workers have in working with disadvantaged groups in assisting disabled people to achieve the goal of independent living. The key issue here, as Finkelstein pointed out, is the influential nature of the helper-helped relationship and what is required is a redefinition of that relationship on the basis of equality and hence participation in the welfare processes.

A recurring theme in this literature is that assessment needs to be an empowering process. This is an argument supported by Ellis (1993) whose research into the participation of users of services in the assessment of their need placed much of the responsibility for achieving this with the professionals involved. She argued that despite the powerless position social workers, occupational therapists and home care organisers may perceive themselves as being in relative to their employing agencies, they do have the discretion to choose between competing models of practice in assessment. Social workers therefore implement the assessment procedures of their agencies and it is they who reinterpret them against the interests of their clients if they so choose. Participation and choice therefore lie to a great extent in their hands.

Holdsworth (1991) takes the argument a stage further by suggesting that it is not only the model of disability within which assessment operates that is important but that the outcomes of that assessment should be geared to services that are empowering. In a similar argument to Doyal and Gough she has equated the needs of disabled people with the right to participate in social life and given that their disability arises from a societal reaction to their impairment, it is this that needs to be overcome. She explains:

> ... much social work practice with disabled people is based on the individual model of disability and seeks to perpetuate predominant societal stereotypes. However, if social workers were to change their way of working, what might be the characteristics of an empowerment model of social work with physically disabled people? Probably the most important of these, having accepted the implications of the social model of disability and the concept of disability as oppression, is the ability to start where the client is, as any individual disabled person could be at any point along a continuum of power and powerlessness and will therefore need a service geared to her specific needs for empowerment. (Holdsworth 1991: 27)

It would be erroneous however to think of empowerment as something that is in the gift of the powerful to the powerless for as Freire (1972) has argued, people can only empower themselves. This appears to have been ignored within social work – as Baistow (1995) has argued, the current trend to incorporate empowerment as an organising principle for institutional change in the public and private sectors is leading to a situation where it not only forms a new tool in the bag of professional social work practice but it may be becoming an obligatory skill. Furthermore she suggests that it is not too far-fetched to imagine a situation in which social work clients might find themselves penalised if they failed to be empowered.

This is easy to see in relation to disability, for if social workers continue to operate in an individual model of disability, empowerment will be seen both in terms of functional independence and as an action of the professionals. Rehabilitation services would be provided to 'empower' people to become functionally independent and those who fail to achieve the goals set for them would be catered for in an institutional manner. The very real danger therefore of much of the practice developments is that unless their adoption is preceded by both an understanding and unambiguous acceptance of the

social model of disability, in which empowerment is integral to the relationship between disabled people, social workers and the welfare state, we may
find that we have turned full circle almost as soon as we have started.

Conclusions

Given its position within the welfare system as a state-sponsored activity,
the forces that shape social work are strong. Finkelstein (1980), Oliver (1990)
and Barnes (1997) have all shown how the hegemony of the individual
model of disability is integral to the development of Western society. While
it may be unrealistic to imagine that social workers can take on and overcome the combined forces of global patriarchy and capitalism that lie at the
roots of oppression (Huntington 1997), they remain the people who are at
the interface of the welfare system and disabled people. We should therefore expect that they will examine the role they play in the perpetuation of
oppression through their relationships with individuals and their employing agencies.

In relation to the former, it is through the nature of the helper-helped
relationship that the concept of care has been constructed and through
which dependency is defined. Social workers need to recognise that independent living is a civil rights issues rather than a functional activity if they
are to effectively incorporate the values of empowerment and the practice of
participation within their everyday activities. While this will not in itself
provide any additional resources for disabled people, it would at least mean
that social workers were working as allies in the cause of independent living
rather than being an impediment to it. Working with disabled people in this
way would be a fundamental step towards changing the social relationships
that have supported the creation of dependency (Oliver and Sapey forthcoming).

While resources are primarily a structural issue that are likely to be
decided at a governmental level, the way in which those currently available
are used is in the control of local authorities. The Community Care (Direct
Payments) Act 1996 provides the infrastructure within which current
resources could be used more effectively in terms of the ideological aims of
independent living and at the same time ensure an increase in the actual
level of personal assistance available because of the economies of this
approach. Local authorities may not have a good record in terms of working within the social model of disability, but it would be wrong to assume
that the blame for this can be attributed to elected members as their policy
decisions are usually made on the advice of their officers. Social workers
occupy a position of privilege in this respect in that they have direct contact

with large numbers of disabled people and are aware of the individual impact of institutional care and segregation, while also being part of the formal hierarchies of the agencies that implement welfare policies. It is therefore the responsibility of social workers who are committed to anti-discriminatory practice, to use the organisational structures through which they report and account for their activities to inform their managers and policy makers of the virtues of the case for independent living.

Acknowledgement

My acknowledgement for his helpful comments on each draft of this chapter to Dr Michael Oliver, Professor of Disability Studies, University of Greenwich, London.

References

Baistow, K. (1995) 'Liberation and Regulation? Some paradoxes of empowerment', *Critical Social Policy*, **42**: 34–46.

Barnes, C. (1991) *Disabled People in Britain and Discrimination; A Case for Anti-Discrimination Legislation*. London: Hurst & Co.

Barnes, C. (1997) 'A Legacy of Oppression: A History of Disability in Western Culture'. In Barton and Oliver (1997).

Barton, L. and Oliver, M. (eds) (1997) *Disability Studies: Past, Present and Future*. Leeds: The Disability Press.

Begum, N. and Fletcher, S. (1995) *Improving Disability Services. The Way Forward for Health and Social Services*. London: Kings Fund Centre.

Campbell, J. and Oliver, M. (1996) *Disability Politics. Understanding Our Past, Changing Our Future*. London: Routledge.

CCETSW (1995) *DipSW: Rules and Requirements for the Diploma in Social Work*. London: Central Council for Education and Training in Social Work.

Department of Health (1989) *Caring for People – Community Care in the Next Decade and Beyond*. London: HMSO.

Department of Health (1996) *Community Care (Direct Payments) Act 1996, Draft Policy Guidance Consultation Paper*. [http://www.open.gov.uk/doh/ccdd-pol.htm] accessed 12/12/96.

Department of Health (1997) *Social Services – Achievement and Challenge*. [http://www.the-stationery-office.co.uk/document/doh/sservice/contents. htm] accessed 12/3/97, or London: HMSO.

Doyal, L. and Gough, I. (1991) *A Theory of Human Need*. Basingstoke: Macmillan.

Ellis, K. (1993) *Squaring the Circle: user and carer participation in needs assessment*. York: Joseph Rowntree Foundation.

Feidler, B. (1988) *Living Options Lottery: Housing and Support Services for People with Severe Physical Disabilities – 1986/88*. London: The Prince of Wales' Advisory Group on Disability.

Finkelstein, V. (1980) *Attitudes and Disabled People: Issues for Discussion.* New York: World Rehabilitation Fund.

Finkelstein, V. (1991) 'Disability: An Administrative Challenge? (The Health and Welfare Heritage)'. In Oliver (1991).

Finkelstein, V. and Stuart, O. (1996) 'Developing new services'. In Hales (1996).

Freire, P. (1972) *Pedagogy of the Oppressed.* Harmondsworth: Penguin.

Froggett, L. and Sapey, B. (1997) 'Communication, Culture and Competence in Social Work Education', *Social Work Education,* **16**(1): 41–53.

Gooding, C. (1996) *Blackstone's Guide to the Disability Discrimination Act 1995.* London: Blackstone Press.

Green, D. (1992) 'Liberty, Poverty and the Underclass: A classical-liberal approach to public policy'. In Smith (1992).

Hales, G. (ed.) (1996) *Beyond Disability.* London: Sage.

Holdsworth, L. (1991) *Empowerment Social Work with Physically Disabled People.* Norwich: Social Work Monographs.

Humphries, B. (1993) 'Are You or Have You Ever Been...?', *Social Work Education,* **12**(3): 6–8.

Huntington, A. (1997) Personal correspondence with Bob Sapey.

Jones, C. (1993) 'Distortion and Demonisation: The Right and Anti-racist Social Work Education', *Social Work Education,* **12**(3): 9–16.

Macfarlane, A. (1996) 'Aspects of intervention: consultation, care, help and support'. In Hales (1996).

Middleton, L. (1997) *The Art of Assessment: Practitioners' Guide.* Birmingham: Venture Press.

Miller, E. and Gwynne, G. (1972) *A Life Apart.* London: Tavistock.

Morris, J. (1993) *Community Care or Independent Living.* York: Joseph Rowntree Foundation.

Morris, J. (1994) *The Shape of Things to Come? User-led Social Services.* London: National Institute for Social Work.

Morris, J. (1995) *The Power to Change. Commissioning Health and Social Services with Disabled People.* London: King's Fund Centre.

Oliver, M. (1983) *Social Work with Disabled People.* Basingstoke: Macmillan.

Oliver, M. (1990) *The Politics of Disablement.* Basingstoke: Macmillan.

Oliver, M. (ed.) (1991) *Social Work, Disabled People and Disabling Environments.* London: Jessica Kingsley.

Oliver, M. (1996) *Understanding Disability. From Theory to Practice.* Basingstoke: Macmillan.

Oliver, M. and Sapey, B. (forthcoming) *Social Work with Disabled People,* 2nd edition. Basingstoke: Macmillan.

Oliver, M and Zarb, G. (1992) *Greenwich Personal Assistance Schemes: An Evaluation.* London: Greenwich Association of Disabled People.

PSW (1997) 'So what would you do with CCETSW?', *Professional Social Work,* September: 6–7.

Sapey, B. (1993) 'Community Care: Reinforcing the Dependency of Disabled People', *Applied Community Studies,* **1**(3): 21–9.

Sapey, B. and Hewitt, N. (1991) 'The Changing Context of Social Work Practice'. In Oliver (1991).

Shapiro, J.P. (1994) *The New Civil Rights.* [http://www.eskimo.com/~dempt/crights.htm] accessed August 1995.

Shearer, A. (1984) *Centres for Independent Living in the US and the UK – an American*

Viewpoint. London: King's Fund Centre.

Smith, D. (ed.) (1992) *Understanding the Underclass*. London: Policy Studies Institute.

Social Services Inspectorate (1991a) *Care Management and Assessment: Managers' Guide*. London: HMSO.

Social Services Inspectorate (1991b) *Care Management and Assessment: Practitioners' Guide*. London: HMSO.

Stevens, A. (1991) *Disability Issues*. London: CCETSW.

Thompson, N. (1993) *Anti-Discriminatory Practice*. Basingstoke: Macmillan.

Zarb, G. and Nadash, P. (1994) *Cashing in on Independence*. London: Policy Studies Institute for the British Council of Disabled People.

5 Facing our Futures: Discrimination in Later Life

Mary Marshall and Cherry Rowlings

Abstract

Although ageism in social work has received less attention than other forms of oppression such as sexism or racism, it exerts a powerful influence on policy and practice. This chapter examines understandings of age, ageing and old age and considers what may lie behind the separation of old age from, in particular, the rest of adulthood. Through focusing on social work with people with dementia, the authors illustrate the ways in which ignorance and negative assumptions can stultify practice. Examples are provided of positive practice which values individuality and inclusion and which seeks to establish social work practice with older people as truly 'person-centred'.

Introduction

Ageism is a powerful and pervasive force in UK society. Strictly speaking, it refers to the negative discrimination, disadvantage and oppression that may be experienced by a person of any age, by virtue of nothing more than their chronology – their 'existence in the passing of time' (Améry 1994: 1). This chapter, however, focuses on ageism in the context of old age, which is how the term is most widely used. We chose the title deliberately, as a reminder that, providing we survive, we will all become old and therefore vulnerable to institutionalised and personal ageism, including the internalisation of ageist beliefs and assumptions. For, like all powerful oppressions, part of the strength of ageism comes from the way in which those who experience it come to believe in the 'truths' on which it is based.

Our starting point is that we have no need to demonstrate the existence of ageism within social work in the UK. Its prevalence is well established and has been a recurring theme of social work research for over twenty years. In order better to understand what lies within this professional history, it is instructive to note what anti-ageist practice has had to struggle against. In a study conducted in 1974–77, the priorities for social work attention were described as 'first child care, second mental health and third the elderly' (DHSS 1978: 142). A far from atypical view of the needs of older service users was expressed by a respondent in the same study as follows:

> The [unqualified staff] get the sort of cases involving gas or electricity accounts because there are set procedures for dealing with them. I think there is also a pattern for dealing with the elderly in the same way. (DHSS 1978: 143)

Social work with older people was not popular with the majority of qualified staff. It was unqualified staff who worked with older people and the problems of older people and the solutions to those problems have been seen in predominantly practical terms (DHSS 1978, Goldberg and Warburton 1979, Howe 1986). In other words, an assessment of need was in effect an assessment of eligibility for a service, such as home help, day care or bathing aids, or for a resource such as sheltered housing or residential care. Within local authorities across the UK, an unqualified worker could be responsible for assessing need for residential care for an older person but would not be allowed to do this for a child; good practice in terms of preliminary visits to the establishment and a carefully planned admission process over time, regarded as essential if a child were coming into care, did not form part of the routine work with older people.

Textbooks on social work with older people by British writers of the time (Brearley 1975; Rowlings 1981; Mortimer 1982; Marshall 1983) may be seen as attempts to convince qualified workers that problems occurring in *old* age were as appropriate for social work attention as problems at any other age; that it was the nature of the problem and the individual's response to it that made social work intervention appropriate, not the age of the person experiencing the difficulty. The worst expressions of the denial of the human experience of older people detailed above are, it is to be hoped, now something of the past, although our concern about attitudes towards and practice with older people with dementia has prompted us to focus the second half of this chapter on anti-discriminatory practice in this aspect of work with older people.

A major step forward in developing an understanding of the professional role came with the experimental research in care or 'case' management, as it was then called (Challis and Davies 1986), which demonstrated the effectiveness of social work in helping to maintain in the community older people who would otherwise have needed residential care. The studies were full of professional optimism about what could be achieved by social workers working collaboratively with the older person, informal carers, voluntary effort and other professionals. It has been argued by Phillips (1996) that the legislation reforming the provision of health and community care in the UK – the National Health Service and Community Care Act 1990 – has continued the process of establishing social work practice with older people on a more secure footing (she is referring to community-based practice here; qualified social workers on the staff of residential or day care centres continue to be few and far between). There may be (some) truth in what she says but there is no cause for complacency. Petch et al. (1996) have raised questions about whether, whatever the rhetoric and the copious official guidance on the importance of involving service users and their carers in both need assessment and the identification of appropriate responses, the end result is really more of the same rather than the creativity and collaborative effort of those early care management experiments. And a further note of caution comes from Hughes (1995) who contrasts the relatively low level of professional attention given to anti-ageist social work practice and policies compared with the greater interest in anti-racism or anti-sexism. We would agree with her and hope this chapter makes a contribution towards a better understanding of the nature of ageism in professional practice and an improved ability to counter it in ourselves and in others.

We continue the chapter with an exploration of age, ageing and ageism. Given that other chapters focus on other oppressions, such as sexism, racism or disablism, we do not deal separately with how these may impact upon older people. We do, however, recognise that ageing and ageism in the UK cannot be considered in isolation – we grow old as a woman or as a man, as a white person who is part of the majority population or as a black person who is not. Ageism is therefore only one of the 'jeopardies' (Norman 1985) that older people are likely to experience and there will be times when it is hard to know whether ageism is the more or the less powerful negative force in their lives. Many older people come to old age with a history of disadvantage and often oppression, not behind them (for that could imply it is past and out of the way) but *inside* them. Their experience of ageism may therefore go unnoticed, no different from what they have been used to throughout their lives by virtue of their sex, the colour of their skin or their sexual orientation. And indeed, being old may be of less significance to them in terms of their identity than other attributes they have lived with for all or most of their lives. As professionals concerned with the impact of ageism on people's lives, we should not fall into the trap of assuming that our consciousness will be shared or even regarded as relevant by those whom we seek to help.

As previously indicated, the chapter concludes with an examination of ageism specifically in respect of social work with people who have dementia. These are the service users who are most likely to attract the adjectives beginning with 'un' that Améry (1994: 68) has identified as associated with old age: 'unable ..., uncoordinated, unfit ..., unteachable, unfruitful, unwelcome, unhealthy'. We take the view, however, that perhaps the test of our capacity to counter ageism in our own and other people's practice is in the way we respond to that minority of older people who express themselves in ways we cannot readily understand and identify with and whose conversations, perceptions and wishes we struggle to respond to in ways that are meaningful to them and to ourselves and respectful of the person whom we may find so hard to recognise as 'one of us'.

Age, ageing and ageism

Ageing is a process that we experience all our lives, in ourselves and in others. It happens 'without effort' as Featherstone and Wernick (1995a: 8) succinctly describe: 'with aging [sic] all we need to do is stick around, time will do the rest.' More accurately, though, ageing is a combination of processes (biological, social and cultural, to name but three) which interact with each other and also with other attributes of ourselves such as 'race', sex and socioeconomic class. What we inherit, in terms of our genes, and how we exist during the passage of time (our diet, lifestyles, whether we are in employment and, if so, what job we do, and where we live), all impact upon the way in which we grow older and, indeed, how long our ageing continues before we die.

Moreover, because ageing is progressive and, at any stage of our life, our age represents a point of transition between what we were and what we will be, ageing enables us to experience and, it may be hoped, better understand the attributes with which we were born and which are unchanging. These are our 'race', our sex (we acknowledge that there are exceptions here, such as people undergoing a sex change, but the point holds true for the great majority of the population) and, for many who believe sexual expression to be a matter of genetics rather than socialisation, our sexual orientation. For what it means to be black, female, gay or any combination of these attributes is experienced through or mediated by our age, just as our experience of ageing, throughout our life, cannot be divorced from, in particular, our sex and our 'race' (as these influence both patterns of ageing and survival into old age) but also from the way we express our social and sexual identity. Macdonald and Rich (1984) illustrated this forcefully when writing about being an older woman and especially an older lesbian, effectively excluded from the contemporary Women's Movement which was the world of women in early and mid-adulthood who ignored the continuities in the experience of being a woman and a sexual being.

Some would argue (for example, Woodward 1995) that being an older woman continues to be largely ignored by feminists and that older women tend either to be 'socially invisible' in society or portrayed through images that are 'demeaning or "disgusting"' (Arber and Ginn 1991: 36). Yet the story of old age is largely the story of women: more than two-thirds of the UK population aged over 75 are women and it is women (often in late middle age or old age) who provide most of the social support for older people and most of the paid and unpaid care when it is needed. Equally important is that the present story is predominantly a *white* woman's story. The black and Asian populations in the UK are still mainly 'young' populations and it is not until the early years of the next century that we will see a significant proportion over retirement age. Even this, however, could be dwarfed by the far greater numbers of the majority white population, with the result that the black and Asian experience of old age in the UK is at risk of being devalued or ignored. Blakemore (1997) has argued persuasively that a better understanding of ageing and being old requires much greater attention to the ageing of minorities – the patterns of ageing within different minority ethnic groups in the UK (both black and white), the attitudes to and images of old age that younger people from minority groups have of the older people in their own cultural or ethnic community, the way in which age and 'race' may be differently experienced when power rests with the doctor, the nurse or the care assistant who is from a minority ethnic group and not with the older person from the majority population who is now dependent on these professionals for daily survival.

The way in which age divides and old age is separated from rather than incorporated in the rest of adulthood has more recently been described by Jeffreys (1997), in relation to continuing to be an academic whilst retired from her tenured university post. 'Distancing' is the word she uses to describe what has been happening between her younger working colleagues and herself, but initiated by them, not her. Professional continuities have been threatened as a consequence of a socially imposed compulsory retirement age. Throughout our lives, we experience similar divisions based on chronological age: it is used to determine when we are legally required to go to school and when we may legally leave, when we can consent to sexual intercourse, marry without parental permission, exercise a political vote or fight for our country. Time, rather than capacity to perform, is the basis upon which tomorrow we are required or allowed to do something which today we are not. Being subject to the external test of time rather than a personal test of capacity has the advantage of avoiding the need continually to 'prove' one's worth or skill, but the disadvantage of imposing homogeneity when, as we age, so heterogeneity increases. Hence, whilst developmental milestones linked to chronological age offer helpful guidance with regard to very young children, to attempt equivalents for middle or old age is an almost meaningless activity.

Although old age is most frequently measured by time, there are other ways which can be used and which reflect our wish or our need to 'place' people according to their stage of life. Bytheway (1997) has identified a further five means by which old age is conferred, or not as the case might be, on people. He refers to what he calls description (the use of words such as old or elderly which convey accepted meanings), relations (the categorisation of people with reference to their belonging to one generation or another), body (what we look like and whether we 'look old' or 'look young'), pressures or expectations (a reference to responsibilities to and for others which come from being a parent or an adult child and which a child or young person will not have) and biography (an account of the national and personal events that someone has lived through and the range of experiences that has been gained over years). Each or all of these means of categorisation can be used instead of or as supplementary to the reference to chronology. Bytheway's discussion shows how chronological age can be either corroborated or minimised by reference to these other ways of defining age. Examples of corroboration appropriate to this chapter are in comments such as 'at your age, don't you think you should' or (a favourite of professionals) 'well, at your age, you have to expect'. Minimising can be seen in the statement 'I know she is 80 this year but she still walks into town every day.'

If we take an historical perspective on age and ageing, we find that a concern with old age as a separate category in the lifespan is of fairly recent origin. So, too, is the association of old age with problems and deficits. Katz describes the shifts from an eighteenth-century optimism over the marvel of old age – an optimism which believed it was possible to uncover the secret of surviving to be over 100 or even 200 years old – to nineteenth-century constructions of old age as a time of malfunction and illness – a clinical problem and the domain of doctors. Developments in medicine and science were responsible for ending the belief in the potential for longevity and instead replacing this by 'gradually separating old age as a special part of the life course, one marked by systematic signs of senescence' (Katz 1995: 61). But as Hareven has pointed out, the isolation and segregation of old age is part of the more general and recent phenomenon in respect of *all* age groups. Until the twentieth century, adulthood 'flowed into old without institutionalised disruptions. The two major adult roles – parenthood and work – generally stretched over an entire lifetime' (Hareven 1995: 126–7). She notes the way that transitions within the life cycle have generally become 'more clearly marked, more rapidly timed and more compressed in their timing', in contrast to the 'more gradual and less rigid' practices of the nineteenth century (Hareven 1995: 129).

The increasing medicalisation of old age and the reliance upon chronological age as the mechanism for structuring and indeed segregating society can therefore be seen as two separate but related forces that have influenced current attitudes towards old age and professional responses to older people. Social measures such as a compulsory retirement age and provision of 'old age' pensions for women at the age of 60 and men at 65 have strengthened the divide between old age and adulthood and emphasised the *dis*continuity rather than the continuity of ageing. In this way, old age and older people are distanced from other ages and other people.

It is perhaps this distancing which lies at the heart of ageism, for it allows disassociation and encourages denial of the fact that our old age is in us and in us increasingly as we grow older. '"She" will be "I"', says Kathleen Woodward (1995: 92), speaking of the older woman, whilst for Améry, old age is achieved by the personal accumulation of time. It is *'lived* time' (1994: 21) and therefore *'our* time which is always *only* ours' (p. 4, italics in original); 'to be old or even just to feel oneself ageing means to have time in one's body' (p. 15).

Ageism therefore begins with seeing the older person always as 'the other', the one who is different, not necessarily subject to the same thoughts, feelings, aspirations and fears as the non-old. The way society responds to the financial needs of older people offers an example. Poverty is a serious problem for many older people in the UK, especially those who are very old. The gap between those in work and those for whom the universal, flat-rate state retirement pension is the main or sole form of income continues to increase because there is no longer a link between earnings and the level of the pension. Poverty restricts participation in normal everyday life (Townsend 1979) and poverty in old age, caused by an inadequate state pension and low levels of benefit for necessities such as heating, has created a dependency amongst many older people which is a direct consequence of the social policies of this century (Walker 1980, Townsend 1981). A mobility allowance, payable to younger disabled people, is not payable to people who become disabled when they are over retirement age. Legislation – the Community Care (Direct Payments) Act 1996 – that enables some service users, if they wish, to become the budget holders for the community care services they need is directed at younger people; those over pensionable age are explicitly excluded. These expressions of social policy convey assumptions about what is needed and wanted when living in old age compared with living at any other age; they are rarely challenged but instead it is seen as acceptable and not all patronising or demeaning for Government to recognise the low income by providing people receiving the state retirement pension with a £10 'bonus' every Christmas. Since its introduction the sum has never been upgraded in line with inflation, thus in our view compounding the indignity by rendering its actual value increasingly worthless.

For older people needing health or social care, the ageism of professionals is a significant barrier to appropriate service. Impaired hearing may not be investigated as it would be if the person were 15, not 75; residents of old people's homes experience restrictions on the way they conduct their daily life which no one else would want and which, indeed, they do not want either (Willcocks et al. 1987). Old age becomes a reason to justify both the actions and the inactions of those who are not old. An interesting example of this is provided by Latimer in her account of the way nursing and medical staff on an acute medical ward responded to a patient, Jessie, who was aged 91. Jessie was admitted following a major stroke but for the ward Sister 'she's been old for a long time. She had been going downhill' (Latimer 1997: 141). In certain circumstances, illness is constituted:

> as the natural consequence of getting older, of decline. Jessie is being put 'outside' one division, a class of patient (the person who is acutely ill) and into another class (that of old person whose difficulties are chronic and the consequence of a natural order of things, a progressive deterioration and decline). (Latimer 1997: 144)

This recategorisation enables staff on the ward to reassess their responsibility towards Jessie, in effect to reduce their medical one and thereby adopt strategies for care and for discharge which have implications for others rather than themselves. Importantly, though, as Latimer is at pains to point out, the response to Jessie, whilst it may be criticised as ageist, is not only this. It also enables staff to cope with meeting the financial and efficiency targets that are required of each hospital, by defining some patients as 'appropriate' and others as not. In this situation, familiar to many professionals, and certainly not confined to health care, the existence of beliefs and attitudes that are evidently ageist facilitates the continued existence of the institution and implicitly or explicitly may be seen as contributing to what could be termed 'the greater good'.

The story of Jessie reminds us that ageism is there for a purpose and within this purpose, both personal and political (institutional) interests may be served. Phillipson (1982) emphasises the benefits for capitalism in defining both old age and our response to it. And it is true that old age as a time of deficit and uselessness is a feature of advanced industrialised societies, although Wada (1995) would argue that this is tempered in Japan by cultural inheritances which remain strong despite the highly developed economy and the situation of older people in the former USSR suggests that ageism is not confined to capitalist societies alone (Hegelson, 1989). An equally powerful, but personal, interest, however, may be associated with death and dying, which increasingly in the twentieth century have become associated with old age rather than part of the normal life cycle from birth onwards. In industrialised societies, death happens in old age and has no place in a society where youth, health and fitness are highly valued. It is old age that brings us face to face with mortality and, as medical practice advances, with the possibility of survival with limitations and disability. The threat of age-related disease, of which dementia is a prime example, becomes greater as we grow older. Yet, unless we die young, we will die old and that offers opportunities as well as risks. However, the opportunities are difficult to believe in when the purpose of old age seems so unclear. It seems highly unlikely, if it is simply to wait for death, that there should be such a long period between the end of reproductive capacity (for women) or its diminution (for men) and the end of life. This is not, after all, true elsewhere in the animal kingdom. In pre-industrialised societies, older people have often been the teachers, the sharers of knowledge, skills and wisdom; they have also usually been the possessors of wealth and property. In rapidly changing technological societies, knowledge, skill and wealth are equally and often more available to the younger generations. Are we who are not yet old able to appreciate and value the broader experience we all have as a result of being part of a multi-generational society? As family members or as professionals, we may all respond with gratitude and relief when grandparents provide substitute child care or move in with an older relative who would otherwise have needed us to provide care during recovery after a hip replacement. But can we also value the understandings we may gain from sharing the perspectives that come from the experience of an (almost) complete life?

Questions such as these lead all of us to ask of ourselves how we view the purpose and the worth of old age and, in particular, how we view the prospect of our own old age. In our work as educators and trainers of social work and social care staff and students, we typically come across situations where the number of negatives in the discussions of this topic far outnumbers the positives. Fear of ageing is a powerful part of what is being said, often, it seems, more so than fear of death. It is tempting on these occasions for group members and we as their tutors to overcompensate for the prevailing negativity by taking comfort from the 'wonder stories' – the centenarian flying the Atlantic, or the person in his or her eighties who continues to walk the local hills. This is not, however, the way forward. Part of the challenge of developing anti-ageist practice is to be at ease with the normal processes of ageing that will impose some, albeit varying, limitations on physical and mental processes and to neither deny their existence nor to medicalise them (there is no disease called 'old age') nor, conversely, to attribute to normal ageing what are in fact signs and symptoms of illness. This challenge exists for both professionals and older people. The failure to recognise symptomatology is a significant barrier to accessing assessment and treatment. Thus a GP said recently to one of our colleagues 'I just thought your mother was getting old, I didn't think it was dementia' (this was in reply to her questions about why her father's visits to the surgery had met with so little response). And, as Crosbie (1977) showed when he asked older people what advice they would give to one of their contemporaries who had recently become too tired to do the shopping, the suggestion of a visit to the GP to check whether this was due to anaemia or to some other dietary deficiency was not amongst their answers. Instead, they viewed this potentially serious and very probably remediable situation as an inevitable consequence of ageing and something to be addressed by asking someone else to do the shopping or getting the shop to deliver.

So, a proper understanding and an acceptance of the normality of the ageing process in old age is a prerequisite for developing anti-ageist practice. So also is an attention to language. Too often, older people are spoken of in depersonalising terms – 'the elderly' or, perhaps even worse, 'elderly', as in 'this day centre provides a service for 100 Elderly each week'. Elderly *what*, one is tempted to ask. Such expressions encourage lack of differentiation and denial of personal difference, yet may be made in respect of a section of the population that incorporates an age difference of thirty years or more. They are more subtle but probably no less powerful than the obviously pejorative terms such as 'geriatric' or 'wrinklies' which are used either as a deliberate term of abuse (older politicians are particularly at risk of being called 'geriatric' by their opponents) or as a simple description. There is of course no law in the UK against ageism and in considering how old age is represented by ourselves, or by others, it is instructive to ask whether, for example, it would be acceptable to write or speak of black people in equivalent terms. As individuals, our language is something we can control – unlike the negative speech or behaviour of others. But because we are part of a society which is ageist, we will have absorbed this, just as we have absorbed the prejudice against black people, disabled people or women. Thus without thinking, we may say 'I do feel old today' when what we mean is that we feel tired or weary; or we compliment an older person on how 'young' he or she looks instead of saying 'you're looking really well' or 'you look really good in those clothes.'

Starting from the personal, we can then move to the professional, examining how we interact with older service users, how we *in*clude rather than exclude them from the decisions about their life and how we argue for services and systems that are the equivalent for older people of the 'child-centred' practice that is required in child care social work. This means going beyond the 'needs-led' approach to assessment and service provision that is currently emphasised in guidance on how to implement the legislation that has reorganised the provision of community care in the UK (Department of Health 1991). Welcome though this is, as a development from the earlier service-led approach it seeks to replace, the real progress must surely be to a practice which is person-led and not dominated by weakness and deficit. Instead of making negative judgements ('Mr X is isolated'), goal-oriented assessments convey a more positive approach ('Mr X would like to meet more people') and lead more easily to shared problem-solving activity (Barrowclough and Fleming 1986). Converting problems into goals is a technique commonly used with success in other areas of social work, but has not been a feature of work with older people, largely because the professional optimism has not been there to sustain it.

We turn now to the concluding section on social work with people with dementia, as an excellent example of the way in which professional negativity, left unchallenged, can stultify practice and exacerbate the very things we could do something to improve.

Dementia, ageism and social work practice

Recently a social worker telephoned one of us to say that he had read that people with dementia can die when they are moved from one location to another (Siddall 1997). He wanted to know how he could minimise the chances of this happening. We found ourselves quite outraged. For a start, he should have read the article properly and he would have realised that such deaths were by no means inevitable. But more important, as a social worker, he will have been trained to understand the importance of traumatic life changes in the well-being of people and the social work skills that are required. Every textbook about work with older people (Rowlings 1981, Marshall and Dixon 1996, Froggatt 1990) has a substantial section on moving into longstay care, including careful planning and consultation, taking time to familiarise yourself with the new environment, taking as much as possible with you from the old environment, and having rituals surrounding saying goodbye to the old and welcome to the new place. These skills are well established in every aspect of social work: child care, work with adolescents and work with older people. So why did he need to ask?

One possibility is that he did not see people with dementia as people. He did not see them as people with the same feelings as you and me. But an impaired intellect does not mean impaired emotions. It may well mean being unable to explain these emotions or to work out what to do about them. It may also mean that the person with dementia has less understanding of what is going on and why. But they will experience the sense of loss as we all do when we are uprooted.

Dementia is best understood as far as social work is concerned as a disability characterised, in very general terms, by:

- impaired memory
- impaired learning
- impaired reasoning
- high levels of stress
- an acute sensitivity to the social and the built environment.

The last of these is no different from any other disability. The more disabled you are, the more you depend on your social and built environment. Other people have to help you do things and the building has to compensate for your disabilities. Thus if you have a spinal injury and are in a wheelchair, you might need other people to assist you in some of your activities of daily living and you might also need to have a house with no stairs and an adapted bathroom.

There is also increasing recognition in the world of disability that it is the social and the built environment which actually exacerbates the extent of disability. The person with the spinal injury might have her confidence eroded by the way she is treated and might be totally immobilised by an unsuitable building. The concept of excess disability is very useful here. In dementia, this would be when the magnitude of the disturbance in functioning is greater than might be accounted for by basic physical illness or cerebral pathology and it can be caused by:

- untreated or chronic conditions
- overuse of psychotropic or other medications
- excessive noise
- lack of stimulation and exercise
- inappropriate care giver responses
- excessive assistance provided.

Some of these causes may need explanation. For example, noise to someone with an impaired intellect is as disabling as stairs are to someone in a wheelchair (Hiatt 1985); people with dementia can lack the ability to sift noise and are consequently overwhelmed by it. Excessive assistance is unhelpful for anyone with a disability because it undermines skills and competence. This is perhaps especially true for people with dementia who have such fragile confidence in the first place and need every opportunity to practise remaining skills if they are to maintain them.

This disability perspective is not the conventional way to approach dementia. Normally it is introduced by the description of brain damage, in often very complex neurological terms such as plaques and tangles. This can be very intimidating to the non-medical person and may, in some way explain the tendency to see people with dementia as another species with something frightening and incomprehensibly wrong with them. Clearly the neurology is important but, for many professionals, it can be a barrier to approaching someone with dementia as a person with a disability. The 'ownership' of dementia is in a state of flux at the moment. In many European countries it remains firmly in the hands of psychiatric or geriatric medicine. In others the social model is in the ascendancy. In Sweden, for example, the main model of care is group housing. In the UK there is a move towards social care as the psychiatric hospitals shrink and the need to contain the costs of care becomes a crucial consideration. The danger now is that people with dementia will not receive adequate psychiatric and medical care. Failing to recognise a person's (relatively expensive) medical and nursing needs is every bit as discriminatory as failing to see their social and personal needs. Achieving holistic care is everybody's aim but it is very difficult as professionals both off-load responsibility for people with chronic and non-urgent conditions and as they defend their own profession. Conversely there are key professional groups with a supposedly holistic remit, such as GPs, who often fail people with dementia and their carers because they have neither the positive attitude nor the training to provide much-needed continuity and coordination of care.

Dementia is, of course, a relatively new phenomenon in several respects. Alzheimer's disease, which is the main cause of dementia, was only diagnosed in 1907 by Alois Alzheimer. The number of people with dementia has only become significant in the last ten years or so as the baby bulge of the Edwardian era ages. The risk of dementia increases with age. This means that staff trained more than ten years ago are unlikely to have had much, if anything in their training about dementia. Dementia has, until recently, been very much owned by the medical profession and the social perspectives are very new indeed. A leader in the field is Kitwood (1997) whose concept of person-centred care to counteract what he has termed a prevailing 'malignant social psychology' is very influential.

The presence of ageism in dementia care has been helpfully explored by

Phair and Good (1995). In addition, the lack of knowledge about dementia and the new perspectives further explain the lack of interest and understanding by some social workers. We want now to look at some examples of the way that this leads to discrimination by looking at some widely held attitudes:

- 'People with dementia cannot communicate.'
- 'People with dementia are not aware of their condition.'
- 'People with dementia have a progressive and terminal condition so can only deteriorate.'
- 'People with dementia cannot give consent.'
- 'People with dementia are a burden to their carers.'

Before looking more closely at some of these discriminatory assumptions, it is important to make the point that everybody's pathway through the disease of dementia is different. In some traditional textbooks, specialists have attempted to outline stages of dementia and whilst in general terms and probably in an institutionalised population there may be some truth in these stages, a closer acquaintance with any one individual reveals their limitations. This is the same with any other attempt to classify behaviour into stages. Take bereavement, for example. How many of us grieve exactly according to the stages we learn about in the textbooks? We all grieve differently, although we may experience some of the stages, some of the time.

The picture is further complicated in that older people with dementia have long and rich life experiences which will have shaped them: we get more and more different one from each other, as we age. They are also people with a high probability of concomitant illnesses, both physical and mental, and all illnesses interact with each other. Thus severe mobility problems will interact with dementia and make it different from how it would be for someone who is physically very fit. Pharmacology too, has a major role to play since many older people are on considerable amounts of medication. People's circumstances are also very different in terms of standard of living, family support, the nature of relationships and so on. The label dementia *on its own* is almost meaningless in reality.

'People with dementia cannot communicate'

The label dementia can have a dramatic effect on professionals. Their expectations of a sensible conversation can diminish and this is conveyed to the person with dementia in subtle and sometimes very unsubtle ways. Our style can quickly become patronising, for example, when we are told that someone has dementia. It is also not unusual to see staff talking about a person with dementia in front of them. The consequence is that someone who is already highly anxious as the world becomes a more bewildering place, is further impaired. We also expect coherent speech and are not always very good at translating what may be allegorical or metaphorical.

As verbal skills diminish we can fail to see attempts at non-verbal communication. Yet people with dementia are experts at non-verbal communication. They can respond to posture, tone of voice and demeanour instantly. As professionals we are highly trained verbally; we know how to listen carefully but we are often much less good at using our eyes. We need to become more sensitive in the non-verbal cues that we give and in how we respond to those we receive. On a more overt level it is now increasingly understood that challenging behaviour may be an attempt to communicate. Allan (1994) lists a whole set of things people might be trying to communicate when they walk a lot (sometimes called wandering). These include the possibility that the person may be too hot, they may be lost, they may be in pain, they may need exercise, they may be unhappy in the unit.

There is now excellent material on communication. Goldsmith's book *Hearing the Voice of Dementia* (1996) is a good place to start for a résumé of the issues. Killick's book *You Are Words* (1997) uses poetry to show us how people with dementia can communicate in pictures and stories.

Ignorance about the issues of communication result in discrimination as people with dementia are left out of processes such as commenting on the services they receive, or participating in the assessment process. Many of our interventions are verbal. We can offer counselling, groupwork and family therapy. If we do not believe that people with dementia can communicate, they are denied these kinds of help. There is an awakening interest in the use of these approaches which deserves to be more widely known. Sutton (1997), for example, has applied psychotherapeutic ideas to help staff in a residential home manage the often apparently bizarre behaviour of one of the residents. Yale (1995) runs groups for people with dementia. There is a continuing concern by many social workers about the extent to which people with dementia are bereaved and the extent to which they can work through it. Mary Dixon (1997) reports on her failure to see the extent of bereavement in a person with dementia. It seems likely that a lot of the preoccupation with past relationships, especially with long-dead parents or siblings, that characterises the conversation of people with dementia is in fact an expression of an abiding sense of loss. Fiel (1992) thinks that a lot of the behaviour of people with dementia relates to unfinished business from the past.

'People with dementia are not aware of their condition'

Believing that people with dementia have no awareness of their condition or indeed of the world around them, has been the way that professionals have tolerated the poor care that is so often offered. Some of the longstay environments result in a diminishing of affect such that it is not difficult to believe that there is no understanding left at all. The tide is turning however. Davis (1993) and McGowin (1993) have written books about their dementia using word processors. Killick's (1997) poetry would seem to suggest that residents of nursing homes are often painfully aware of their condition. Barnet's (1997) interviews of people with dementia in a longstay NHS unit would seem to confirm this impression. Social workers and other care workers have traditionally taken their cue from psychiatry, where it is true that people with dementia do not have 'insight' as such. However this does not mean that they are unaware of their predicament.

'People with dementia have a progressive and terminal condition which can only deteriorate'

Negative expectations are widespread in dementia care. It is common for professionals to blame challenging behaviour and failures in day-to-day competence on the dementia without thinking whether it might instead be a result of poor care. A simple example is the labelling of bedroom doors. We are often told that Mrs A or Mr B cannot find their own bedroom in a residential home because of their mental deterioration. It may be that Mrs A can no longer read the label on her door but she could recognise a picture of her cat. Mr B might not be able to remember a number but he might remember that his room was beside the bookcase. In one sense it is not wrong to blame deterioration, but what is wrong is to assume that, because of the deterioration, no functioning brain is left. The reality is that deterioration is always patchy. Some capacity remains and it is our job to find out what this is and organise our care to build on remaining capacity. Quite remarkable strides have been made in the last ten years or so in providing care regimes which enhance or maintain skills and competence. Many of these are described in the excellent *Journal of Dementia Care*.

'People with dementia cannot give consent'

There are a great many ethical issues in dementia care which are well described in Hope and Oppenheimer (1997). Consent is a key issue. As Hope and Oppenheimer point out, the reality is that people with dementia will be able to consent on some issues but not on others. Mrs C, for example, may be well able to decide who is going to inherit her teapots but she may not be able to decide whether or not she should have an operation. Mr D might have a good understanding of the assessment undertaken by a social worker but no understanding at all about the financial implications. Langan and Means (1996) have published widely on some of the ways that social services departments may be acting improperly in their financial dealings with people with dementia.

'People with dementia are a burden to their carers'

Professionals tend to find it easier to empathise with carers, sometimes at the expense of people with dementia. This is understandable. They are often more similar in age. Carers are usually more articulate than people with dementia. Social workers and nurses are only too aware that the whole system depends on carers being willing to go on caring and their well-being is therefore paramount. They are also often acutely aware of the heavy price carers pay in terms of their mental and physical health (Schultz et al. 1995).

Whilst being understandable, this can be highly discriminatory as the needs of carers are put ahead of people with dementia. What is needed is much greater attention to conflict resolution techniques. Many professionals regard the use of mediation and negotiation as quite unrealistic if one of the parties has dementia. Yet without this kind of technique a fair compromise is rarely achieved.

This one-sided attitude also distorts the reality for many families. Caring can be life enhancing especially since dementia can make people more emotional and affectionate. Charlotte Clarke (1997) reports on how unhelpful some social work intervention is which plays up the negative consequences of dementia, when families are trying to hold on to relationships and to adjust themselves to the changes. The very limited view of the capacity of people with dementia also sometimes results in care workers being unaware of issues such as sexual problems in relationships.

The roots of discrimination

So where does this brief examination of some forms of discrimination leave us in working with people with dementia? What understanding of its origins may help us to confront and deal with it? One source is clearly the dread we all have about ageing and death, which is infinitely worse if we lose our minds as well. Another is that these things are self-perpetuating. Because poor, unskilled care results in unnecessary dependence, we see more dependence. We need more examples of what can be achieved with skills and appropriate attitudes.

Another possible explanation of discriminatory attitudes is that this is an area of social work where social work itself is relatively powerless. We have to work alongside other professional groups such as doctors and nurses. Multidisciplinary work does not suit everyone and many are unprepared for the style of the medical approach with its certainties and hegemony.

A final explanation may be that with dementia we are working in a field full of questions but with few answers. This is both at the fundamental level of whether people with dementia have a soul, and at the more prosaic level of whether the new drugs are going to make any significant difference to their competence. This is not an easy field to work in. Discriminatory practice is probably an easy way of coping. As we saw in the preceding section in relation to Jessie, discrimination and ageism can perform useful functions. But then social workers miss out on the very real discoveries that are taking place about the potential of people with dementia.

Good practice

Good, non-discriminatory social work practice with people with dementia and the people who care for them is no different from good practice with any other minority group. It requires social workers first to be sensitive to the existence and nature of the discrimination. It requires social workers capable of feeling outrage yet acting with tactical sense and discretion.

At the interpersonal level, social workers need to believe the potential in everyone. Dementia will always only affect part of the brain; even near the end some of the brain will be functioning. Like any other professional working in this field, the approach should be to focus on remaining memory and skills. In making assessments, too, we can demonstrate this conviction. Some people with dementia will be able to participate. Some may need advocates. People with dementia can have views about services. Where they have been effectively listened to they seem to be stressing the quality of the social aspects of services rather than the merely practical. In planning care it is really important not to cause unnecessary disability by, for example, undermining remaining skills or moving people too often.

People with dementia already experience discrimination as older people and dementia adds another layer. It is sometimes useful to think of people with dementia as a cultural minority in our midst: one where people have a different language, different ways of expressing themselves and a high level of emotional interaction. Given this understanding, many of the lessons from discrimination against other minorities apply.

Social workers may be said to have two very special roles with people with dementia. One is our resolute commitment to self-determination as a principle of practice. This makes us very preoccupied with ethical and legal practice. We have much to contribute to multidisciplinary practice in this respect. The second is our focus on communication as a means of resolving or at least ameliorating, personal problems. At its best, this is the way to practise with discriminatory social work with people with dementia and those who care for them. The skills of communicating with people with dementia are developing very fast indeed at the moment. There are opportunities, with our help, for people with dementia to be treated as citizens, a part of rather than apart from society. This surely must be the goal of our practice.

References

Allan, K. (1994) *Wandering*. Stirling: Dementia Services Development Centre.
Améry, J. (1994) *On Ageing. Revolt and Resignation*. Bloomington, IN: Indiana University Press. (English translation by John D. Barlow of Über des Altern Revolte und Resignation (1968) Stuttgart: Ernst Klett Verlag fur Wissen and Bilddung GmbH.)
Arber, S. and Ginn, J. (1991) *Gender and Later Life*. London: Sage.
Barnet, E. (1997) 'Collaboration and Interdependence: Care as a Two-Way Street'. In Marshall (1997).
Barrowclough, C. and Fleming, I. (1986) *Goal Planning with Elderly People*. Manchester: Manchester University Press.
Blakemore, K. (1997) 'From minorities to majorities: perspectives on culture ethnicity and ageing in British gerontology'. In Jamieson et al. (1997).
Brearley, C.P. (1975) *Social Work, Ageing and Society*. London: Routledge and Kegan Paul.
Butcher, H. and Crosbie, D. (1977) *Pensioned Off – A Study of the Needs of Elderly People in Cleator Moor*. York: University of York.
Bytheway, B. (1997) 'Talking about age: the theoretical basis of social gerontology'. In Jamieson et al. (1997).
Challis, D. and Davies, B. (1986) *Case Management in Community Care*. Aldershot: Gower.
Clarke, C. (1997) 'In sickness and in health: remembering the relationship in family caregiving for people with dementia'. In Marshall (1997).
Crosbie, D. (1977) 'The concept of need – an analytical model'. In Butcher and Crosbie (1977).
Davis, R. (1993) *My Journey into Alzheimer's Disease*. Amersham-on-the-Hill: Scripture Press.
Department of Health (1991) *Care Management and Assessment: Practitioners' Guide*. London: HMSO.
DHSS (1978) *Social Service Teams: The Practitioner's View*. London: HMSO.
Dixon, M. (1997) 'Talking about death'. In Marshall (1997).
Featherstone, M. and Wernick, A. (1995a) 'Introduction'. In Featherstone and Wernick (1995b).
Featherstone, M. and Wernick, A. (eds) (1995b) *Images of Ageing*. London: Routledge.

Feil, N. (1992) *Validation: The Feil Method*. Ohio: Edward Feil Productions.

Froggatt, A. (1990) *Family Work with Elderly People*. London: Macmillan.

Goldberg, E. and Warburton, W. (1979) *Ends and Means in Social Work*. London: Allen & Unwin.

Goldsmith, M. (1996) *Hearing the Voice of People with Dementia: Opportunities and Obstacles*. London: Jessica Kingsley Publishers Ltd.

Hareven, I. (1995) 'Changing images of aging and the social construction of the life course'. In Featherstone and Wernick (1995b).

Hegelson, A. (1989) 'USSR – the implications of *glasnost* and *perestroika*?'. In Munday (1989).

Hiatt, L.G. (1985) 'Understanding the Physical Environment', *Pride Institute Journal of Long Term Care*, **4**(2): 12–22.

Hope, T. and Oppenheimer, C. (1997) 'Ethics and the psychiatry of old age'. In Jacoby and Oppenheimer (1997).

Howe, D. (1986) *Social Workers and their Practice in Welfare Bureaucracies* Aldershot: Gower.

Hughes, B. (1995) *Older People and Community Care*. Buckingham: Open University Press.

Hunt, L., Marshall, M. and Rowlings, C. (eds) (1997) *Past Trauma in Late Life: European Perspectives on Therapeutic Work with Older People*. London: Jessica Kingsley.

Jacoby, R. and Oppenheimer, C. (eds) (1997) *Psychiatry in the Elderly*. Oxford: Oxford University Press.

Jamieson, A., Harper, S. and Victor, C. (eds) (1997) *Critical Approaches to Ageing and Later Life*. Buckingham: Open University Press.

Jeffreys, M. (1997) 'Intergenerational relationships: an autobiographical perspective'. In Jamieson et al. (1997).

Katz, S. (1995) 'Imagining the Life Span: From premodern miracles to postmodern fantasies'. In Featherstone and Wernick (1995b).

Killick, J. (1997) *'You are Words' Dementia Poems*. London: Hawker Publications.

Kitwood, T. (1997) *Dementia Reconsidered: The Person Comes First*. Buckingham: Open University Press.

Langan, J. and Means, R. (1996) 'Financial Management and Elderly People with Dementia in the UK: As much a question of confusion as abuse?', *Ageing and Society*, **16**: 287–314.

Latimer, J. (1997) 'Figuring identities: older people, medicine and time'. In Jamieson (1997).

Macdonald, B. and Rich, C. (1984) *Look Me in the Eye*. London: The Women's Press.

Marshall, M. (1983) *Social Work with Old People*. London: Macmillan.

Marshall, M. (1997) *State of the Art in Dementia Care*. London: Centre for Policy on Ageing.

Marshall, M. and Dixon, M. (1996) *Social Work with Old People*. London: Macmillan.

McGowin, D.F. (1993) *Living in the Labyrinth: A Personal Journey through the Maze of Alzheimer's*. USA: Elder Books.

Mortimer, E. (1982) *Working with the Elderly*. London: Heinemann.

Munday, B. (ed.) (1989) *The Crisis in Welfare*. Hemel Hempstead: Harvester Wheatsheaf.

Norman, A. (1985) *Triple Jeopardy: Growing Old in a Second Homeland* London: Centre for Policy on Ageing.

Petch, A., Cheetham, J., Fuller, R. MacDonald, C. and Myers, F. (1996) *Delivering Community Care: Initial Implementations of Care Management in Scotland*. Edinburgh: The Stationery Office.

Phair, L. and Good, V. (1995) *Dementia: A Positive Approach*. London: Scutari Press.

Phillips, J. (1996) 'Reviewing the literature on care management'. In Phillips, J. and Penhale, B. (eds) *Reviewing Care Management for Older People*. London: Jessica Kingsley Publishers Ltd.

Phillipson, C. (1982) *Capitalism and the Construction of Old Age*. London: Macmillan.

Rowlings, C. (1981) *Social Work with Elderly People*. London: Allen & Unwin.

Schulz, R., O'Brien, A.T., Bookwala, J. and Fleissner, K. (1995) 'Psychiatric and Physical Morbidity Effects of Dementia Caregiving: Prevalence, Correlates, and Causes', *The Gerontologist*, **35**(6): 771–91.

Siddall, R. (1997) 'Road to Success', *Community Care*, **1179**: 20–21.

Sutton, L. (1997) ' "Out of the Silence" When People Can't Talk About It'. In Hunt et al. (1997).

Townsend, P. (1979) *Poverty*. Harmondsworth: Penguin Books.

Townsend, P. (1981) 'The structured dependency of the elderly: A creation of social policy in the twentieth century', *Ageing and Society*, **1**(1): 5–28.

Wada, S. (1995) 'The status and image of the elderly in Japan: Understanding the paternalistic ideology'. In Featherstone and Wernick (1995b).

Walker, A. (1980) 'The social creation of poverty and dependency in old age', *Journal of Social Policy*, **9**: 49–75.

Willcocks, D., Peace, S. and Kellaher, L. (1987) *Private Lives in Public Places*. London: Tavistock.

Woodward, K. (1995) 'Tribute to the older woman: Psychoanalysis, feminism and ageism'. In Featherstone and Wernick (1995b).

Yale, R. (1995) *Developing Support Groups for Individuals with Early-stage Alzheimer's Disease: Planning, Implementation and Evaluation*. London: Jessica Kingsley.

6 Lesbians and Gay Men: Social Work and Discrimination

Helen Cosis Brown

Abstract

This chapter sets out to contextualise social work practice with lesbians and gay men both within the history of lesbian and gay politics and social movements as well as within social work.

The chapter is divided into five sections: an historical and international overview of lesbian and gay oppression, lesbian and gay identity, the social/political context of social work with lesbians and gay men, social work education and training and, finally possible ways forward. The first part of the chapter is necessary to enable the contextualisation of the second. The chapter addresses the complexity of looking at the international context but argues that we must have social work with lesbians and gay men on the international agenda.

Introduction

'Same-sex love is a phenomenon common to almost every culture, one occurring throughout history. The ways in which people have understood this attraction, however, have varied widely' (Blasius and Phelan 1997: 2). The ways people have responded to the phenomenon have also been varied. Both understandings and responses to homosexuality within different cultural, historical and geographical contexts have profoundly influenced the provision of social work and social care to lesbian and gay individuals and communities.

This chapter focuses on social work with and social care provision for lesbians and gay men. As the chapter is written by an English social work academic it inevitably draws heavily on an English and 'Western' context.

However it is hoped that the developments within this context may reflect those in other parts of the world and be useful to reflect upon. At the time of writing Britain is in the perceived throes of social and ideological change. Although the changes are seemingly negligible compared to the social and political upheavals that half of Europe have been engaged in for over ten years, for Britain these changes are significant. British newspapers, since the change to a Labour Government in May from nearly twenty years of Conservative administration, are full of stories of a new Britain: 'More Open and Tolerant, Less Macho and Miserable. Welcome to New Britain' (Freedland 1997). Clearly changes in perception do not necessarily mean there have been real changes in material conditions. However, there has been the development of some feelings of optimism, which political and governmental change do seem to have stimulated.

This optimism has the politics of inclusion integral within it. The death of Diana, Princess of Wales and the resulting national mourning exposed some fundamental changes in British culture and society. The news coverage included the interviewing of significant numbers of black men and women on the streets who spoke, as did white people, about their personal response to her death. This was the first time black Britons had been so 'normally' included in media coverage of an event affecting everyone. The streets and parks in the aftermath of her death were full of crowds with the visible presence of gay men and black men and women within them. There was a feeling of inclusion, one where it seemed that Britain had managed to create an inclusive society, one where oppressed groups were now part of the wider whole. Historical political analysis will make sense of the meaning of the events and representation of those events over time. However, the reality of many hundreds of 'out' gay men lining the streets of London along with the rest of a whole cross-section of the public to attend the funeral of a member of the aristocracy, even ten years ago would have been inconceivable. Although the Princess herself carried personal and symbolic meaning for individuals and the wider culture, her death also exposed fundamental social changes that have occurred in recent British history, and have impacted on the lives of lesbians and gay men.

Despite the last twenty years in Britain having been marked by a Conservative government intent on limiting the rights and life chances of lesbians and gay men, they have also been the years where we have seen the improvement of the conditions of many lesbians and gay men in Britain, with the development of a more vociferous, visible and celebratory presence. This is not the case for all parts of the world. Amnesty Internationals recent survey on human rights violations based on sexual orientation (Amnesty International 1997) acts as a sobering reminder that the experience of being lesbian and gay is fundamentally dependent on context:

Attitudes towards homosexual behaviour are ... culturally specific and have varied enormously across different cultures and through various historical periods. What is less obvious ... is the realization not only that attitudes towards same sex activity have varied but that the social and subjective meanings given to homosexuality have similarly been culturally specific. (Weeks 1996: 42)

Social work has to grapple with this head on as its activities are related to the individual in relation to their social context. It is therefore difficult to develop 'truths' about social work with lesbians and gay men as practice will be utterly dependent on the individual, the cultural context and the political and national setting. However, we can argue that for social work to be relevant and effective it has to be about working with specific and unique individuals within their own context. Postmodern thinking, although criticised for its tendency towards meaningless fragmentation, has for the purposes of social work been helpful in moving the profession away from notions of binary opposite general categories such as crude categorisations of men and women as if all individuals within the women category would have a shared reality and subjective experience. For lesbians and gay men these theoretical developments have been important to better reflect the complexity of their individual and community experience.

Lesbian and gay oppression – an historical and international overview

The international perspective

A significant factor in lesbian and gay culture has been its internationalism. In the later part of this century there has been considerable movement of lesbians and, particularly, gay men between 'gay cities' across the world, which has undoubtedly impacted on both lesbian and gay culture as well as political movements, and has gained momentum. The International Lesbian and Gay Association founded in 1978 initially had a predominately western European membership whereas it now has a membership that encompasses Europe, Africa, Asia-Pacific, Latin and North America (Ramakers 1997). However this internationalism or globalisation of gayness should not be overstated:

There are many countries – particularly in the African, Arabian, and Asian continents - where the globalization of gayness has hardly moved. And, although barriers are breaking down between East and West as I write, there are still many questions to be posed about homosexuality in the former Soviet Union. It would be dangerous to suggest a convergence in homosexual life-styles across the world – into one true universal gayness. Further, each national and local culture brings its own richness, its own political strategies, its own uniqueness. (Plummer 1992: 17)

Despite the increasing linking of lesbians and gay men across the world and the consequential strengthening of a sense of international community, the reality for the vast majority of lesbians and gay men is one of isolation and vulnerability. Amnesty International's survey into human rights violations based on sexual orientation found that out of the countries they looked at, in 65 homosexuality was illegal. In many countries lesbianism was not recognised. The punishments for the 'crime' of homosexuality ranged from execution or imprisonment to fines:

> In countries all over the world, individuals are being targeted for imprisonment, torture and even murder, simply on the grounds of their sexual orientation. Gay men, lesbians, transvestites, transsexuals any person who doesn't adhere to the dictates of what passes for 'normal' sexuality may be subject to such persecution at the hands of private individuals or government agents. (Amnesty International 1997: 7)

Alongside the 'legal' persecution of lesbians and gay men goes the unregulated and informal persecution through such activities as queer-bashing, an activity as prevalent in countries where homosexuality is legal as in those where it is not.

There have been considerable legislative changes in the countries of the former Soviet Union and Eastern Europe since the fall of the Berlin Wall in 1989: 'In most of the countries of the former Soviet Union and other Warsaw Pact countries, anti-gay laws have been repealed and organisations fighting for gay rights have been recognised officially' (Amnesty International 1997: 33). Lesbian and gay activity and resistance pre-dated 1989 within these countries. Schenck writes of the development of a lesbian and gay movement within the German Democratic Republic from the beginning of the 1970s. Many private groups were set up to offer support, however:

> It was also the declared aim of these groups to draw public attention to the situation of homosexuals and to demand changes. Given that at that time homosexuality was generally portrayed not only as a pathological condition but also as a crime, and prejudice against homosexuals continued to be endemic, these activities were of great importance for the self-confidence and self-image of lesbians and gay men. (Schenck 1997: 818)

Despite positive moves forward in many of these countries many lesbians and gay men face attitudes that have not changed at the same pace as legislative progress. For lesbians in Lithuania:

> Lesbianism is only now beginning to be discussed in the press. Because homosexuality was not spoken about for so long, public opinion is shaped by misinformation and stereotyping ... Nijole Steponkute, an advocate for women and mothers, explains that to be a lesbian in Lithuania is 'a shame, and a mental sickness. You are seen as dirty and immoral.' Understandably then, lesbians are very closeted – so much so that many people do not believe they exist. (Sharp 1997: 153)

Very few countries have protective legislation relating to lesbians and gay men. In 1996 South Africa included lesbian and gay rights within its new constitution and in New South Wales, the Anti-Discrimination Act 1977 made discrimination illegal on a number of counts including sexual orientation, as is also the case in a number of North American states. These examples are the exception. In Britain there is no such protective legislation.

Lesbian and gay activism

The responses to homosexuality historically have generally, but not always, been hostile. Why such a degree of hostility exists has been much debated. The idea that homosexuals have to be made 'other' for heterosexuals to disassociate themselves from their own homosexual desires is often accepted. Homophobia (the fear and hatred of homosexuality) has often, across cultures and time, used the formal vehicles of the law, medicine and the Church to propagate and regulate hatred towards lesbians and gay men and others who fail to conform to the rigid categorisations of heterosexuality and gender. Weeks argues that homosexuality: 'has also, as an inevitable effect of the hostility it has evoked, produced the most substantial forms of resistance to hostile categorisation and has, consequently, a long cultural and subcultural history' (Weeks 1997: 41). It is this history that has led eventually to the inclusion of lesbians and gay men onto the anti-discriminatory agenda in social work.

Blasius and Phelan's (1997) historical sourcebook of gay and lesbian politics offers a useful international historical perspective on the development of lesbian and gay politics, cultures and movements. Lesbians and gay men have been organising for political and social change for a very long time and the nature of that organisation has changed. The perceived watershed of the development of a new lesbian and gay political movement is often described as 'Stonewall'. 'Stonewall' refers to the Stonewall riots in New York City, in June 1969, which were the result of police raids on a gay club. What marked out this particular raid was that the police were met with resistance, and the resulting 'riots' are seen as the symbolic conception of 'gay pride' and the beginning of the Gay Liberation movement.

Stonewall acted as a catalyst for lesbian and gay organisations across the world: in Britain the Gay Liberation Front was born in 1970. Lesbian and gay politics has, like many other politics, been noted for its two main forms of political organisation: first, reformist lesbians and the gay rights movement which in the British context would include such organisations as the Campaign for Homosexual Equality in the 1970s and Stonewall (a political lobbying organisation) in the 1990s, and second, transformationist politics represented by the Gay Liberation Front in the 1970s and Outrage (a direct action group) in the 1990s. Both types of political organisation have been crucial to the social and cultural changes that have taken place within lesbian and gay communities but also in their influence on the wider community's attitudes towards them.

Another watershed in lesbian and gay politics in the late twentieth century was the onset of the AIDS epidemic. It offered a convenient vehicle onto which could be hitched the ideologies of fear and hatred. One of the historical ironies of the AIDS epidemic was that rather than weakening the lesbian and gay movement it strengthened it. Gay men and lesbians came together to resist both the disease itself and also the ideological aftermath that came with it. AIDS has carried with it terrible personal meaning but also symbolic resonance for a community of lesbians and gay men:

> The epidemic caught us as a community in full adolescent abandon, deservedly and delightedly letting off steam less than 10 years after the 1969 Stonewall riots. It has travelled with us through the past years, marking our passage from over a century of oppressed oblivion ... to the beginnings of a proud and defiantly visible culture of our own. (King 1995: 16)

Many have linked the AIDS epidemic and the political and social responses to it to the development of 'Queer' politics:

> Both the backlash and the AIDS crisis prompted a renewal of radical activism, of a politics of confrontation, coalition building, and a need for a critical theory that links gay affirmation to broad institutional change. (Seidman 1996: 10)

'Queer' has an intimate relationship with postmodernism, but is primarily about resistance, rebellion and transformation. It argues for the deconstruction of gender as well as sexuality, that homosexuality can not be understood outside understandings of gender and all sexual practices.

Social work with lesbians and gay men and the quality of that work is an area of concern that has been given voice in Britain from the early 1980s (Hart 1980; Hart and Richardson 1981). The process of placing these debates onto the social work profession's agenda is inseparable from the history of lesbian and gay activism since 1969.

Lesbian and gay identity

Same-sex sexual activity does not necessarily lead to a person identifying as lesbian or gay. Social workers, particularity those engaged in the criminal justice system, will work with men prosecuted in Britain for 'cottaging' where those men have a clear sense of themselves as heterosexual. The identity of 'the homosexual' is a recent phenomenon which McIntosh dates from the end of the seventeenth century (McIntosh 1968), whereas the recording of same-sex sexual relationships pre-dates that by a very long way.

Homosexuality has been problematised through various means, but predominantly via religion, medicine and the law. It has been seen as immoral, sick, deviant and unlawful. Heterosexuals have been fascinated and frightened by homosexuality and have expended much energy in trying to either annihilate it or regulate its activities and influence. It has often been linked in the public imagination with contagion, disease, treachery and treason. How it has been viewed has been intrinsically linked with a particular culture's perception of gender. An example of this has been the relative invisibility of lesbians within many cultures and throughout history. Notions of gender have been fundamental to this invisibility:

> Several intertwined elements determined attitudes to lesbianism, and consequent possibilities for lesbian identity: the roles that society assigned women; the ideology which articulated, organised, and regulated this; the dominant notions of female sexuality in the ideology; and the actual possibilities for the development by women of an autonomous sexuality. The prevailing definitions of female sexuality in terms of the 'maternal instinct', or necessarily responsive to the stimulation of the male, were overwhelming barriers in attempts to conceptualise the subject. (Weeks 1996: 58)

Lesbian visibility within many countries coincided and increased with female independence and economic security. The second wave of the women's movement from the 1960s saw the beginning of lesbian visibility and autonomy, as we see it within many countries today.

The legal, religious and medical frameworks of homosexuality have not just influenced societies' attitudes towards lesbians and gay men but have also influenced lesbians' and gay men's attitudes towards themselves. Lesbians and gay men have often internalised or identified with negative views about themselves, as well as having differing views as to the 'causation' of homosexuality. At the risk of being simplistic there are commonly two views of 'causation' prevalent among lesbians and gay men: that homosexuality is socially constructed and that it is biologically determined. These two views carry with them political and social consequences. If homosexuality is constructed then so is heterosexuality and gender. Nothing then is 'normal', we can only talk of a majority activity. If nothing is 'normal', there is no reason why all sexualities and genders would not have equal status unless a political ideology evolved to privilege one sexuality above all others. Within most settings heterosexuality is privileged above all others.

Genetic predisposition arguments about homosexuality have found favour amongst many gay men, particularly in the United States. One can only guess, at the present time, why this should be the case. Such writing as that by Kus is common:

> Very little is known about gay and lesbian children, and virtually nothing is known about gay and lesbian infants. Biological advances will, undoubtedly, go far in helping us understand more as we learn how gays are different biologically from other males, and how lesbians are different biologically from other females. (Kus 1990: 31)

The belief in biological determinism has been located within a predominantly conservative politics. The political and social consequences of the two positions, social construction of homosexuality versus biologically determined homosexuality, carry social consequences and are well articulated in two related essays by Nussbaum (1996) and Scruton (1996). The arguments in response to these two positions are crudely as follows: if gays 'can't help it' they should be protected but if gays 'choose' to be different then they are deviant and should be controlled and sometimes punished.

'Coming out', the process of acknowledging to oneself and to the public world that you are lesbian or gay, is a particularly difficult process for the majority of lesbians and gay men. Many never publicly acknowledge their sexuality publicly for fear of recrimination as a result of the discrimination and oppression experienced by lesbians and gay men. The relative ease or difficulty of coming out will be dependent on an individual's circumstances and personal history but will also be highly dependent on their national and cultural location.

From the Gay Liberation Movement in the 1970s onwards in 'the West', great emphasis has been placed on being 'out', both for reasons of psychological health as well as those of political and social visibility: such slogans as 'out and proud' were common. However, it took black lesbian and gay writers to point out the cultural specificity of the 'out is good' position. Black writers have argued that black lesbians and gay men are not just lesbian or gay having only to deal with homophobia. Hayfield, a black lesbian, writes:

> In any examination of the discrimination the Black lesbians experience in Britain, we must examine the racism that exists against all Black people, the sexism against all women and the homophobia against all lesbians and gay men. These discriminations are inseparable; as black lesbians we belong to all three categories and therefore experience these oppressions simultaneously. (Hayfield 1995: 186)

Black lesbians and gay men may choose for very good reasons not to be out in a given situation, feeling that at a particular moment tackling racism has to be the priority. Black writers have been central to alerting 'Western' lesbians and gay men to the specific relative privilege of white lesbians and gay men in North America, western Europe, and Australia, as compared to lesbians and gay men living within nations and cultures that have far more repressive attitudes and laws, where the question of being out or not carries with it very serious personal consequences.

For social work in Britain, the 'coming out' of social workers has been central to the improvement of service provision for lesbians and gay men. However, this process happened within a political climate of relative tolerance. For social work providers within very repressive regimes in relation to lesbians and gay men this is a complex area.

Lesbian and gay identity has been central to the development of a political and social movement of lesbians and gay men since the 1960s. Those identities are as varied as are the individuals involved, have changed over time and are dependent on the individual's context. A possible 'universal truth', however, relevant to social work with lesbians and gay men, is that individuals need to feel content with themselves as lesbian or gay, for there not to be the likelihood of negative psychological consequences for them as individuals and in how they are able to relate to their social world. Social work is about interventions in relation to the individual and the social.

Social work with lesbians and gay men: the social and political context

The social and political context

This section uses the British context to look at some of the detail of social work with lesbians and gay men. Ironically the period within social work where this has been addressed has coincided with a period where central government focused on lesbians and gay men as the scapegoats for all Britain's moral ills. The period from 1979 saw a central government trying to limit lesbian and gay life chances at the same time as many Labour-controlled local authorities were trying to enhance them.

Social work was radically affected by the political and social movements involving groups experiencing discrimination from the 1960s onwards, and had to engage in much soul-searching as to the part it had and did play in contributing towards and supporting that discrimination. This was the case for social work in relation to lesbians and gay men. Social work in Britain historically had been both a passive onlooker and an active participant in supporting discrimination against, and the oppression of, lesbians and gay men. Homosexuality had been pathologised within social work and at best clients might have been 'helped to overcome their homosexual urges'. From the early 1970s onwards the speed of change was considerable as the lesbian and gay community became more assertive and visible and started making demands for change. Lesbian and gay involvement in local politics (in particular local Labour parties), trade unions and professional organisations as well as community groups put increasing pressure on social work from both outside and from within for a better, more appropriate and sensitive service provision for lesbians and gay men. This culminated in the majority of local authorities placing sexual orientation within their equal opportunities policies as both providers of services and as employers. By the end of the 1980s the Central Council of Social Work Education and Training had included sexual orientation within its policies regulating social work education (CCETSW, 1989).

Social work, during the 1980s and 1990s, found itself in the peculiar position of being caught between many local authorities (at that time the major employers of social workers) that were trying to address issues related to social work and social care with lesbians and gay men, and a Conservative government that tried on several occasions to limit the rights of lesbians and gay men. The Conservative government focused its concerns on two areas, first, male same-sex sexual activity and second, lesbians' and gay men's capacity to act as carers for children. Ironically, however, in relation to the first it was the Conservative administration that enacted the Criminal Justice and Public Order Act 1994 that lowered the age of consent for gay men to 18 (but not 16) from 21. The Government partly focused on the second as its concerns grew at the increasing visibility of lesbian mothers (Harne and Rights of Women 1997). They were also aware that as a consequence of increasing lesbian and gay confidence, lesbians and gay men were putting themselves forward to fostering and adoption agencies as potential substitute carers.

The Government made three separate but unsuccessful attempts to limit lesbians' and gay men's right to parent, during the drafting of the foster placement, guidance and regulations of the Children Act 1989, the Human Fertilisation and Embryology Act 1990 and the white paper *Adoption: The Future* (Department of Health 1993). On each attempt the childcare lobby refuted the Government's arguments, that lesbians and gay men should not be allowed to act as parents, and the Government had to back down. The childcare lobbies were cognisant of the increasing research base indicating that the sexual orientation of homosexual parents had no detrimental impact on developing children (Brown 1998a: 90). However the Conservative government did successfully enact Section 28 of the Local Government Act 1988. This was the Act that forbade local authorities to use resources in such a way that might 'intentionally promote' homosexuality. It also stopped schools from 'promoting the teaching in any maintained school of homosexuality as a pretended family relationship'. Designed to limit lesbian and gay activity it in fact did the reverse. In the process of resisting the legislation the lesbian and gay community was strengthened (Carter 1992).

It was within this climate that some social work agencies and social work educators started looking at the detail of social work and social care with lesbians and gay men.

Social work and social care with lesbians and gay men

Lesbians and gay men become service users for as many varied reasons as do heterosexuals, most of which will not be specific to their sexual orientation. The exception to this is within the criminal justice system where probation officers may be working with a gay man who has committed a victimless crime by, for example, having had consensual sex at 17 with another 17-year-old. Probation is the area of social work-related activity where probation officers do work with gay men, specifically because of their sexual orientation; because at the present time in Britain some areas of male same-sex sexual activity are still illegal. However for the majority of social work activity with lesbians and gay men, the sexuality of the individual will be only one part of a complex whole and not the focus of the intervention. Despite this there is still a tendency in social work, if the practitioner is aware of a person's homosexuality, for there typically to be two responses; either an inappropriate over-emphasis on sexuality, or ignoring sexuality where it may be relevant. Because our sexuality is an integral part of our private and domestic lives, a person's sexuality is often relevant to the social worker who is frequently engaged with the private and the domestic. In such activities as community care assessments – drawing up a care plan for a person in need of domicilary assistance, for example – the sexuality of the individual may be important. If it is ignored, in the absence of an obvious

heterosexual husband or wife, the social worker may inadvertently overlook a caring partner who might need to be an integral part of a care package, to enable the person to remain at home.

Given the political sensitivity of social work with lesbians and gay men, and the considerable level of anxiety this area arouses for practitioners and agencies, a helpful development has been the focusing on 'competence' as an organising concept in social work practice and education. The Central Council for Education and Training in Social Work's (CCETSW) emphasis on competence and its three component parts – knowledge, values and skills – in its reconfiguration of social work education in the late 1980s (CCETSW 1989, 1995) was helpful to the process of thinking about social work with lesbians and gay men. This emphasis on competence has been criticised for its mechanistic nature and limited potential however:

> There are many reasons why knowledge, values and skills are of paramount importance, but at this stage we may concern ourselves only with the most obvious: social work is complex and hazardous, and part of the origin of tragic outcome of so much of social work action of the past is nearly always traceable to a lack of knowledge values and skills, or, an inability to apply them. (O'Hagan 1996: 8)

Certainly this has been the case for much work with lesbians and gay men, where workers did not have relevant knowledge, had not reflected on their own values sufficiently and lacked appropriate skills. Critical reflection on all three aspects of competence has led to a rethinking of the assumptions that were often made about lesbians and gay men, of the theoretical base upon which social workers drew and the appropriateness of this base. Social work knowledge, and its use, and discriminatory practice are closely linked, social workers often seeking out knowledge that will back and reinforce their own personal values (Brown 1996).

Not only was the social work profession's selective use of knowledge problematic but the knowledge itself was sometimes lacking, as it drew on research material that had used heterosexual subjects with the overriding heterosexist assumption that that was the social reality of all human experience. Lesbians and gay men rarely appeared in research other than that which specifically addressed homosexuality. They rarely entered the realm of the 'ordinary' either in social work research or publications with a few noteworthy exceptions (Davis 1993, Oliviere et al. 1998).

The requirement in British social work education of focusing on knowledge, values and skills, has meant that social workers have needed to think about the knowledge they use that informs them about; their clients' lives and circumstances, about their social work interventions and the legislative context of their work. The social worker has also needed to reflect upon their own values, their clients' values, those of the agency and the legislative framework's underpinning value system. In addition, they have had to consider the applicability of their skills to all service users and clients.

The activity of social work takes place within a specific organisational context. However reflective and competent an individual social worker may be when working with lesbians and gay men, the organisational ethos is likely to impact on their work. An important aspect of the political activities that British trade unions, relevant to social workers, were engaged in when looking at lesbian and gay rights, was that there was never a separation between the campaigning about the conditions and rights of the lesbian and gay workers and those of the service users and clients. It was understood that the positions of both groups were intrinsically linked. For example, it would be unlikely for sophisticated and competent work to be undertaken with a lesbian who had injured her child in an agency where equal opportunities for the lesbian and gay workforce were denied. Where lesbian and gay social workers are able to feel more confident as a result of their organisation having a proper policy of protection towards them, and where they can be 'out' if they so wish, those agencies are more likely to reflect on other organisational aspects that may impact on their service delivery to lesbians and gay men. In organisations where social workers have benefited from protective policies, those same organisations often have policies that state that an equal service will be given to service users irrespective of their sexuality. This 'equal service' involves having to address many areas within the organisation including 'welcome' language and images.

Lesbians and gay men may assume that a social work organisation will be homophobic, partly, as a reflection of the quality of provision social work has meted out to lesbians and gay men in the past. How 'welcoming' an agency is has a profound impact on how groups who experience discrimination form their first impressions of that organisation and how easy it will be for them to develop a helping relationship. The receptionist's, the telephonist's and the duty staff's ability to utilise the skills of engagement with service users will be crucial to the outcome of whether a lesbian or gay man returns to that agency or not. The use of language is important as it is one of the ways we convey our organisational culture to others. For example if an agency only ever refers to 'husbands' and 'wives' rather than the more neutral term of 'partner', which does not assume the sexual orientation of the individual, a lesbian or gay man may be made to feel rendered invisible. Similarly the images we display within social work agencies convey whether or not there is a recognition, on the organisation's part, of the diversity of the service user group. Lesbian and gay social workers and probation officers have been at the forefront of these sorts of organisational considerations, working towards enabling an agency to convey a culture that is both welcoming and respectful of diversity.

Fostering and adoption

For the purposes of this chapter I am focusing on one aspect of social work activity, fostering and adoption. It is the area of social work practice with lesbians and gay men that has attracted much attention from both the media and the government in Britain, and has consequently been an area of practice that has raised anxieties for social work agencies. The deep-seated beliefs that children must have a mummy and a daddy to develop into healthy and well-functioning adults was a 'common-sense' belief that much of the public had never been required to analyse. Campion, commenting on the increased tolerance towards lesbians and gay men that has developed in the recent past, writes:

> However, any suggestion of openly gay or lesbian adults as parents seems to produce a huge outcry – somehow, having children brings parents into the public arena where their personal lives can be justifiably criticised. All the age-old arguments come flying forth: homosexuality is sinful, perverted, unnatural. (Campion 1995: 177)

Lesbian and gay applicants coming forward to become substitute parents are a recent phenomenon. It is generally accepted that lesbians and gay men have acted as substitute carers for many years, but these carers would not have been 'out'. The growing confidence of the lesbian and gay communities and the increasing research base showing that children were not detrimentally affected by the homosexual sexual orientation of their parents (Patterson 1992), culminated in some fostering and adoption agencies accepting lesbians and gay men as applicants. In Britain it was within the social and political context outlined above that these moves took place. Lesbians and gay men have also become more visible as substitute carers in North America and Australia. Griffin and Mulholland (1997) offer a useful survey of the current state of play within European countries as to whether or not they accept lesbians as foster and adoptive carers. Their survey showed considerable differences between European countries. These differences do not neatly fall into what used to be referred to as 'East' and 'West', as many 'Western' countries still bar lesbians from fostering and adoption, for example France (Griffin and Mulholland 1997: 113).

Social work practice for agencies that do welcome lesbian and gay applicants as substitute families has had to focus on the following areas: assessment, placing children, working with birth parents and carer support.

Whether or not assessments of lesbian and gay carers should take the same form as assessments of all carers has been a complicated question, one argument being that to assess lesbian and gay applicants differently would be discriminatory, the other, that not to take account of how homophobia had and might in the future impact on the applicants, would be irresponsible. Many lesbians and gay men have been approved as suitable foster and adoptive parents but far fewer have been actually used. The tendency has been to place children with specific needs, often being categorised as hard to place, with lesbian and gay carers. Children need to be placed with the best possible carers whether they be heterosexual or homosexual. When agencies have difficulties using lesbian and gay carers it might be more honest not to assess them in the first place.

Working with birth parents is often used as an argument as to why a lesbian or gay carer should not be used. A number of cases have attracted great publicity in Britain, because of the attention they have received at the hands of the media, where a birth parent has voiced an objection to their child being placed with a lesbian or gay carer. This negative publicity has resulted in anxiety being raised for social work agencies. However where birth parents are worked with and helped to understand that a particular placement may be the best to meet their child's particular needs there is often not the same resistance.

A major criticism arising from lesbian and gay substitute carers towards social work agencies is that of the ineffective support they receive once they have been approved as carers. They often feel abandoned and isolated. Again, if agencies do recruit lesbian and gay carers, they need to make sure they have proper support structures in place to enable these foster and adoptive parents to offer a competent service as carers.

Social work has the responsibility to make sure that their practitioners offer the best possible outcomes for clients and service users including lesbians and gay men. Part of this responsibility lies with the social work educators who equip the qualifying social worker with relevant knowledge, the ability to consider values and the applicable skills as well as the ability to reflect critically upon all three in addition to their own practice.

Social work education and training

Little has been written about lesbians and gay men and social work education and training. Woodman's book (1992), an American text, was one of the very few relevant publications that was applicable to the international context for some time. In the last two years there has been a small flurry of relevant publications in Britain, (Logan et al. 1996; Brown 1998a,

1998b), all of which are again transferable to the international context. Given that lesbians and gay men have remained an invisible group within both social work and social work education and that it was not until the late 1980s that in Britain social work education was required to address the area at all, the small amount of literature is of little surprise. What has been more surprising is that amongst the anti-discrimination in social work publications there has been so little written specifically in relation to lesbians and gay men:

> There has been, over the last twenty years, an increasing awareness of inequalities in society resulting in legislative reform, particularly in relation to race and gender, which has aimed to alleviate the discrimination experienced by people on an individual level ... The situation is very different, however, for lesbians and gay men, and the belief that it is right to discriminate on the grounds of sexual orientation is not only widespread but is also sanctioned in law. (Logan et al. 1996: 3)

In Britain sexual orientation often still remains invisible on many social work courses despite CCETSW's direction that it should be considered. Invisible in that lesbian and gay students often still feel vulnerable being out on their courses; that the content of the teaching lacks any material directly relevant to social work practice with lesbians and gay men, and that the agencies in which the students are placed for their practice experience frequently do not address the area directly. Social work education is a vehicle by which the culture of social work is transferred from one generation of social work practitioners to another. This 'silence' within social work education conveys much of social work's historic hostility towards lesbians and gay men as service users and clients, as well as its current apathy.

Social work knowledge

Social work draws from a wide knowledge base, being primarily dependent on other disciplines to inform its practice. I have elsewhere, for the sake of simplicity, described the knowledge base of social work as falling into three broad areas: first, knowledge relating to the client's experience and context, second, that which relates to social work intervention and third the legislative and organisational context (Brown 1996: 10).

The second category draws on literature and ideas that social work has made the most significant contribution towards, that of theories, models and methods of intervention. The history of this arena of social work knowledge draws as it did, in social work's development into a profession from the 1920s onwards, on psychoanalytic ideas that were traditionally not renowned for their sympathetic treatment of homosexuality either theoretically or on the couch.

The first, knowledge that informs the practitioner about the client's experience and context, is highly dependent on other disciplines, for example, psychology and sociology. Social work has little control or impact on these disciplines. Psychology has been central to the propagation of negative attitudes and beliefs towards homosexuality. It has only been more recently that psychological ideas have begun to be deconstructed and reconsidered as to their relevance and applicability for lesbians and gay men (Greene and Herek 1994). Sociology has had quite a different relationship with homosexuality, which is well documented by Seidman (1996). The social construction theorists of the 1970s and 1980s played a significant part in furthering our understandings of homosexual desire and practice as well as sexuality more generally. Interestingly the development of 'Queer' theory during the 1990s has been located more inside the humanities within the fields of cultural theory, with sociology catching up at the end of the 1990s (Seidman 1996).

Much of social work's use of psychological and sociological ideas has traditionally been quite conservative, and failed to contextualise material. This necessary contextualisation would enable students to make critical use in practice of ideas that they may see as lacking relevance. One of the more negative consequences of some anti-discriminatory developments within social work education has been the sometimes fashionable rejection of some ideas such as the work of, for example, Bowlby, due in part to the language and the normative fashion in which much of his early work was written. However, the majority of his work on attachment and loss, is still fundamentally important to social work practice and can be used usefully if his work is placed within its cultural, historic, economic and geographical context and then critically applied.

The flip side of this fashionable rejection of sometimes useful ideas is the uncritical acceptance of ideas that are intrinsically problematic in developing anti-discriminatory social work education. A case in point would be the still widespread use of Erikson's model of the life-cycle approach to human development. In Erikson's sixth developmental stage 'intimacy versus isolation' covering the period of young adulthood, he describes the ideal as:

> ... mutuality of orgasm, with a loved partner, of the other sex, with whom one is able to share a mutual trust, and with whom one is able and willing to regulate the cycles of work, procreation and recreation so as to secure to the offspring, too, all the stages of a satisfactory development. (Erikson 1965: 257)

It seems that by definition lesbians and gay men who are not having sex with a member of the 'other sex' are excluded. It would be churlish to reject or ignore Erikson's ideas within social work education because of their inbuilt homophobia, as they still have a great deal to offer. However it would also be negligent for the social work educator not to point out the problematic areas of his thinking, to thus enable the student social worker to think and apply the ideas in a critical way.

The final category, knowledge that clarifies the practitioner's understanding of the legal, policy, procedural and organisational context is of particular significance in relation to preparing social work students to work with lesbians and gay men. The national context of the social work practice will dictate exactly what 'knowledge' needs to be made available. Because there are laws within most countries that restrict the activities of lesbians and gay men, both socially and sexually, social workers need to be aware of the legal and policy framework in which they are trying to deliver an anti-discriminatory practice. Where there are protective laws (as in New South Wales, South Africa and some North American states) towards lesbians and gay men, and protective policies (as in Britain in relation to young people under the Children Act 1989), social work students need to be equally aware of these and how they can be utilised in the interests of their clients.

Values and skills

Traditionally much of the thinking in social work education about the delivery of an anti-discriminatory social work practice has been located under the umbrella of values. However, as indicated above, much discriminatory practice is as the result of an inability to contextualise and critically apply knowledge. Knowledge and values are intimately connected in social work. There is a tendency amongst many practitioners and academics to be more critically alert when faced with knowledge that challenges our personal beliefs than when it reinforces them. One of the central tasks of the educational process within social work is to develop and nurture students' ability to make conscious values in relation to the work they are engaged in, as part of their everyday competent practice. I have argued elsewhere that values need to be considered at four levels: those of the social worker, the client/service-user, the social work agency and those of the social and legal framework (Brown 1998a: 20).

Social work with and social care delivery to lesbians and gay men necessitates all four levels being reflected upon. Sometimes the different levels of values may be in harmony, but they may just as likely be in conflict. For example, a social worker might be in sympathy with a young man of 17 (for whom she has some social work responsibility) moving into his 20-year-old boyfriend's flat. However, this social worker may be located in a national context where same-sex sexual practice is illegal until 18 or where it is illegal whatever the age. If she encouraged the young man's desired move this would place the social worker in direct conflict with the criminal justice system. The legal context is of great significance for both the social worker as well as their employing agency and the lesbians and gay men involved as service users and clients. The delivery of a truly anti-discriminatory social work practice to lesbians and gay men internationally is a complex arena, given the varied national and legal contexts within which that practice takes place. It may be that the best that can be hoped for within some contexts is that the conflicting values are made explicit, and the social worker does the best they can within their own context.

When working with lesbians and gay men, the area of interpersonal skills is fundamental to effective practice. Lesbians and gay men approaching a social work agency may well be apprehensive about their reception. Earlier in the chapter I outlined some organisational considerations about an agency's 'welcome'. The individual social worker also has a key role in facilitating an atmosphere in which a lesbian or gay service user can feel that there might be the possibility of developing a relationship of trust. Student social workers, in preparation for qualification, need to focus on the skills of engagement to enable a trusting relationship to be established that enables the service user or client to be able to explain the detail of their domestic and personal lives, where that is necessary for productive social work intervention to take place. The teaching of skills is an important aspect of social work education and training, and one where there needs to be the realisation that interpersonal skills should be deployed in a discriminatory way. Certain groups, lesbians and gay men being amongst them, may need to be engaged with in such a way that strongly conveys warmth, trust and integrity, to overcome their potential fear of rejection or discrimination at the hands of the social work agency (Brown 1998a: 20).

Practice teaching

Social work education takes place within both the college and the practice placement setting. Within the latter the practice teacher or practice super-visor plays a key role in enabling the student to make sense of what is learnt in the college setting in relation to practice. The practice teacher helps the student reflect on social work 'theory' and examine its applicability to the practice setting and real cases. The practice teacher also has a key role in reassuring lesbian and gay male students that their sexual orientation will not detrimentally impact on their assessment as social work students. Earlier in the chapter I outlined some areas for organisations to consider in relation to how welcoming they would be to service users and clients. These apply equally to lesbian and gay students whether they be out or not. In particular the practice teacher needs to spend time establishing a trusting and productive relationship with the student, one in which they will feel safe and comfortable enough to learn and develop.

Many social work agencies now have equal opportunity policies that include sexual orientation both as employers and service providers. Where these exist students should be made aware of them and where they are absent the practice teacher needs to contextualise the lack.

Social work education and training holds the key role in the preparation of competent practitioners who are able to deliver an anti-discriminatory service. This involves facilitating students, both within the college and practice placement setting, critically appraising the knowledge base of social work, reflecting on relevant values and appraising their skills.

For there to be effective and competent practice with lesbians and gay men, all three components have to be in place.

Ways forward

The development of international perspectives on competent social work practice with lesbians and gay men is a complex task. The varied national, cultural and legal contexts within which social work practice takes place makes any generalisations somewhat irrelevant. Within many countries homosexuality is illegal and within others (for example New South Wales, South Africa and a number of North American states) lesbians and gay men have protective legislation at their disposal. These differences are considerable and impact on social work practice. However, it is possible to draw out some points that have international relevance to the enterprise of social work.

A belief that social work should operate in the best interests of the specific, unique individuals that it works with within their own familial, social, cultural, social and political context, is universally applicable for social work. To be able to do this social workers have to critically appraise their knowledge base as to its relevance and applicability to lesbians and gay men and contextualise the knowledge from which they draw. They have also to reflect on the values that impinge on their work and make conscious their relevance. They need also to deploy discriminately their skills in such a way that enables different individuals in need of social work intervention or services to be able to establish productive and effective relationships.

Social work is not single-handedly responsible for the liberation of lesbians and gay men. However it is responsible for the quality and the effectiveness of the social work and social care services to that group.

International perspectives on social work policies and practice are helpful in contextualising the national and local. It enables us hopefully to move beyond the parochial and learn from different contexts, perspectives and experiences. Social work student and academic and practice staff exchanges have been important in furthering the development of alternative perspectives. Given where the very different stages different countries are in the furtherance of lesbian and gay rights, exchanges within this area may be particularly fruitful in placing the improvement of social work practice with lesbians and gay men permanently on the international social work agenda.

References

Amnesty International (1997) *Breaking the Silence: Human Rights Violations Based on Sexual Orientation*. London: Amnesty International.

Blasius, M. and Phelan, S.P. (eds) (1997) *We are Everywhere: a Historical Sourcebook of Gay and Lesbian Politics*. London: Routledge.

Brake, M. and Bailey, R. (eds) (1980) *Radical Social Work and Practice*. London: Edward Arnold.

Brown, H.C. (1996) 'The Knowledge Base of Social Work'. In Vass (1996): 8–35.

Brown, H.C. (1998a) *Social Work and Sexuality: Working with Lesbians and Gay Men*. Basingstoke: Macmillan.

Brown, H.C. (1998b) 'Working with Lesbians and Gay Men: Sexuality and Practice Teaching'. In Lawson (1998).

Campion, M.J. (1995) *Who's Fit to be a Parent?* London: Routledge.

Carter, V. (1992) 'Abseil Makes the Heart Grow Fonder: Lesbian and Gay Campaigning Tactics and Section 28'. In Plummer (1992b): 217–26.

CCETSW (1989), *DipSW Requirements and Regulations for the Diploma in Social Work, Paper 30*. London: CCETSW.

CCETSW (1995) *DipSW: Rules and Requirements for the Diploma in Social Work, Paper 30*, rev. edn. London: CCETSW.

Davis, L. (1993) *Sex and the Social Worker*, new edn. London: Janus Publishing Company.

Department of Health (1993) *Adoption: The Future*. London: HMSO.

Erikson, E. (1965) *Childhood and Society*. Harmondsworth: Penguin.

Freedland, J. (1997) 'More Open and Tolerant, Less Macho and Miserable. Welcome to New Britain', *The Guardian*, 18.9.97.

Greene, B. and Herek, G.M. (1994) *Lesbian and Gay Psychology: Theory, Research and Clinical Application*. London: Sage.

Griffin, K. and Mulholland, L.A. (1997) *Lesbian Motherhood in Europe*. London: Cassell.

Harne, L. and Rights of Women (1997) *Valued Families: The Lesbian Mothers' Legal Handbook*, rev. edn. London: The Women's Press.

Hart, J. (1980) 'It's Just a Stage We're Going Through: The Sexual Politics of Casework'. In Brake and Bailey (1980): 43–63.

Hart, J. and Richardson, D. (eds) (1981) *The Theory and Practice of Homosexuality*. London: Routledge & Kegan Paul.

Hayfield, A. (1995) 'Several Faces of Discrimination'. In Mason-John (1995): 186–206.

Herek, G.M. and Greene, B. (eds) (1995) *AIDS, Identity and Community: The HIV Epidemic and Lesbians and Gay Men.* London: Sage. 1–18.

King, N. (1995) 'HIV and the Gay Male Community: One Clinician's Reflections Over the Years'. In Herek and Greene (1995).

Kus, R.J. (ed.) (1990) 'Coming out: Its Nature, Stage, and Health Concerns'. In Kus, R.J. (ed.), *Keys to Caring: Assisting Your Gay and Lesbian Clients.* Boston: Alyson. 30–44.

Lawson, H. (ed.) (1998) *Practice Teaching – Changing Social Work.* London: Jessica Kingsley.

Leahy, M. and Cohn-Sherbok, D. (1996) *The Liberation Debate: Rights at Issue.* London: Routledge.

Logan, J., Kershaw, S., Karban, K., Mills, S., Trotter, J. and Sinclair, M. (1996) *Confronting Prejudice: Lesbian and Gay Issues in Social Work Education.* Aldershot: Arena.

Mason-John, V. (1995) *Talking Black: Lesbians of African and Asian Descent Speak Out.* London: Cassell.

McIntosh, M. (1968) 'The Homosexual Role', *Social Problems,* 16(2): 182–92.

Nussbaum, M. (1996) 'Lesbians and Gay Rights: Pro'. In Leahy and Cohn-Sherbok (1996): 89–107.

O'Hagan, K. (1996) *Competence in Social Work Practice: A Practical Guide for Professionals.* London: Jessica Kingsley.

Oliviere, D., Hargreaves, R. and Monroe, B. (1998) *Good Practices in Palliative Care: A Psychosocial Perspective.* Aldershot: Ashgate.

Patterson, C.J. (1992) 'Children of Lesbian and Gay Parents', *Child Development,* 63: 1025–42.

Plummer, K. (1992a) 'Speaking its Name: Inventing a Lesbian and Gay Studies'. In Plummer (1992b): 3–28.

Plummer, K. (ed.) (1992b) *Modern Homosexualities: Fragments of Lesbian and Gay Experience.* London: Routledge.

Ramakers, M, (1997) 'The International Lesbians and Gay Association Five Years Later'. In Blasius and Phelan (1997): 134–39.

Schenck, C. (1997) 'Lesbians and their Emancipation in the Former German Democratic Republic: Past and Future'. In Blasius and Phelan (1997): 817–22.

Scruton, R. (1996) 'Gay Reservations'. In Leahy and Cohn-Sherbok (1996): 108–24.

Seidman, S. (1996) *Queer Theory/Sociology.* Oxford: Blackwell.

Sharp, M. (1997) 'Lithuania'. In Griffin and Mulholland (1997): 152–7.

Vass, A.A. (ed.) (1996) *Social Work Competences: Core Knowledge, Values and Skills.* London: Sage.

Weeks, J. (1996) 'The Construction of Homosexuality'. In Seidman (1996): 41–63.

Woodman, N.J. (ed.) (1992) *Lesbian and Gay Lifestyles: A Guide for Counseling and Education.* New York: Irvington Publishers.

7 Intellectual Disability, Oppression and Difference

Tim Stainton

Abstract

This chapter considers the issue of oppression of people who have been labelled as having an intellectual disability. It considers the basis for that oppression in the intellectual heritage of modernity, particularly the association of reason with goodness and value, and then considers how this has manifest itself in specific oppressive practices such as segregation, abuse, socioeconomic deprivation, legal inequality, euthanasia and elimination. We will also consider briefly some possible pathways for emancipation and the role of social work both in the oppression and emancipation of people with intellectual disabilities. Finally it considers the more general question of difference and oppression and the commonality of the process of oppression across marginalised groups. In general the chapter deals with practices that have been consistent throughout western societies, although some variation will inevitably occur in degree and time scales. Examples will be largely drawn from the West, primarily the English-speaking countries. The basic ideas are, however, relevant not only to the West, but to modernity in its broadest sense.

Introduction

This chapter will look at the oppression of people who have been labelled as having an intellectual disability. It will consider the basis for that oppression in the intellectual heritage of modernity and how this has manifested itself in specific oppressive practices. We will also consider briefly some possible pathways for emancipation and the role of social work both in the oppression and emancipation of people with intellectual disabilities. In general the chapter will deal with practices that have been consistent throughout western societies, although some variation will inevitably occur in degree and time scales. Examples will be largely drawn from the West, primarily the English-speaking countries. The basic ideas are however, relevant not only to the West, but to modernity in its broadest sense. Before we can begin to look at the specific forms of oppression, we need to consider a more subtle, but critical factor in the oppression of people with intellectual disability: the question of naming and categories.

Names and categories

To name something is to exercise power. Sometimes this power is explicit, as when a social worker names a given individual 'disabled', thus entitling them to resources and services attached to the category. It is a mechanism of inclusion/exclusion. At other times the name or label carries with it a host of identity features and stereotypes which threaten to overpower the specific identity of the subject: the *child abuser*, the *drug dealer*, the *psychiatric case*, the *cripple*, the *lesbian* and so on *ad infinitum*. These names and labels are powerful constructs which the individual must struggle against to have their identity as a person recognised. Names and labels serve to consolidate the power of others. If there were no *psychiatric patients* there could be no psychiatry, thus the power to name and label is crucial to the very existence of all psychosocial professions, a power they guard jealously. In light of this it is no surprise that most emancipation struggles begin by shedding the names given them by others and taking back the power to control the language of their identity: 'Negroes' became black or African people; 'ladies' and 'girls' became women or wimmin; 'homosexuals', 'queers' and 'faggots' became 'gay' in a riot of identity reclamation.

People who have been labelled 'mentally handicapped', 'retarded', 'defectives' and so on have also tried to shed their externally imposed labels. 'Label jars not people' has been a core slogan of the movement of people who have been so labelled. Indeed, the power inherent in the labels attributed to them has repeatedly transformed these terms from allegedly scientific ones into colloquial derisives. *Idiot, moron, imbecile, retard, defective* all began their modern semiotic life as 'scientific' categories but have all been transformed into popular terms of derision in the English language. Such is the power of the construct that whatever term is used it almost inevitably takes on an oppressive, derisory meaning. So it is appropriate to begin our discussion of oppression and intellectual disability with the name.

The name chosen by the self-advocacy movement of people with intellectual disability is simple and instructive: *People First*, attempts to directly challenge the exclusion and categorical stereotyping which masks their common humanity. Interestingly though they have not, as other liberation movements have done, tried to either reclaim the labels as the gay movement has done with 'queer' or physically disabled people in Britain have done by insisting on the use of 'disabled person' as a positive identity affirmation. This has left something of a vacuum when one seeks to refer to this labelled group and has contributed to often acrimonious debate, a large dose of political correctness (Race 1995) and at times, absurd and awkward constructions in an ultimately futile attempt to find a neutral terminology. In the UK *learning difficulty* or *disability* are the current 'correct' terms, while in the US the use of 'people first language' is *de rigeur*, resulting in long complex designations such as 'people who have been labelled mentally retarded'. One rather absurd but instructive example comes from one of the leading US journals in the field which in its instructions to authors insists on 'people first language'; however, the title of the journal remains *Mental Retardation* which few would find acceptable terminology today.

The reality is of course that there is no such thing as a neutral term, nor is any term perceived today to be 'correct' likely to remain so. Language is power and so will always reflect the shifting sands of power dialectics. For the purposes of this chapter I have chosen to use the term *intellectual disability*. This is not to suggest that it avoids the above-mentioned pitfalls, but as a contingent response to current reality it has some advantages. It is not particularly associated with one country such as learning disability or developmental disabilities, and it is consistent with the disability movement's use of *disability* to refer to a social construct as distinct from a specific impairment such as Down's syndrome (see Oliver 1990, Race 1995).

While the simple task of naming has proven complex, identifying exactly who we are talking about within whatever label we choose is equally complex and even more directly related to the issue of oppression. The question of 'what is intellectual disability?' is a subject of much debate. At one end there is an exclusive or predominant emphasis on the biological facts, for example, the presence of a specific impairment such as Down's syndrome. The main problem with this type of definition is its exclusive focus on intellectual disability as a 'disease', an individual pathology, with little or no reference to the practical or social consequences which may vary greatly given the severity, the individual and the social context. A more specific problem is the magnitude of possibilities and the range of degrees that may be present in a given case. Most intellectual disabilities cannot be attributed to a specific biological factor. Down's syndrome represents the largest single identified cause and yet includes only 10 per cent of the entire putative class. On the level of sub-classes alone there are: inborn errors of metabolism, chromosomal disorders, gross neurological defects, as well as infections and exposure to toxic agents during pregnancy and brain damage during delivery (Ryan 1987). This is further differentiated by the degree of deviation from the 'norm' in a given case.

Other definitions have focused on adaptive functioning such as the widely used definition of the American Association of Mental Deficiency (AAMD): '... significantly sub average general intellectual functioning existing concurrently with deficits in adaptive behaviour, and manifested during the developmental period' (Grossman 1977: 27).

Intelligence testing is central to these definitions which rely heavily on normative assumptions about what constitutes average functioning or adaptive behaviour. The sociocultural bias in IQ testing is also well documented (see Gould 1981). Its arbitrary nature can also be seen in the fact that when the AAMD reclassified its IQ levels, 'thousands of people were cured of mental handicaps overnight' (Blatt quoted in Bogdan and Taylor 1982).

These first two types of definitions generally are underpinned by what Oliver (1990) has termed the 'personal tragedy theory of disability', where disability is seen exclusively as an individual problem, thus encouraging a focus on the elimination of the impairment and a predominantly bio-psychological approach to policy and practice. Alternatively, a 'social model' of disability has begun to emerge, spurred largely by the work of people with disabilities themselves and focusing not on the individual with a disability as the problem, but on social arrangements which 'construct disabilities'.

In this vein some have attempted to deal with the problem by the conceptualisation of intellectual disability as purely a social construct. (See Liachiawitz 1988; Ferguson 1987; also Berger and Luckmann 1966 for social construction theory.) The central idea is that through processes such as labelling and segregation we have constructed the disability. While these ideas seem relevant, they fail to give us the whole picture, and they do not seem to deal adequately with physical or intellectual difference. One may well be disabled because, as a wheelchair user, you cannot enter a building that does not have a ramp, but the fact still remains that physiological difference must be acknowledged if it is to be addressed.

None of these conceptions seem to provide, in and of themselves, an adequate definition of intellectual disability. None seem to allow for some notion of difference without encouraging a devaluing of the person, or without leaving us with a counter-factual denial of biological difference. We need a conception that allows for some identification of difference if we are to justify differential treatment in terms of social policy and resource division within society and further, allows us to engage in a process of empowerment and collective emancipation but does not itself engender social devaluation and discrimination.

St. Claire (1989) argues that we need to view three dimensions interactionally: impairments (i.e. Down's syndrome), subnormal performance and role failures, that is, failure to adequately fulfil socially defined roles or achieve a status consistent with valued social roles. Social construction is seen as overlaying all three dimensions encouraging an interaction between elements. That is, identification of an impairment, and consequent labelling, may lead to inadequate education, stigmatisation and segregation thus inhibiting development of social skill development resulting in devaluation and role failures. This seems to be the most plausible approach to definition which requires attention to each of the spheres and more critically their interaction. This is also a useful conception for looking at the issue of oppression as it allows us to examine the interplay between alleged scientific factors and the social meaning applied to them. This is crucial as there is a long history of oppression justified by the reification of social phenomena into 'scientific fact' in order to justify oppressive practices. We will consider examples of how science was used and abused to justify oppressive practices shortly, but before we begin to look at specific forms of oppression we need to look at what lies at the root of the oppression of people with intellectual disabilities. I will argue that the central idea in their oppression lies at the heart of the idea of modernity, that is, the association of reason and value and this accounts for the pervasiveness and consistency of oppression of people with intellectual disabilities in modern societies.

Reason's other

The *otherness* of intellectual disability seems to be a consistent phenomenon over time and states. As far back as classical Greece we have evidence of infanticide of disabled newborns (Garland 1995). The practice of keeping intellectually disabled people as slaves and fools goes back at least as far as ancient Rome where they were so highly prized they commanded higher prices in the slave market than the non-disabled (Stainton 1994). What lies at the heart of their otherness and why has it been such a consistent and potent force for oppression? Quite simply, intellectual disability strikes at the very heart of classical and modern ideas of value and humanness. Shakespeare at his most Aristotelian sums up this central plank in the modernist project: 'What a piece of work is man! how noble in reason! how infinite in faculty! ... the paragon of animals!' [*Hamlet*, II.ii].

It is reason from which classical and modernist ideas of value stem and underpin our putative preeminence over the beast; hence, those that lack these qualities will naturally lack both nobility and value and be associated with animals, that is, something less than fully human. This basic argument can be seen in the natural philosophy of both Plato and Aristotle as well as their social and ethical writings. Aristotle's argument for justifying the inferior position of women and his justification of slavery as a natural institution are particularly instructive. Slaves and women were said not to possess, or at least not to a sufficient degree, reason which justified their social position and *naturally* precluded them from citizenship. Aristotle discussing the rule of freemen over slaves, males over females and men over children notes

> while parts of the soul are present in each, the distribution is different. Thus the deliberative faculty in the soul is not present at all in the slave; in a female it is present but ineffective, in a child present but undeveloped. (*Politics, Ixiii*)

This theme of exclusion and inferiority based on a perceived degree of reason was reasserted with the coming of modernity. John Locke, perhaps the central figure in modern political thought, was clear that participation in the liberal state was contingent upon reason. In his *Two Treatises of Government* he states:

> But if through defects that may happen out of the ordinary course of Nature, any one comes not to such a degree of reason wherein he might be supposed capable of knowing the law ... he is never capable of being a free man ... So lunatics and idiots are never set free from the government of their parents. (Locke 1690: 145)

In this Locke was following in the natural law tradition. Samuel Pufendorf (1717) notes: 'To make a Man capable of (I) giving a ferious and firm *Confent*, tis above all things necessary that he be mafter of his Reafon ...' (p. 56). He goes on to state that if one is incurably lacking in reason that he 'is in all Legal and Moral Confideration to be accounted *Dead*'. The latter reference is to the notion of civil death, an exclusion from society and civil life.

While these citations may seem of little relevance today, they represent the very basis upon which people with intellectual disabilities have been excluded from social and civil equality. We will consider some of these exclusions shortly, but there is another, more damning way in which this idea of reason and value has been interpreted. This strain found its most vigorous exponents in the eugenics movement of the end of the nineteenth and the first half of the twentieth centuries.

Spurred on by Darwin's theory of evolution, scientists began to consider the role humans could take in their own evolution. Francis Galton (1822–1911) coined the term *eugenics* which he defined as 'the study of agencies under social control which may improve or impair the racial qualities of future generations' (1909). Numerous factors contributed to the currency of eugenicist thought during this period. Stedman Jones (1971) has argued that there was an increased fear of the 'underclass' within the middle classes and concern that they had not responded to legislative and charitable attempts to 'raise them up'. Concern with national degeneration caused by the alleged relative fecundity of the lower classes was heightened in Britain by the vast number of recruits for the Boer war who were unfit for service and worries over 'national efficiency' in the face of increasing international competition (Searle 1976). Similar fears contributed to the rise and currency of eugenics elsewhere in Europe and North America (see Paul 1995; McLaren 1990).

Tredgold, a leading specialist in mental deficiency and exponent of eugenics put the case clearly:

> There is not the slightest doubt that the decline [in the birth rate] is chiefly incident in – indeed, one may say practically confined to – the best and most fit elements of the community, whilst loafers, the incompetents, the insane and feeble-minded, continue to breed with unabated and unrestrained vigour. (quoted in Searle 1976: 21)

In 1895, the first lobby group was founded for the control of the feeble-minded: the *National Association for Promoting the Welfare of the Feeble-Minded* (NAPWF), a Charity Organisation Society (COS) (one of the founding organisations of social work) offshoot. The goals of NAPWF were anything but ambiguous. At a meeting of the association Lord Herschell moved a resolution affirming that:

> The existence of large classes of feeble-minded persons is a danger to the moral and physical welfare of society and calls for immediate attention both on the part of public authorities and charitable enterprise. (*The Times*, 1898)

Similar organisations for the control of the 'feebleminded' and the promotion of eugenics were also formed around the same time elsewhere in Europe and North America (see Paul 1995, McLaren 1990). The above quote suggests another aspect of eugenicist thought: the tendency to both expand the category and to associate perceived deficits in intellectual ability with virtually all moral and social ills. This is clearly evident in the following quote from Goddard (1866–1957), who was the director of the first psychological research laboratory for the study of mental deficiency at the Vineland Training School in the US. Goddard wrote:

> For many generations we have recognized and pitied the idiot. Of late we have recognized a higher type of defective, the moron, and have discovered he is a burden ... a menace to society and civilization, that he is responsible in large measure, for many, if not all, our social problems ... (Quoted in Abbot and Sapsford 1987: 25)

The eugenicist had essentially four strategies for controlling the 'spread and menace of the feeble-minded': elimination, sterilisation, marriage regulation and segregation. All would be utilised, and to some extent continue to be used today. On a less direct level, it is the legacy of the eugenics movement which has shaped many of our institutions and policies towards intellectual disability today. In the following section we will consider this legacy, and that of the preceding discussion on the exclusion of people with intellectual disability from full civil and social rights.

Practices of oppression

In this section we will look at some of the specific practices which have resulted in the oppression of people with intellectual disabilities. While this section will deal with specific examples it is important to remember that many of the oppressive practices are intimately interrelated, often with the outcome of one practice being used to justify others. For example, the diagnosis of someone as severely intellectually disabled may lead to institutionalisation, which in turn engenders a retardation of the development of social skills which then may be used to justify further interventions. Or, segregated education may encourage the perception of people as different or dangerous, thus reinforcing a broader social exclusion.

Segregation and isolation

The segregation and isolation of people with intellectual disabilities is one of the most pervasive forms of oppression throughout the past hundred years. The most dramatic and obvious form is of course the institution. While institutions pre-date the eugenics movement, the degree of institutionalisation and the nature of the institutions themselves changed dramatically with the advent of eugenics from pedagogical facilities to ones explicitly for segregation (Wolfensberger 1975; Stainton 1994). While rationales would change again in the post-war era to a quasi-medical one, the basic nature – and outcomes – of institutionalisation remains the same. Goffman's *Asylums* (1961) is perhaps the best known of numerous studies and critiques of institutions. A breeding ground for abuse, isolation and desocialisation, institutions reached their peak in most western countries in the late 1960s, but remain a common feature of most countries' service systems despite their widely acknowledged inherent oppressive nature. Indeed one of the most common features of institutions is the consistency of scandal associated with them across time and jurisdiction. From Abendberg, the 'first' institution for the intellectually disabled in the mid-nineteenth century, through the contemporary reports of conditions in institutions in Romania and other former Soviet Bloc countries, scandal, abuse and oppression are endemic to the very structure of institutions. (See for example: Cohen and Scull 1985; Kanner 1960; Martin 1984; Stainton 1994.)

Most Western countries are now involved in a process of deinstitutionalisation, but isolation does not necessarily end with the closure of the institution. Institutionalisation is as much a process as a specific locale (Paul et al. 1977), and there is evidence of the transfer of institutional practices to community residential services (Williams 1995). It is common in many jurisdictions for staff from the institutions themselves to set up private for-profit homes for those coming out of institutions as an easy way of achieving deinstitutionalisation and deflecting staff opposition to closures.

Deinstitutionalisation is not just a process of leaving a facility. Too often the process stops at the address change but isolation in the community can be even greater than within the confines of the institution. The commodification of people with intellectual disabilities as fodder for the social service industry also encourages a minimalist approach to deinstitutionalisation in many jurisdictions (Wolfensberger 1989).

The exclusion of people with intellectual disabilities from mainstream education is one of the most insidious forms of segregation. Not only does it result in an inferior education but contributes to the disabling of the broader community. Children grow up with the message that people with intellectual disabilities are somehow fundamentally different than themselves, they do not grow up to see them as a normal part of the rich fabric of community life and thus are trained to be unwitting accomplices in the oppression and marginalisation of people with intellectual disabilities. Children with intellectual disabilities grow up to see themselves as different, thus encouraging the internalisation of their *spoiled identity* (Goffman 1968).

The basic reality is virtually the same for all areas of social life be it work, leisure or even transportation. For the majority of people with intellectual disabilities, regardless of whether they are in a formal institution or not, they live a life isolated and segregated from the mainstream of the community. We may pass them on the street as they ride by in special buses or have them as neighbours in 'the group home down the road' which we may have heard about because other neighbours organised a NIMBY (not in my back yard) campaign to try and stop it, but we are unlikely to live, work and play with the other unless we do some voluntary work as our bit to 'help out the poor unfortunates' or are paid to be there. Progress is being made in all these areas; it is no longer the case that we 'don't know better', but the gap between our rhetoric of inclusion and the reality of people's lives remains enormous.

Sex, relationships and families

The regulation of the sexual life of people with intellectual disabilities, particularly women, was one of the key obsessions of the eugenics movement. Strict sexual segregation was, and to some degree still is, a key aspect of institutional regimes. The attitude towards the sexuality of people with intellectual disabilities is somewhat paradoxical. On the one hand the belief that they tended to be less sexually restrained and hence more prolific in their procreation led to the kinds of sexual segregation noted above, restrictive marriage and sexual offence legislation and widespread sterilisation of women, which for many years was legally mandated in many western countries. On the other hand the view of people with intellectual disabilities as childlike has often resulted in a lack of any kind of sex education or even recognition of them as sexual beings, leaving them vulnerable to abuse, disease and exploitation.

While laws prohibiting sexual contact and marriage of people with intellectual disabilities are generally being repealed or revised in most western countries, sterilisation remains a common feature of the lives of women with intellectual disabilities, with some countries still having eugenically inspired sterilisation laws on their statute books (Paul 1995). For many years services and institutions would sterilise women as a matter of course, now there is some protection in many countries but the practice is still common. Two similar cases on the non-therapeutic sterilisation of women with intellectual disabilities illustrate both the progress and the tenacity of the belief in the efficacy of sterilisation. The 'Eve' case in Canada ruled that a non-therapeutic sterilisation without consent could not be performed despite the wishes of a legal guardian, her mother. This case became something of a test of the degree to which fundamental citizenship rights of individuals with intellectual disabilities overrode any paternalist instincts. It came after the 1982 passing of The Canada Act which included The Canadian Charter of Rights and Freedoms, which specifically includes mental disability in the equality rights sections. This case provides an almost direct comparison with a case in the UK, *Re* 'B' in which the judgment went in favour of the guardian. The contrast of the two judgments is clearly one between the paternalism of the welfare principle as cited by Lord Hailsham and the rights of the citizen as noted in *Re* 'Eve'. In a review of the UK case, in which he contrasts the Canadian and UK decisions, M.D.A. Freeman (1988; 78–9) notes that 'at the very least the Lords' decision helps to foster an ideology which denies human rights and, in doing so, denies the humanity of an already disadvantaged group' and criticises the Lords for 'putting what they conceived to be Jeanette's best interest before her rights ... [and] giving too little consideration to Jeanette's rights'.

But for those fortunate enough to retain their ability to have children, it remains difficult to marry and even more so to have and keep children. Despite the fact that recent research has shown that having parents with an intellectual disability results in no more problems for the children than those of non-disabled parents (Booth and Booth 1997), social services', parents' and care workers' most common response is to advise against having children. If they proceed, the child is almost automatically put on the child protection register and in many cases is removed by social services.

Abuse

One of the most direct forms of oppression is the widespread physical, sexual and psychological abuse of people with intellectual and other disabilities (Roeher Institute 1995; Brown and Craft 1989). While little research was carried out in this area until the past decade, studies indicate that not only does abuse of all types occur, but the prevalence rates are much higher than in the general population. This is a prime example of how oppressive practices interact. As with all types of abuse, isolation tends to be a key predisposing factor; as noted above, this is also a key outcome of much of our social and structural response to people with disabilities so the higher prevalence rates are not surprising.

Compounding this is the difficulty people have in communicating their abuse and having it taken seriously when often the abusers are the people they are dependent upon for care and support. In some cases abuse is disguised as treatment, such as long periods of isolation and electric shocks (Roeher Institute 1988a). If it does come to legal proceeding, which is rare as systems tend to try to address these issues internally without involving legal authorities, people with intellectual disabilities often are not taken seriously by the police or in court as they are often deemed by the court as incompetent to give evidence or are confused by aggressive defense lawyers (Keays-Bryne 1997; Gunn 1989). So once again we have a clear interaction of oppressive practice which creates a synergistic effect, compounding the oppression experienced by people with intellectual disabilities.

Socioeconomic oppression

One of the many features that people with intellectual disability share with other marginalised groups is poverty. This is not surprising since the vast majority rely on state benefits and real unemployment rates tend to be anywhere from 70–90 per cent. (See for example Statistic Canada 1986; Roeher Institute 1988b.) Many jurisdictions in fact require people to be declared unable to work in order to qualify for benefits or set up poverty traps wherein the loss of benefit outweighs the economic gains which could be had by low-paid employment. Substituted for real work is endless training, day centres or workshops where their labour is exploited, working for little or no remuneration. Yet again we see the system reinforcing the isolation and marginalisation of people with intellectual disabilities.

Structural and legal oppression

As noted previously, the tradition in liberal jurisprudence is that a person must be deemed competent to be ascribed rights and citizenship. Hence, many jurisdictions have actively excluded people with intellectual disabilities from equal citizenship. We have previously noted several examples with regard to sterilisation and competency to testify. Until 1985 the Canada Elections Act denied people whose 'liberty was restrained' or whose property was under the control of a trustee because of 'mental disease' the right to vote. The denial of the rights to enter into contracts, refuse treatment and to have basic liberty of movement, both within one's own country and across borders, is common. This denial of basic rights has been common throughout western countries with the state or families having virtually unlimited proxy rights with regards to major decisions.

On a more structural level, our service systems have been designed not around the needs of individuals, but around a class conception of need. In other words, we have developed a range of 'services for the intellectually disabled' on the assumption that somehow a broad class of need can be identified without regard for individual preference, autonomy, race, ethnicity or gender. Thus people that have to rely on supports and services to meet their daily needs and to support their participation in the community are forced into predetermined categories of need whether these fit with their individual needs or not (Stainton 1994). This has generally resulted in a lowest common denominator approach to services, at once enforcing and reinforcing the stereotype.

Life and death

As noted above, extermination was one of the four main strategies of the eugenicist. With the coming of the Nazis in Germany this became a state-enforced reality. In 1939 Hitler began what was to become known as the Holocaust by ordering that anyone who, in the opinion of a physician, was incurable to be authorised for release by euthanasia. Later that year Aktion T4 ordered a more formal programme which eventually would result in the gassing of tens of thousands of people with an intellectual and other disabilities (Scheerenberger 1983; Paul 1995). We generally like to feel those days are behind us; however, with the new genetics and the introduction of genetic screening for various disabilities coupled with the increasing debate on the right to treatment and euthanasia, we find ourselves facing many of the same questions. With the new genetics has come a new eugenics.

While a complete discussion of these complex issues is beyond the scope of this chapter, a few areas for concern can be highlighted. With increasing pressure on health care systems there is a growing concern with both the rationing of treatment and the efficacy of treating people whose quality of life is deemed by others to be below the norm. Quality Adjusted Life Years or QALYs is one means by which medical ethicists are suggesting resource allocation can be 'rationalised'. Inevitably people with an intellectual or other disability will virtually always be assumed to have a lower quality of life and thus be less eligible for treatment which would use up scarce resources. In the most dramatic cases, this will involve euthanasia, which is commonplace whether or not it is formally legalised (Bueckert 1993). In other cases we see murder covered up as 'mercy killing' because the victim was intellectually disabled and their life was deemed not worth living (Calder 1994).

As threatening as the above developments are, by far the greatest threat to people with and intellectual disability is the new genetics. It is now commonplace to screen prenatally for Down's syndrome and other disabilities and to recommend abortion of the foetus. What does this say about the value of people who are part of our community who have Down's syndrome or about the future for others that do not quite fit the normative ideal of society? Already genetic research has returned to the eugenic Holy Grail in a search for genes which determine intelligence, despite the fact that intelligence is not a fixed identifiable quantity but a socially determined normative judgement. It is even more disturbing given the obvious links to the eugenic past that researchers refuse to even acknowledge let alone debate the ethics of the potential uses of their research. One leading researcher, Robert Plomin is quoted in the *Guardian* as saying 'I am not worried about the ethics of what I am doing, and I don't want to discuss it in a public forum ... I want to get on with the science of it.' (1 February 1996) So once again we have potentially enormously oppressive practices hiding behind the cloak of science, as they did with the first wave of eugenics. While this brief review of the topic does not do it justice, it is crucial we recognise the profundity of such practices and their potential for the ultimate oppression of any subject group. (See International League of Societies for Persons With Mental Handicap 1994; King 1997; Shakespeare 1995).

Towards emancipation?

While the above only provides a brief overview of some of the forms of oppression experienced by people with intellectual disabilities, there is a certain epistemological consistency, despite the wide variation in specific forms of oppression. While each form will to some degree require a specific response in order to counteract the oppression, the current chapter does not allow for a complete discussion on this. We can however consider an emancipatory project on this more general epistemological basis. As argued earlier, the oppression of people with intellectual disabilities stems from a fundamental association of reason with value. This has taken on two key forms: a juridical form resulting in a denial of basic rights, exclusionary competency requirements and a diminished citizenship; and, a psycho-social form, most paradigmatically in the mental testing and eugenics movement. It follows then that an emancipatory project must focus on breaking this link between reason and the value of persons in these two spheres.

On a practical level, it must focus on obtaining basic legal equality and securing equality of rights. There has been some progress in this regard. The introduction of the Canadian Charter demonstrated the force of this in both the 'Eve' case and in the overturning of the discriminatory section of the Canada Elections Act noted above. The introduction of the wide-ranging and strongly enforceable Americans with Disabilities Act 1989 (ADA) is another good example and demonstrated its worth when it was used to declare an Oregon plan to distribute health care resources on the basis of quality of life indicators as contravening the rights of disabled people. Australia and Britain have also passed disability discrimination legislation, although in the latter case the efficacy of the Act is seriously questioned.

Legal equality is, however, only one step towards equal citizenship for people with intellectual disabilities. To achieve a truly participatory citizenship both a change in social policy structures and in public attitude is required. To a degree the two are linked, but let us deal with the social policy issues first. The tradition in social policy regarding people with intellectual disabilities has been largely based on this paternalist model. The assumption has been that they lack the basis of participation and require care at best, and at worst, control or elimination as the eugenics movement has advocated. The assumption behind most social policy is that people with an intellectual disability are a unitary body, or at best a set of collectives defined by levels of intellectual impairment. Hence the bulk of social policy has specifically precluded participation through segregation, isolation and low expectations and provided support based on this specious class of need. There is little room in this equation for the person with intellectual disability to emerge as either a specific individual citizen or as a participant in the state or civil society. If we are to reverse this historical trend in social policy we must reverse these assumptions, we must assume participation, individuality and equality. To this end some positive signs are emerging. The now well-established trend towards inclusion in schools, work and social life are important parts of this process but ones with a long way to go before they are realities. On a more structural level, policy must begin to allow for individually made choices about the how, when and where support is provided. This is why policy developments like service brokerage, individualised funding, more flexible approaches to consent and access to advocacy which allow the individual to choose how their needs are to be met are so critical to building equal citizenship (Stainton 1994). They provide the means for the individual citizen to emerge, participate and grow as an individual citizen rather than a part of some excluded putative class.

A change in attitudes is somewhat more difficult to approach directly, although we have made some progress on this issue in the past decades. When people are allowed to be full participants in life, when they share the same rights, schools, workplaces and communities as any other citizen, they are more likely to be seen and treated as equals. It is not surprising that in societies which have excluded, vilified and labelled people with intellectual disabilities that they have come to have a negative value in those societies. We have created a fertile bed for negative attitudes. It is only by reversing this legal, structural and social exclusion that attitudes will change and the social basis of citizenship – mutual respect – will emerge.

Social work: part of the problem or the solution?

Thus far we have not dealt directly with social work as a profession. To some degree this reflects the fact that it has historically been a somewhat marginal actor in the area of intellectual disability, which has been dominated and fiercely protected by the medical and psychological professions. As noted above though, from the early beginnings of social work through COS, the profession has been a part of the oppression of people with intellectual disabilities and certainly has not been a major voice in their emancipation. While institutions remained the dominant form of social support, the social worker's role was generally to deal with the family, often to convince them of the need for their son or daughter to be segregated. In this role social work often tried to extend the pathology beyond the individual to include the entire family. 'Chronic sorrow' was the professional interpretation of the families' response (Olshansky 1962) and any positive responses of the family were attributed to denial (Behr 1990).

With the advent of deinstitutionalisation and community-based support, social work has become a much more integral part of the social response to intellectual disability. As case managers they are often the key link between the individual and the support system and as such have an enormous capacity to influence the way society responds to people with an intellectual disability. There is however nothing inherent in case management that ensures an emancipatory approach. Like all technologies, it can be used equally to enforce oppressive practice as to emancipate (Stainton 1997).

The profession's multidimensional focus does however give it a unique perspective on the individual's situation, being able to look not only at the person but the mezzo and macro socioeconomic factors which affect the quality of their lives. The profession's ethical base, founded on equality of persons and self-determination of the individual, also provides strong incentive to eschew the false categories and labels and the insidious link between reason and value in order to work towards a new equality in partnership with the individual. To do this, social work must use its broad focus to challenge the social and structural basis of oppression and to ensure that their involvement with people with intellectual disabilities is a relationship of equality. Social workers must be prepared to share their power and to challenge oppressive practices within their own agencies and authorities, and to accept their role as a support to the individual rather than an agent of the state (Stainton 1991). This presents unique challenges and opportunities for the profession both in defining its own stance towards the oppression of people with intellectual disabilities and to consolidate its identity as an autonomous profession rather than as a secondary adjunct to the medical and psychological fields or as merely gatekeepers for the state. In the end, social workers must decide if they are to be part of the problem and remain agents of the oppressive state or take their ethical and epistemological foundations seriously and join with people with intellectual disabilities and their families and advocates to end the pervasive oppression.

Conclusion: identity, difference and solidarity

This chapter has tried to broadly outline the epistemological basis of the oppression of people with intellectual disabilities and provide some examples of the more blatant oppressions which stem from it. While we have only briefly considered some of the ways an emancipatory practice might be undertaken and the role of social work, it is hoped that the basis for a debate on how social work should respond has been laid. While this chapter has focused on intellectual disability, many of the arguments and examples would apply equally well to other oppressed and marginalised groups. Oppression is rooted in the manipulation of identities, the translation of difference into otherness in order to reinforce the power of the dominant identity in a given society. So it is not surprising that the technologies of oppression are similar across groups. In conclusion then, it is useful to consider briefly this broader question of identity and difference and the implications for an emancipatory social work. If social work is to challenge oppression it must begin by challenging the very categories of difference.

There are numerous examples of oppression based on claims to objective differences and the reification of social phenomena as 'natural facts' (Noel 1994). Women were routinely excluded from the public sphere on the grounds of their natural association with the private realm (Pateman 1989); black people were said to be genetically inferior to whites (Shipman 1994), and as we have seen, people with disabilities were seen to have a natural tendency to profligate sexuality and socially deviant behaviour. All of these were legitimated by claims of objective, empirical truth. The invisibility of the One – the dominant normative subject – is continually reinforced by claims to objective knowledge as the basis of difference (Noel 1994). When we accept the existence of an objective empirical state as a basis for difference, we assist the dominant group in masking its own power. Such a strategy allows the dominant group to retain a claim to 'truth', thus ensuring its ability to regulate the process, degree and impact of emancipation.

There is of course the idea of a value-neutral difference which suggests that while differences may well be socially constructed they do not necessarily imply any imbalance of power or the existence of a dominant group. This is usually invoked to provide a basis for liberal equality of opportunity where differences are essentially ignored in the public sphere. There are two serious problems associated with this view, paradoxically, the minimising of difference and the overemphasis of difference. Minimising difference has been the dominant liberal social work tradition, which leads to an emphasis on sameness – the idea that 'deep down we are all the same' (Pinderhughes 1989). This approach legitimates social work practice that ignores diversity. It also legitimates policies which provide a superficial equality that, in the end, comes to reinforce the power of the dominant group.

This position also ignores the essential role of difference in identity formation, both collective and individual. Connolly, in his closely argued book *Identity/Difference*, expresses this necessary relationship well:

An identity is established in relation to series of differences that have become socially recognized. These differences are essential to its being. If they did not coexist as differences, it would not exist in its distinctness and solidity ...

Identity requires difference in order to be, and it converts difference into otherness in order to secure its own self-certainty. (Connolly 1991: 64)

Hence, an approach based on ignoring differences or treating them as value neutral ignores the necessity of value judgements in identity formation.

While the focus on sameness is problematic, so too is an overemphasis on difference as a positive affirmation of socially determined groups. This approach provides ample justification for stereotyping, 'separate but equal policies' and a subjugation of the individual to the group. This overemphasis on difference reinforces a reductionism which serves to confine the individual to roles predetermined by the dominant group such as 'a black person', 'a disabled person', 'an Italian'. With regard to intellectual disability, this often results in a denial or minimising of other identity features such as race, class or gender. What both the proponents and critics of the liberal approach ignore is the role of the dominant group in defining the other, which again masks the hegemonic aspects of difference.

On a more personal level, this overemphasis on the difference of the group ignores the role of the individual in autonomous self-definition. Identity is ultimately an individual process; by overemphasising difference we limit the individual's ability to define herself no less than by enforcing sameness. Also ignored in this formulation is the issue of multiple self-identification. We all have multiple attachments to social categories which define us. While it is true that we may be forced to attach greater significance to a given identify feature by the experience of oppression, identity definition is ultimately an individual process. We may choose to emphasise one set of attachments such as our sexual orientation or our cultural associations at a given time, but these need to be placed in a broader and infinitely more complex identity of the particular self if a person is to be fully understood and appreciated. This idea is not meant to minimise the importance of the group or the social context as the forum in which this process occurs. It is the group which provides the main context for an individual's struggle for emancipation and self-actualisation:

Even though emancipation begins and ends with the individual, he or she has only collective means of ensuring its progress. (Noel 1994: 192)

If we reject the 'neutral' approach to the idea of difference, we are left with a conception entailing the notions of inequality and oppression. Difference is defined by the exercise of power by a dominant group. Difference always entails an other and always involves the exercise of power. It is only by conceiving of difference in terms of oppression that we can begin the process of unmasking the dominant One and identifying the technologies of oppression employed to maintain this power. Further, it is only through an oppression-based definition of difference that we can begin to articulate the processes of emancipation.

On a somewhat more practical level, this conception of difference allows us to explore the commonalities of experience across groups, including both the means by which apparently diverse groups are oppressed and common means of emancipation (Noel 1994; Stainton and Swift 1996). Such a definition of difference allows for a more generalised approach, one which minimises competition among oppressed groups and maximises the possibility of collective action. When the mechanisms of oppression and emancipation rather than the particular identity features become the focus of analysis, we have a means of encouraging solidarity rather than fostering competing claims. In other words, this approach allows an analysis which retains the otherness without accepting the dominant construction.

If social work is to truly undertake an emancipatory project then it must take this broader view of difference and oppression. While individual workers may practise with one particular group, they must recognise that the 'group' is itself to some degree a social construction and that the ultimate goal must be to support the emancipation of all people regardless of the definitions and labels applied to them. To ignore this is to risk reinforcing the oppressive construction and unwittingly support oppression rather than emancipation.

References

Abbott, Pamela and Sapsford, Roger (1987) *Community Care For Mentally Handicapped Children*. Milton Keynes: Open University Press.
Barton, L. (ed.) (1989) *Disability and Dependency*. London: Falmer.
Behr, S. (1990) *Literature Review: Positive Contributions of Persons With Disabilities to their Families*, Robert Hoyt (ed.) Lawrence, KA: Beach Centre on Families and Disability.
Berger, Peter L. and Luckmann, Thomas (1966) *The Social Construction of Reality*, Harmondsworth: Penguin.
Bogdan, R. and Taylor, S. (1982) *Inside Out: The Social Meaning of Mental Retardation*. Toronto: University of Toronto Press.
Booth T. and Booth W. (1997) *Exceptional Childhoods, Unexceptional Children: Growing Up with Parents who Have Learning Difficulties*. London: Family Policy Studies Centre.
Brown, H. and Craft, A. (eds) (1989) *Thinking the Unthinkable: Papers on Sexual Abuse and People with Learning Difficulties*. London: FBA Education Unit.
Bueckert, D. (1993) 'Euthanasia common but it's kept secret, MD's told', *The Montreal Gazette*, August 25: B1.

Calder, M. (1994) 'Mercy or Murder', *The Montreal Gazette* November 24: B3.

Cohen, Stanley and Scull, Andrew (eds) (1985) *Social Control and the State*. Oxford: Basil Blackwell.

Connolly, W.E. (1991) *Identity/Difference: Democratic Negotiations of Political Paradox*. Ithaca: Cornell University Press.

Ferguson, Philip M. (1987) 'The Social Construction of Mental Retardation', *Social Policy*, Summer.

Freeman, M.D.A. (1988) 'Sterilising the Mentally Handicapped'. In Freeman, M.D.A. (ed.) *Medicine, Ethics and the Law*. London: Stevens and Sons.

Galton, Francis [1909] (1985), 'Probability: The Foundation of Eugenics'. In *Essays in Eugenics*, Reprint. New York: Garland.

Goffman, Erving (1968) *Stigma: Notes on the Management of Spoiled Identity*. Harmondsworth: Penguin.

Goffman, Erving (1961) *Asylums: Essays on the Social Situation of Mental Patients and Other Inmates*. Garden City, NJ: Anchor Books.

Gould, Stephen J. (1981) *The Mismeasure of Man*. Harmondsworth: Penguin.

Grossman, H.J. (ed.) (1977) *Manual in Terminology and Classification in Mental Retardation*, rev. edn. Washington, DC: AAMD.

Guardian (1996) 'The search for the clever stuff', February 1: 2.

Gunn, M. (1989) 'Sexual abuse and Adults with Mental handicap: Can the law help?'. In Brown and Craft (1989).

International League of Societies for Persons With Mental Handicap (1994) *Just Technology?* North York: Roeher Institute.

Kanner, Leo (1960) 'Johann Jakob Guggenbuhl and the Abendberg', *Bulletin of the History of Medicine*. XXXiii.

Keays-Bryne, S. (1997) 'People With Intellectual Disability and the Criminal Justice System', *Interaction*, **10**(3).

King, D. (1997) 'Testing Times', *The New Internationalist*, 293: 12–14.

Liachowitz, Claire H. (1988), *The Social Construction of Disability*. Philadelphia: University of Pennsylvania Press.

Locke, John [1690] (1924) *Two Treatises of Government*. London: J.M. Dent.

Malin, N. (ed.) (1995) *Services for People with Learning Disabilities*. London: Routledge.

Martin, J.P. (1984) *Hospitals in Trouble*. Oxford: Basil Blackwell.

McLaren, Angus (1990) *Our Own Master Race*. Toronto: McClelland & Stewart.

Noel, Lise (1994), *Intolerance: A General Survey*. Montreal: McGill-Queen's.

Oliver, Michael (1990) *The Politics of Disablement*. London: Macmillan.

Olshansky, S. (1962) 'Chronic Sorrow: A Response to Having a Mentally Defective Child', *Social Casework*, 43: 190–3.

Pateman, Carole (1989) *The Disorder of Women*. Oxford: Polity Press.

Paul, Diane B. (1995), *Controlling Human Heredity: 1865 to the Present*. New Jersey: Humanities Press.

Paul, James L., Stedman, D.J. and Neufeld, R. (eds) (1977) *Deinstitutionalization: Program and Policy Development*. Syracuse, NY: Syracuse University Press.

Pinderhughes, E. (1989) *Understanding Race, Ethnicity and Power*. New York: Free Press.

Pufendorf, Samuel (1717) *Of the Laws of Nature and Nations*, 3rd ed. Basil Kennet, translator with the notes of Jean Barbeyrac. London.

Race, David (1995) 'Classification of people with learning disabilities.' In Malin (1995).

Roeher Institute (1988a) *The Language of Pain*. Downsview: Roeher.

Roeher Institute (1988b) *Income Insecurity*. Downsview: Roeher.
Roeher Institute (1995) *Harm's Way: The Many Faces of Violence Against Persons with Disabilities in Canada*. North York: Roeher.
Ryan, Joanna (1987) *The Politics of Mental Handicap*, rev. edn. London: Free Association Books.
Scheerenberger, R.C. (1983) *A History of Mental Retardation*. Baltimore: Paul H. Brookes.
Searle, R. (1976) *Eugenics and Politics in Britain: 1900–1914*. Leyden: Noordhoff.
Shakespeare, Tom (1995) 'Back to the future? New genetics and disabled people', *Critical Social Policy*, **44/45**: 22–35.
Shipman, Pat (1994) *The Evolution of Racism*. New York: Simon and Schuster.
St. Clair, Lindsay (1989) 'A Multidimensional Model of Mental Retardation: Impairment, Subnormal Behaviour, Role Failures, and Socially Constructed Retardation', *American Journal on Mental Retardation*, **94**(1).
Stainton, Tim (1997) 'Rights and Rhetoric in Community Care Policy and Practice: Contradictions and Conundrums for Practitioners'. In Symonds and Kelly (1997).
Stainton, Tim and Swift, K. (1996) '"Difference" and Social Work Curriculum', *Canadian Social Work Review*, **13**(1): 75–87.
Stainton, Tim (1995) 'Bureaucracy and Ideology: A Case Study of the Rise of the Community Living Movement in Ontario in the 1970s', *Ontario Journal on Developmental Disabilities*, **4**(1): 75–87.
Stainton, Tim (1994) *Autonomy and Social Policy: Rights, Mental Handicap and Community Care*. Aldershot: Avebury.
Stainton, Tim (1991) 'Rights Based Social Policy: The Role of Consumers, Advocates, Brokers and Individualized Funding'. In Taylor and Devereux (1991): 45–60.
Statistic Canada (1986) *Health Activity Limitation Survey*. Ottawa: Statistics Canada.
Stedman Jones, Gareth (1971) *Outcast London*. Harmondsworth: Penguin.
Symonds, A. and Kelly A. (eds) (1997) *The Social Construction of Community Care*. London: Macmillan.
Taylor, P. and Devereux, J. (eds) (1991) *Social Work Administrative Practice in Health Care Settings*. Toronto: Canadian Scholars' Press.
Williams, Paul (1995), 'Residential and day services'. In Malin (1995).
Wolfensberger, Wolf (1975) *The Origin and Nature of Our Institutional Models*. Syracuse, NY: Human Policy Press.
Wolfensberger, Wolf (1989) 'Human Service Policies: The Rhetoric versus the Reality'. In Barton (1989).

8 Strategies of Empowerment: Taking Account of Protests by People

Robert Adams

Abstract

The concept of empowerment has had its share of exponents of its virtues. Theoreticians, researchers and, in the UK, official guidance on the implementation of the NHS and Community Care Act 1990, contribute to the rhetoric concerning its use. But there are significant constraints on its practice. These provide a counterpoint for the opportunities for empowerment alleged to exist by officials and professionals, in the domains of politics, policies, service organisations, professions, individual workers, service users and carers.

Two such constraints are examined in this chapter. First, a notable schism exists between the literature concerning anti-oppression and anti-discrimination, and that on empowerment. The former, whilst not always being 'top-down', focuses often enough on the impact of structural inequalities and divisions; the latter, while not always beginning with the individual, deals exhaustively with individual and group-based empowerment. Second, the literature concerning individual and collective empowerment relates at best tangentially, and more often not at all to the area of challenges or protests by people. Such happenings are routinely ignored, misrepresented, under-explained, or subsumed under other phenomena.

This chapter explores the case for reconceptualising the contribution of the person receiving services, so as to make individual and collective challenges by people, and in particular collective protest, part of the mainstream of the agency's activities, rather than constituting the periphery, or even being treated as an excluded activity.

The final section of this chapter considers strategies by which those engaged in social work may address these shortcomings.

Introduction

Since the 1980s social work educators in the UK have shown great enthusiasm for, and commitment to, the linked goals of anti-oppressive practice and empowerment of clients. In contrast, there is no evidence that any significant democratisation of people receiving personal social services has taken place, or that any significant enhancement of participation by people receiving these services has occurred in global, national, regional or local politics, through their engagement in radical, social and collective action. The reasons for the stark contrast between rhetoric and reality are not entirely clear. Perhaps the concept of empowerment is too challenging and dangerous to be contained in most political and social environments. Perhaps it is difficult for powerful people not to resist the power they have worked so hard to attain being taken away from them. This chapter does not examine the political theories embedded in such speculations, but restricts itself to discussing links between the idea of empowerment and the traditions of collective protest which are evident from time to time in many parts of the criminal justice, education, health and social services. It divides into three sections, first considering the concept of empowerment; second making brief notes on some relevant social and historical aspects of protests; and third, examining how the two ideas can be linked viably together. In this way, there is a good chance that the robustness, vigour and criticality of the concept of empowerment will be preserved, thereby preventing it being diluted and incorporated into official and professional practice.

Some problems of the concept of empowerment

Vulnerability to professional and official encroachment

Empowerment is a concept well-rooted in traditions of social development and mutual aid (Tax 1976) in many parts of the world. These traditions by far predate its accelerating professionalisation in Western countries during the late twentieth century. Stokes notes that more than four-fifths of people in Europe belong to at least one networking group or organisation, many of which relate to a tradition or culture of self-help and mutual aid (Stokes 1981). Western concepts of empowerment and mutual aid have developed in the predominantly Judeo-Christian, individualistic and pluralistic political and social culture of the West (Oka 1994: 73). This does not mean, as Oka notes of Japan, that such ideas are absent from countries where there may seem to be little similarity in cultural terms, but rather that there is a need to remove the specifically Western cultural factors and attempt to identify those features which are universal to all cultures. Such comparative work is rare, but very important. Through it, links between empowerment in Western and other countries are being made more readily than before the 1980s (Craig and Mayo 1995; Yuval 1994; Parsloe 1997). However, the burgeoning literature on empowerment does not correlate positively with increased numbers of people experiencing being empowered. In South Asia, for example, which includes countries such as Bangladesh – according to Carr et al. (1996a: 1) the only part of the world where female life expectancies are lower than those of males – half the poor people of the world are living in conditions which are getting worse, absolute poverty rising by 50 per cent among women as opposed to 30 per cent among men (Carr et al. 1996a: 1).

Empowerment has the advantage of being a plastic concept, which can be fashioned to suit many different settings. Popular publications on self-management and self-care are replete with references to empowerment. The importation from the US into the UK of the concept of downshifting, for example, has been accompanied by books providing guidance to self-empowerment through simpler, and cheaper, living (see Ghazi and Jones 1997). The disadvantage of the pliability of the concept of empowerment is its liability to be appropriated by those wishing to define, or even carry out, other people's empowering for them. Allied with this is the confusion between related and sometimes overlapping concepts such as community action (Jacobs and Popple 1994), social movements (Barker 1997), advocacy and consumerism and empowerment (Beresford 1992: 17).

As yet, in some Western countries, notably the US, social work occupies conceptual territory which, despite the long-standing currency of ideas about empowerment in the wider context of work with people (Kieffer 1984), is largely segregated from these. It is also cut off from broader ideas about participatory methodologies, transformational activity and social development and community action in many other parts of the world. In the UK, in contrast, empowerment has taken a strong hold in the professional social work literature since the late 1980s (Adams 1996b). The application of concepts of empowerment across professional boundaries – notably education, health and nursing – has been furthered by the development in different professional areas of similar debates about empowering people (Gibson 1991; Sines 1995; Labonte 1994; Braye and Preston-Shoot 1993; Malterud 1993; Wallerstein and Bernstein 1988, 1994).

According to Ted Gurr, however, empowerment is already largely circumscribed by a particular style of political ideology and democracy (Gurr 1989a: 113). Whether or not we accept this pessimistic view, there is little doubt that empowerment is vulnerable to cooption by professionals (Smale et al. 1993) and in the UK in work with people (Clarke and Stewart

1992). In the area of community care in particular, empowerment has already been heavily colonised by the authorities (Adams 1996b: 181–2).

Diversity of perspectives on empowerment masking common commitment to non-oppression

Empowerment is not a unitary, homogeneous concept. Empowerment strategies develop in the context of a variety of different perspectives and theoretical constructs, which may not be made manifest, but which embody a diversity of assumptions informing actions. First, there is a vast range of radical positions from which action may be undertaken: feminist, Marxist and other socialist positions, and other radical viewpoints. Second, there is a number of participative approaches linked, more or less explicitly, with social democratic and liberal positions. Third, in the health and personal social services fields at any rate, some organisations and groups are aligned with the focus on a particular category of client or service user. In mental health (Rose and Black 1985), these include the Patients' Association; in the disability movement, there are self-advocacy groups such as Survivors Speak Out and voluntary organisations such as MIND. Such groups tend to draw on a variety of perspectives associated with personal rights and social justice.

The development of the scope of political, policy and practice studies to incorporate this diversity of perspectives has been most marked since the late 1960s, though many of them would legitimately claim much longer histories. It is arguable, however, that they have only reached a critical mass in the second half of the twentieth century as broad social movements associated with empowering people. This is not to underestimate the diversity and sometimes conflict which may arise between individuals and groups. Despite such differences, various attempts have been made (see Dominelli 1997; Adams 1996b) to set out features of this change in terms of a paradigmatic shift, in so far as it involves professionals, community action, social movements and people. Irrespective of the irregularities and gaps in this analysis, there seems to be a widespread academic and public consensus that 'something happened in the 1960s' and this is often linked with social protests by students and other groups, as well as with the development of divergent lifestyles associated with hippies, popular culture, pop music and fashion. In the arena of ideas, Auckland (1997: 9) refers to a breaching of the dualism of enlightenment philosophies underpinning liberalism, notably the core dichotomy of nature and culture so closely bound up with constructions such as masculine and feminine, order and disorder, which furthered the development from the late 1960s of the sociology of deviance. Key contributions to research and theorising have been made, as Barker

(1997) discusses – from Durkheim (1961, 1965) to James C. Scott (1985, 1990) – which point up rather than solve the problematic of how individuals and groups make the transformation from dissatisfaction to revolt, from creating and joining social movements to actually taking collective action. In social work, from the same period, there were growing debates about the respective merits of, and connections – or rather, tensions and incompatibilities between – individual casework, groupwork and community work. From the late 1980s, there were growing challenges from approaches based on empowerment rather than, for example, on medico-treatment (Adams 1996b: 36).

Since all ideas are socially constructed and produced at particular points in time, it is unrealistic to develop a statement concerning the mainstreams of ideas about oppression and empowerment in social work which is segregated from their historical locations. Radical stances in relation to oppression and empowerment draw on Marxist, feminist and ecologically inspired ideas. The schisms between these are as significant as areas of convergence. Rojek and colleagues are careful to hold back from an overoptimistic view of social workers' contribution to work with people in a capitalist society. They distinguish progressive, reproductive and contradictory perspectives (Rojek et al. 1988: 52–5). Ecological views have contributed increasingly since the anti-nuclear protests of the late 1950s to an environmentally-sensitive movement using largely non-violent tactics of resistance of growing sophistication. Feminist critiques have played a unique part in extending the repertoire of protest. There is, of course, no single strand of feminist ideas and activism. The struggle of women to establish the legitimacy of debates about feminist issues beyond the workplace, such as in the home, was advanced by analysis of the work of the housewife, such as in the publication by Mariarosa Dalla Costa of the Trivenito Committee for Wages for Housework and Selma James of the London Wages for Housework Committee (Dalla Costa and James 1972). They refer to the way women organise their protests collectively, in such periods as the time after work finishes on Friday:

> With the experience they have in managing things and with the aid of the other women in their groups, they know what to do when they want to take action. The women in a housing project in San Fransisco got together to halt the rise in prices. They saw the government wasn't doing anything so they took matters into their own hands. They held meetings and demonstrations and distributed leaflets. No one person organized it. After living with their neighbors in a housing project for so long they knew each other intimately; each other's weaknesses and strengths. The women made price lists up of every store in town and bought at only those stores that had the lowest prices. The whole city knew about 'Mana's OPA' and the papers had many articles on it. (Dalla Costa and James 1972: 70)

But just as significant are women's protests which do not receive mass media coverage:

> Women will barricade streets so that their children will have a place to play. The police with tear gas bombs can not drive them away. Women will pass the word along to other women that on a certain day no woman is to buy meat. They would just walk up to strange women and say 'Don't buy meat on such a day'. Women know each other so well that they can talk to a perfect stranger and be sure of being understood. The miners' wives went out on strike to protest at the company selling their homes and again to protest the dust in the air of the mining towns. They got the support of their husbands in both cases. Their husbands refused to cross their picket lines. (Dalla Costa and James 1972: 70–1)

Lack of theorisation of perspectives on empowerment

However, the range of perspectives on empowerment remains unevenly and imperfectly theorised. The reasons for this contribute to the particular form this deficit takes. For example, there is a notable lack in the UK of a forum giving all contributors to the personal social services an equal stake in debates about the ideas and practices of empowerment. Empowerment has emerged as a widespread preoccupation of professionals in the health and social services in the UK since the 1980s, with significant support from professional bodies such as CCETSW and, ironically, in areas such as community care, from the Department of Health in its official guidance on practice (see Department of Health 1991, for instance). These developments have occurred largely in the absence of a theoretically grounded literature, or arenas for political, policy, professional and public debates about the concepts and practices which are regarded as empowering and dis-empowering. The concept of citizen participation has come to the fore in the UK since the espousal by John Major, Prime Minister of the Conservative Government defeated in the landslide Labour victory of the General Election of May 1997, of the idea of active citizenship. This emphasised 'positive' contributions to the status quo rather than a critical view of available policies and services. It also did not envisage significantly extending the domain of citizenship to people traditionally excluded equal consideration by virtue of disability, mental illness or other forms of social stigma. Unsurprisingly, in the UK, after 18 years of Conservative government, there is a lack of articulation of theories embedded in the ideas about empowerment held by government ministers and civil servants, professional staff in the Department of Health and, specifically the Social Services Inspectorate, senior managers in social services and social work departments in the four countries of the UK: Wales, Scotland, Northern Ireland and England, based on an inclusive, non-oppressive view of the citizen.

In practical terms, the ideas debates, such as they are, have been colonised by officials preparing guidance, in consultation with professionals in higher education, with some involvement of clients, service users and carers, and by researchers and commentators in higher education in their own right. Some of these contributions claim links with, or even roots in, the experiences and perspectives of people receiving services (Beresford and Croft 1984, 1993; Croft and Beresford 1990a, 1990b, 1992; Mullender and Ward 1991; Ward and Mullender 1991), whilst others do not. Whilst in fields such as disability, some notable contributions have been made by disabled people who are also academics, researchers, teachers and writers, it can be argued that the perspective of disabled people is still relatively under-represented. For example, whilst protest is mentioned by Brandon, it tends to be in the context of the advocate protesting for the client (Brandon 1995: 9).

The consequence is that the lack of debate about key areas of empowerment, such as protest by people and challenges to the services, derives from the distance between two contrasting discourses Croft and Beresford identify (1995: 60): first, that of politicians, policy makers, service providers, consultants and researchers; second, that of people receiving services, their organisations and allies. In order to achieve the redistribution of power and resources, and the inclusion of people, the unequal competition between these two discourses would need to be equalised, that is, people receiving services should be fully involved in conceptualising and formulating empowering policies and practices (Croft and Beresford 1995: 72).

But the notion of 'equalising discourses' in itself seems unlikely to reconcile the differences between powerful professionals and relatively powerless clients. This is because it is difficult to shift power and because some citizens claim the right to remain outside the system and criticise from an excluded position, rather than participate on the terms of the authorities. The prisoner is the archetypal excluded person. In the groundbreaking book *The Politics of Abolition* (1974) – in terms of its non-positivistic narrative style of analysis as well as its content – the sociologist Thomas Mathiesen, reflects critically on his work with the Scandinavian prisoners' rights movement. He notes that threats to the purposes, or even the existence, of collective protests by prisoners come not only directly from the authorities at the point of direct confrontation, but also through out-flanking by the authorities, once the full extent of the demands from the prisoners are known. This is a major reason why he emphasises 'the unfinished': the necessity for the manifesto of the prisoners to remain essentially incomplete.

Much more than in the human services, in the field of direct action and pressure groups, there are many which, though refusing to engage with mainstream policy and practice on the terms of the authorities such as Friends of the Earth and Greenpeace, do not necessarily lack influence. But inclusion of them in discourse about empowerment means that the concept of democratic participation should fit comfortably with the perceptions and circumstances of people who take direct action against the system. Most writing about empowerment and citizenship is astoundingly complacent and non-activist. The threefold categorisation of approaches to empowerment by Robin Means and Randall Smith, into empowerment by voice (exemplified in the question: 'How much say do you have in decisions?'), exit (exemplified by the market approach: 'You can choose a different service if you dislike this one') and rights (exemplified in the statement: 'The State needs to recognise that you have the right to pursue your own goals and objectives, perhaps independently of the State') (Means and Smith 1994: 81). The peace, environmental and animal liberation movements are replete with examples of those who reject state grants yet enjoy considerable influence.

The imperfectly theorised field of empowerment derives also from underresearching in some key areas, notably in the relationships between personal transformation, collective action and social movements. In other words, crucial questions require further research, such as: how do people become activist? How does one person's activist state of mind become translated into individual, let alone collective action? The absence of research into such questions in the human services in general and social work in particular does not prevent 'empowerment' – as an assumedly worked-out theoretical construct, as a clearly articulated basis for action and as a major contribution to practice – from occupying a position of growing prominence in official guidance and in all areas of training courses and the literature. However, this is unhelpful to the extent that it sanctions an array of simplified, deproblematised models of empowerment to gain ascendancy in social work, for example. At best, these refer to respectable but dated 'gurus' such as Paolo Freire (1972), whose work is widely instanced (see, for example, Dominelli 1997: 52), but which needs updating in the light of the changes which have occurred, for example, in the Marxist theories and practices to which they relate, particularly since the late 1980s. Attempts to make such links (see Fleming 1997, for example) are not universally made. Undeniably, theorisation of empowerment in social work has not captured the complexities of people's transformations. For example, there is a dearth of research linking theories and practices, ideologies, consciousness, language and actions. This makes it difficult or even impossible to establish connections between social work and empowerment, as concrete reality, description, interpretation and evaluation.

Constraints of concepts and terminology: what to call 'the people'

Empowerment is very largely a term associated with practices, in the absence of a worked-out body of theoretical positions, discourses, approaches, methods or practices. The work of Clarke and Stewart to develop a framework for empowerment is typical of approaches which in attempting to get across to practitioners principles – for example, the use of questioning and exchange 'models' of assessment (Clarke and Stewart 1992: 16–18) – disconnect practice from theory and present models as alternatives without reference to their theoretical contexts.

A significant clue to a problematic at the heart of the debates about empowerment in the health and social services is the lack of a satisfactory word to use, in English at any rate, to refer to the receiver of services. This is ironic in the light of the fact that they are now anticipated as experiencing empowerment partly as a consequence of being in contact with these very services. This points to the problematic status of the person receiving services. The rhetoric concerning empowering people in community care in the UK uses, but does not define and distinguish between the many words for the person receiving services: consumer, customer, client, recipient, citizen, survivor and so on (Hoyes et al. 1993). In the UK, terms such as 'client', in widespread use until the 1980s, have been dislodged from their central position, apparently without any widespread debate in the professional literature or by people receiving services, and largely replaced by such terms as 'user' and 'service user'. This is extraordinary because it cannot be assumed that it is more empowering to be called a service user than a client. At the same time, such terms as 'consumer' and 'customer' have begun to be used by some agencies. These terms imply different relationships between people and their social services, in a policy environment which in the UK until mid-1997 under the Conservative government has been increasingly management-led and which 'in its use of the tools of the market – customer surveys, complaints procedures, standard setting, customer panels and public attitude testing – takes an individualistic rather than a collective approach' (Taylor et al. 1992: 7).

Empowerment and the political context: vulnerability to depoliticisation

Ironically, the concept of empowerment has been expropriated notably by officials in the Department of Health in guidance for the implementation of the NHS and Community Care Act 1990, as well as by the professional regulating body for social workers, the Central Council for Education and Training in Social Work (CCETSW). This has contributed to the widespread publication of a sanitised concept of empowerment which seems superficially to fit non-controversially and apolitically into the marketised contract culture established in the health and social services by the Conservative government of 1979 to 1997. The tendency towards mutual segregation of knowledges in some fields, notably social work and popular protest, has not facilitated such a ready interchange of concepts and experiences as is desirable. This contrasts with the environmental area, for example. Organisations such as Greenpeace have benefited from synergy between researchers and broader connections between activists in different aspects of environmental and other community and social action movements in the UK and many other countries.

One difficulty which forces voluntary organisations in the UK to proceed warily, is the restriction on political activity which accompanies having charitable status. The advantages of charitable status include the maintenance of a public image as a not-for-profit organisation dependent on fund-raising for its activities. They are also financial, in that the organisation does not attract taxation normally applicable in the commercial sector. The constraint, however, is that the charity is not supposed to engage in activities which are deemed political. But the almost inevitable connection between politics and most social issues – from homelessness and child abuse to poverty and unemployment – puts voluntary organisations in the UK in the position of manoeuvring carefully between maintaining their credibility with networks of activists and campaigning organisations, and sustaining charitable status, through the Charity Commissioners.

Unsurprisingly, the points of conjuncture between user movements, protests and mainstream politics, policies and practice within the human services involve collisions of values. They reflect, for example, divergences between groups struggling to sustain non-oppressive activity and those which do not, between user-led activities and those initiated and led by professionals.

User-led initiatives with an interest in engaging in any or all of politics, policy change and practice development are caught in a double bind. If they act autonomously, then they are likely to remain pure in their principles, but outside established politics, policy and practice. If they get involved, they risk being coopted into networks of consultation which may give them the right to make a token rather than a substantial contribution, and may grant them a symbolic rather than a real presence.

Consequential continued exploitation of oppressed people

The consequences of these theoretical shortcomings described above have been noted by critical commentators. For example, Servian notes that psychological and sociological theories of power and empowerment do not of themselves improve the power situation of users 'unless they are enabled to take advantage of the theoretical insights' (Servian 1996: 57). Again, Humphries observes the contradictory dominance of a discourse of empowerment in the 1990s, displayed in the themes of containment, collusion, dominance and nihilism. Containment operates by accommodating the interests of oppressed groups within a restricted framework defined in the interests of patriarchy. Thus, the discourse of empowerment cloaks continued exploitation on the basis of social class, race and gender and other divisions 'and works towards containing challenges to such exploitation' (Humphries 1996a: 13). Collusion works to sustain the interests of some exploited groups, in collaboration with dominant interests, at the expense of others who are even more marginalised and excluded. Dominance is achieved through the 'construction of empowerment by dominant minorities' (Humphries 1996a: 13), again to the exclusion of others. Finally, an empowering nihilism may exist, in which people may be attributed their uniqueness, but through the recognition of the identity of the 'other'. Thus, their characteristics are viewed as confirming 'the essence of their alien nature ... [which therefore requires] containment. They are thus kept very neatly in their place in the class and racial hierarchy' (Humphries 1996a: 14).

Empowerment, discrimination and non-oppressive practice

It is ironic that the concept of empowerment overlaps so little into the territory of anti-discriminatory theorisation and practice. Empowerment remains almost entirely dominated by literature concerning personal development, personal growth and consciousness raising. Much of the examination of structural features of oppression and discrimination are not considered in the field of empowerment theory and practice. In a rare exception to this trend, the primary mover for action is not just difference but inequality. Malcolm Payne (1997: 258–9) is rightly impressed with the conceptual robustness with which anti-oppressive theory and practice and empowerment are brought together in a comprehensive framework by Dalrymple and Burke (1995).

The rationale for empowerment is the oppression of many groups on the basis of disability, age, youth, race, gender, class and many other divisions and categories. It is not cancelled out by the token elevation of one person by their writing and/or direct action. They simply 'escape' into the dominant reality at the expense of all those left behind. We should beware, therefore, of adopting a mistaken post-oppressive, postmodern perspective, which downplays these pervasive themes of inequality and discrimination (Adams, Dominelli and Payne 1998: Introduction).

Fragmentation of socialist and feminist politics: the search for transcendence

The book *Beyond the Fragments: Feminism and the Making of Socialism*, which Sheila Rowbotham and colleagues wrote in the late 1970s, acted as a magnet for debates concerning the relationship between feminist anti-capitalist ideas and practices and male-dominated socialist movements, notably those informed by Marxism. This book focused on the fragmentation of socialist politics and how to transcend this (Rowbotham et al. 1979: 211). It significantly foreshadows the centrality of the concept of fragmentation in postmodernism. However, this demands a sophisticated rather than simplistic analysis. What unites women in the protests illustrated above is their common experience: 'Women act as a group because they are treated like one. They live the same way on the whole, no matter how different the individual situation may be' (Dalla Costa and James 1970: 71). Best and Kellner strengthen the case for searching for a perspective which does not argue one-sidedly for fragmentation, but is a more rounded social analysis. It incorporates trends towards economic concentration, globalisation, centralisation and homogenisation and new forms of social organisation as well (Best and Kellner 1991: 222–3).

This highlights a further limitation of some postmodern theory, which allows for an unrealistically amplified view of the power of individuals and groups to influence the status quo. For postmodernism

> tends to throw out the very concept of social system and society for more fragmentary analysis, for microanalysis of discrete institutions, discourses or practices ... few post-modern theorists have a theory of capitalism, nor do they develop theories of the state and the ways in which state, economy, and culture interact and mutually determine each other ... power is more dispersed, plural and decentred than in the neo-Marxian analysis of the Frankfurt School. (Best and Kellner 1991: 220)

Postmodern theory

> tends to obscure the continuing constitutive role of capitalism in the production and reproduction of contemporary social formations and splinters power and domination into an amorphous multiplicity of institutions, discourses, and practices ... For example, while much post-modern theory correctly points to the power of media and information, it downplays the extent to which ruling groups control and shape these new social forces. (Best and Kellner 1991: 221)

If postmodernism is prone to understating the oppressive power of the state and structural factors, the social work literature sometimes overstates the empowering potential of practice. Baroness Wootton criticises the arrogance of claims that casework can enable a person to deal with the problems of the social environment. This is a reminder of the tendency for social work professionals to make exaggerated claims to effectiveness and influence. She states that 'modern definitions of "social casework" if taken at their face value, involve claims to powers which verge upon omniscience and omnipotence' (Wootton et al. 1959: 271). The literature on user-led initiatives in group work (Mullender and Ward, 1991), if anything, overplays their potential contribution to empowerment. They claim that 'groupwork can be immensely powerful if it is affiliated to a purpose which explicitly rejects the "splintering" of the public and private, of person and society' (Mullender and Ward 1991: 73). But as Baistow notes, the suggestion that groupwork can be an empowering anti-oppressive strategy assumes that the 'problem' can be 'solved' by psychological means: 'In this case the proposed solution is groupwork, in another, counselling' (Baistow 1994: 36).

Empowerment theory and practice should not be left to the experts to study and discuss, but should be democratised to the point where the subjects of research – service users and their carers – play as full a part as the professionals. This assertion has its counterpart in the literature concerning postmodernism. Featherstone observes that leaving aside arguments about whether postmodernism is simply an aspect of modernity (Featherstone 1991: 4), the key point is that discussion should not be the sole preserve of intellectuals, but should 'focus upon the actual cultural practices and changing power balances of those groups engaged in the production, classification, circulation and consumption of post-modern cultural goods' (Featherstone 1991: 5). Ironically, of course, such discussions are invariably couched in language which excludes the very individuals and groups who use such goods.

Protest: some notes on relevant social and historical aspects

The second part of this chapter uses the key activity of protest – notably in the form of collective challenges to the status quo by poor and unemployed people, as well as by pupils in schools and prisoners in penal institutions – to highlight the gap between the rhetoric and the realities of empowerment. This is intended as a brief reminder of the great body of empirical research in the field of protest, to which a more adequate analysis of the concept of empowerment than exists to date needs to relate.

The broader context of social political issues which have aroused collective protest in Britain in the past two centuries demonstrates that it makes little sense to expect social work in the UK to rest on a consensus about the appropriateness of professional values which challenge discrimination and oppression. Whilst there are many examples of movements to oppose many social policies and practices which may be regarded as discriminatory, such opposition is often fragmentary and short-lived, and its supporters diverse in their backgrounds, motives for supporting it and in the diversity of their protests. A focus on a single case study of the history of agitation on behalf of unemployed and poor people illustrates this. The anti-Poor Law movement of the 1830s was 'an uneasy alliance of local middle-class ratepayers and trade unionists, with various independent radical politicians of often nonconformist religious persuasion, rather than of the poor or the unemployed' (Bagguley 1991: 73). The campaigns of the Land and Labour League of the 1860s and 1870s represented an early recognition by trade unionists of the need for unemployed people to be regarded as a sector of the working class with the potential to play an activist role in politics (Bagguley 1991: 76). The history of the National Unemployed Workers' Movement, from its formation in 1920 to its decline in the years immediately before 1940, shows the complex relationship between changing social policy in relation to relief for unemployed people, and organised protest (Bagguley 1991: 87–98). It demonstrates the shift from the large-scale challenge represented by the hunger marches of the 1930s to the individual casework which was the main activity of the organisation in its declining years.

The history of protests by unemployed people provides clues to factors shaping the nature and level of political and social action. Bagguley shows how in the mid-nineteenth century, the virtual exclusion of unemployed people themselves from the political arena contributed to protests on behalf of, rather than by, unemployed people. Working-class people by and large did not have the vote and relief for paupers was regulated by locally elected Boards of Guardians. In the twentieth century, the setting up of the Unemployed Assistance Board, and the subsequent introduction of various forms of national assistance and unemployment benefit, amounted to the nationalisation of all forms of unemployment relief, thereby insulating them from immediate popular democratic control. Bagguley notes:

> political movements of the unemployed can only occur in anything more than the most marginal fashion when they can influence in some visible, direct and substantial way the levels and/or forms of unemployment relief, through a combination of the franchise and collective action. (Bagguley 1991: 113)

Over and above the changing relationship between potential protesters and the state, organisational and cultural resources, as well as different local forms of political organisation and culture, affect the incidence of protest

(Bagguley 1991: 113). Protests occurred in settings where there was a sufficiency of consciousness, associated with radical or class-based activism (Bagguley 1991: 202). The key question which illuminates this issue is not why people protest so much as, given the widespread incidence of hardship through unemployment, why more people do not protest. Through counterpointing this historical analysis with interviews with unemployed people, Bagguley inquires into the factors contributing to political quiescence among unemployed people, during the 1980s, in contrast with the widespread, often mass, protests of earlier decades. In the 1980s, whilst the state was virtually immune to collective action for improved benefits and unemployed people in general lacked 'the requisite organisational and cultural resources for mobilisation', Bagguley observes that 'like most people the unemployed are highly fatalistic about the efficacy of collective action' (Bagguley 1991: 203).

In the area of schooling, centuries of exploitation, oppression and abuse of children (Aries 1962) have been underlain by relatively unchanging structural arrangements for their disciplining and pedagogy (Donzelot 1979). These factors reinforce control and punishment of children by adults (Adams 1997a) rather than encouraging, educating and liberating or empowering children. The histories of protests by pupils which could have been collated and written remain largely hidden (Adams 1991).

Again, in the penal system protests by prisoners remain central to issues concerning penal reform, have been largely ignored as a collective phenomenon by the authorities, save for their implications for the need to improve discipline and control (Adams 1994).

The issues over which protests arise are often not agreed, but are matters for debate and contention. Many commentators have remarked on the paradoxical nature of concepts of empowerment and protest. Self-help has both a radical – often socialist and collectivist – as well as a reactionary – individualist – dimension; community work is rooted in imperialist traditions of community development as well as those of community action; the history of peace activism shows the tensions between themes of nationalism and imperialism as well as internationalism and socialism, in the range of stances on peace, war and violence adopted by the diversity of people who have called themselves 'pacifist' (Hinton 1989).

Protests by recipients of human services

A significant contribution to the quality of the personal social services has been made by activists from among those receiving services, notably in the fields of mental health (Brandon 1995) and criminal justice (Adams 1994: 169). In theory, it is unquestionable that the most vital contributions to the 'personal' and the 'social' aspects of the personal social services are to be made by service users themselves. But as noted above, this cannot be taken for granted. In particular, the space has not been made in theoretical or practice terms for the difficult, the challenging client, who resists. Such a person is more likely than the conforming or apathetic person to be perceived as difficult or deviant and to receive less of a quality service as a consequence. One reason for this is the subservience of knowledges, theorising and research into resistance and protest to the dominant political, policy and social culture in the UK, which rewards compliance or conformity more readily than questioning or rejection of dominant realities. The complainant and the whistleblower are as vulnerable as the rebel to being punished (Adams 1998: Ch. 6).

Need to incorporate challenges by the receiver of services into the mainstream of theory and practice

The protesting person tends to be portrayed as deviant, whilst the conceptualisation of the client remains remarkably tame. The gap between these desperately needs closing. There is a lack of conceptual linkage between collective protest and prevalent ideas about empowering individuals as recipients of services. The notion of citizenship developed in the UK during the Conservative government of 1979–1997 was one of encouraging active citizens to participate, rather than to legitimate challenges to the system, or the status quo. A view of the citizen as a positive critic needs legitimating. The literature concerning individual and collective empowerment relates imperfectly or not at all to challenges to the status quo of services, or protests by people about aspects of them. Such happenings are routinely ignored, misrepresented, underexplained or subsumed under other phenomena. Theorising about these kinds of resistance in the human services remains as much outside popular and academic discourse in the Western countries as are protesters themselves (Adams 1997a: 208). Despite the growing popularity of the term empowerment in social work, much of the social work literature employs a truncated, or taken for granted, concept of empowerment to refer to procedures for involving people, consulting them, rather than achieving transformational changes in the personal, organisational, social and political domains, through their participation. Much of the literature on empowerment in social work is neutered, classless, depoliticised, ablist, ageist in its implications. The empowerment literature tends to represent activity on a linear continuum, from individual to collective activity, or from self to other. Thus, it replicates the very features of dominant realities which should be challenged in the furtherance of empowerment.

The two most obvious illustrations of this are the organisational, group and individual sanctions applied to whistleblowers (people who call public attention to deficits in services) and receivers of services who criticise them. The expulsion of a pupil from a school in Nottinghamshire, England, in July 1997 for refusing to retract a criticism of the school, underlines the vulnerability of the client as critic of services and the tokenism which often accompanies rhetoric about user participation and consumer charters. In contrast, there is a need to reconceptualise the contribution of the person receiving services, so as to make individual and collective challenges by people, and in particular collective protest, part of the mainstream of the agency's activities, rather than protests by people constituting the periphery, or even being treated as an excluded activity.

Conditions for empowerment: reframing protest

This, the final part of this chapter, examines ways of surmounting the difficulties this produces. This entails shifting the discourse about empowerment and anti-discriminatory practice to centre; creating the space for legitimate protest; reconceptualising the person as capable of non-acquiescence/protest and developing inclusive policies and practices for excluded people – disabled people/non-persons – pupils (*qua* prisoners).

One of the constraints on people – whether managers, practitioners, clients or service users, carers or other members of the public – is the language of dominant social work reality, which, in the UK at any rate, despite the growing interest in empowerment and anti-discrimination increasingly is driven by consumerism, contracts, finances and outcomes. A prerequisite for action, therefore, is to set out to empower people through extending the vocabulary and therefore radicalising the concepts embedded in action. There are many different ways of applying this. Clearly, it implies challenging the general limitations of research noted above. But an example is given here of a methodology which has been employed by anthropologists and sociologists (Willis 1978) and commentators on reflective practice (Schön 1991), but which is receiving renewed attention currently, for example, by Laurence Cox of the Centre for Research on Environment and Community at Waterford Institute of Technology in the Republic of Ireland. Cox argues that the concept of reflexivity provides means of transcending dominant materially and technically dominated realities by creating contexts and rationales for a variety of alternative political and cultural projects which rest on local rationalities and thereby can be legitimised in their own terms, institutionalised and extended autonomously to other settings (Cox 1997: 3).

Jacobs and Popple provide a theoretical rationale for community work in the 1990s which uses Gramsci (1971) and Freire (1972) as key reference points for developing a critical understanding of the means by which dominant interests maintain and reproduce their ascendancy and subordinated people and groups can challenge and achieve change, through education and consciousness raising (Jacobs and Popple 1994: 31). They identify the crucial role of a middle stratum of workers – such as community workers – in enabling working-class people and oppressed groups to build up a significant level of cohesion and activism (Jacobs and Popple 1994: 30).

Reflexivity, protest and empowerment

Reflexivity is a term which refers to the process of monitoring one's own feelings and actions in a dialogic way, and creatively using the interaction between self and external realities to sustain or even transform social relations. To the extent that empowerment associated with protest involves social movements from below, it provides a means of challenging impositions from above. Of course, reflexive activity does not escape the ambiguities which are inherent in other areas. Thus, it may contribute to such impositions, and the containing of personal and social conflicts, or to radicalising and transformational activity (Cox 1997: 15). Reflexivity is a powerful methodology, however, since it provides a means of self-reflection on this dichotomous position, bringing together the domains of the self, the group, the organisation and the community (Adams 1996b). Cox notes that the concept of reflexivity can be radicalised, in that it involves not simply self-monitoring but also changing our construction of 'our selves, our actions and our lifeworlds' (Cox 1997: 15). Cox refers to contextualising local rationalities, which means that people's actions – in organising and responding to their situations – depend on local circumstances in which they create contexts which are appropriate to, and justification for, what they choose to do (Cox 1997: 13). He offers three ways in which reflexivity may contribute to the attempts of people to develop such a basis for action: by distancing themselves from surrounding norms (Cox 1997: 4–5), such as the dominant classist and gender-based assumptions made by people, groups and organisations surrounding them; by raising awareness of alternative cultural possibilities (Cox 1997: 7), such as through taking the freedom and the space to experiment; by symbolic and expressive activity, such as aspiring to practical alternatives to surrounding reality by doing things which are not intended to fulfil practical, goal-led functions, but make them feel better. Cox uses the example of playing mind games (Cox 1997: 8), but in this connection the creative variety of collective protests by pupils identified in a previous research project is relevant (Adams 1991).

Enhancing strategies and tactics of protest

Significant empowerment entails the commitment of the authorities to enabling people to develop enhanced strategies and tactics of protest. Strategies adopted by different groups and organisations cannot be considered in isolation from the prevailing political and policy culture. In the environmental area, for instance, a significant shift towards repressive measures by government in the UK, towards travellers and community music such as raves, is exemplified in the Public Order Act of 1994, which put severe restrictions on these people and activities.

Danny Burns' analysis of the success of the rebellion – involving a claimed 17 million people (Burns 1992: 183) – against the poll tax foreshadows the sea change which has overtaken British politics since the Labour Party came into power in the General Election of 1 May 1997. The protests against the poll tax illustrate the argument that

> to fight the forces of oppression it is necessary to have a counter force with which to resist them. Promises, policies, negotiation and even legislation don't constitute a force. The only force we have is people and their power to take collective action. This was what non-payment was all about. Because the community was withholding something which the state needed, it was exercising power. Because it was based in local neighbourhoods, and authority was not vested in the representative structures, that power was not diluted, and it couldn't be corrupted. (Burns 1992: 187)

The increasing tendency for social work professionals to ally themselves with anti-discriminatory causes and protest movements on behalf of poor and excluded groups of people, is a distinctive feature of social work in the UK since the 1980s. It is understandable, in historical terms, that this locates the social work profession as a whole in a comparable situation to the somewhat precarious, and generally short-lived, political and social movements promoting protests on issues concerning poverty and unemployment, which have come and gone over the past two centuries.

A feature of the espousement of the anti-discriminatory and empowerment causes by professional social work organisations such as BASW (British Association of Social Workers) is the enhanced motivation it provides to the workforce of the personal social services as a whole. Burns comments that

> the most effective leadership will not tell people what to do – they usually know what needs to be done – but will give people the confidence to do it. This means providing information and ideas so that people can make choices, and helping them to set up groups so that they can share experiences and provide each other

with solidarity. It means leaders making themselves dispensable and making groups so autonomous and strong that they don't need external direction. This leadership depends on trust, and trust is dependent on the personal and political integrity of leaders. It can only be maintained through openness in decision-making and it is only possible where people are consulted so that they continue to feel involved in the process. When a group is seen to want 'control' it is not trusted ... Because of the grass roots nature of the Anti-Poll Tax movement it was able to support the emergence of different centres of national leadership, encouraging those with specific skills or expertise to organise autonomously. Local Anti-Poll Tax Unions were able to choose which national initiatives to support and from where they got the information and technical support that they needed. This prevented the core of the movement from stagnating, because people moved to where the strongest energy for action lay. (Burns 1992: 19–34)

Local democratisation and power

Danny Burns draws from the analysis of the anti-poll tax campaigns the insight that a highly centralised focus of leadership would have made them more vulnerable to attack from the state and the media:

> In most political movements instructions and information travel up and down the organisational hierarchy; key decisions and debates are carried out by regional and national executives. What was unique about the Anti-Poll Tax campaign was the degree of direct interaction and decision-making which occurred at local level. There was, for example, no need for a policy directive to establish the various strategies of non-co-operation. People understood the need for it – many had no choice. This is illustrated by the fact that it was sometimes in the places where the Anti-Poll Tax Unions were weakest that resistance was strongest. (Burns 1992: 193)

Building on strengths

The development of empowering strategies requires a shift from criticising deficits to focusing on positives (for work in this area, see Winn 1992). Beresford and Campbell (1994) show how the issue of representativeness tends to be used to emphasise the 'unrepresentativeness' of disabled people as service users, rather than developing the inclusive and empowering approaches employed by some service providers and disabled people.

Paradoxically, people's diversity should be regarded as a sign of strength, rather than an obstacle to collective action. Despite the use of tactics such as 'divide and rule' by managers and professionals, and the stereotyping of people in dispossessed groups who contribute particularly energetically to campaigns, solidarity across divisions such as gender, age, social class and so on contributes greatly to the strength of collective protests. Consensus decision making is very important where people's diversity is a feature of the situation (Auckland 1997: 8). There is a necessity to sustain the lowest common denominator of agreement.

The positive aspect of this is diversity itself and the associated virtues of non-hierarchical decision making, which encourages spontaneity and freedom.

The negative aspect of it may include chaotic, disorderly meetings and a haphazard approach to the flow of information (Auckland 1997: 8). It may be argued that even if such approaches are not ideal, they are preferable to the alternatives, such as giving up freedom to a so-called strong leader.

Starting from people's own demands

Protests by people receiving services may come about because they are frustrated, or from a variety of other reasons. Fundamentally, though, they want something they are not getting. It is common, for instance, for people to demand more practical help than they can get from services. In the mental health field, Peter Campbell, a founder of Survivors Speak Out – the organisation for people who have experienced mental health services – notes several things many mental health service users and survivors want from crisis services: more control over crisis situations, more understanding of their crises, to be treated with respect and dignity and 24-hour non-medical crisis services (Campbell 1996: 181–2).

In order to develop a critical appreciation of why such statements all too often are not addressed, we need to recognise the structural barriers which exclude many people receiving services from the policy process. Croft and Beresford argue that one way of challenging the profoundly disempowering experience of being poor is for research and debates about poverty to become more participatory (Croft and Beresford 1990b: 23). This leads logically to the view that participation in social policy making should not be treated as the forum for debates about marginalising policies and services, but also as a contributor to a participatory social policy, en route to a more participatory politics (Croft and Beresford 1992: 41).

Consulting people receiving services: developing a systematic approach

Guidelines for empowering people may be practice-based rather than rooted in a conceptual framework. The framework for empowerment Rees sets out in fact is a checklist of 10 stages:

- understanding themes
- evaluating self-image and knowledge

- specifying problems
- developing awareness of policies
- developing the notion of choice
- experiencing solidarity with others
- acquiring and using language
- resisting a return to powerlessness
- developing interactive and political skills and
- evaluation (Rees 1991: 89).

Again, at the practical level the pace of policy and practice change is so rapid that it runs ahead continually of the analysis and prescriptions of commentators. Thus, much of the detail in the case studies of empowering strategies in the social services set out in the book by Darvill and Smale were already outdated when published in 1990, by the imminent creation of markets in the delivery of personal social services. However, they emphasised – and this emerges for instance, in the paper in that collection, by Andrew Cooper – the importance of regarding clients and carers as part of the resource network alongside professionals (Cooper 1990: 36–7). Wertheimer has documented the practical process of consulting with users about their perceptions and needs in community care, showing how time consuming and resource-intensive this is (Wertheimer, 1991). The consultation process is based on the 'search conference' method pioneered at the Tavistock Institute of Human Relations (London) in the 1960s and consists of a workshop approach giving all participants an equal opportunity to contribute their views, in five stages grouped in two main phases:

Phase 1: Search
    Stage 1   Scanning the environment
    Stage 2   Exploring the probable future
    Stage 3   Defining the desirable future
Phase 2: Action
    Stage 4   Analysis of opportunities and constraints and ways forward
    Stage 5   Identification of issues, tasks and ways forward (Wertheimer 1991: 8).

Learning from experience

In the 1960s, student protests and political action such as squatting converged in many areas. In the 1970s, radical – including feminist and community action – protest groups coalesced around environmental and anti-nuclear issues, for example. In the 1980s, issues in the UK such as animal rights campaigns and anti-poll tax protests were examples of issues which led to demonstrations and other forms of direct action. At the same time, they raised controversy and debate and still attracted widespread attention and support, concerning the appropriateness of physical force either as a protest technique or as a response by the authorities to protesters. In the 1990s, growing public concern about the failures of governments to address the issue of the harmful global impact of the deteriorating ozone layer and the 'greenhouse effect' led to a convergence between broad-based environmental issues and specific issues. Examples include the protracted resistance by campaigners to the Newbury bypass, to the motorway through countryside at Twyford Down in the south of England and to the new runway at Manchester Airport in the north of England.

Sustaining a non-discriminatory practice

Beatrix Campbell maintains that communal rioting in Britain – notably the waves of riots in London, Liverpool and other cities in 1981 and in Tyneside in 1991 – should be explained in terms of theories which recognise an economic emergency in many neighbourhoods, 'where the difference between what women and men do with their troubles and with their anger shapes their strategies of survival and solidarity on the one hand, danger and destruction on the other' (Campbell 1993: 303). Campbell argues that it is mistaken to reduce explanations of the causes of crime and violence in society to single-factor causes such as the existence of an unemployed, fatalistic and feckless category of miscreants. (See Murray 1990, 1994, for an unsympathetic view of the underclass and Field 1989 for a sympathetic view.) In penetrating the realities of life in the underclass – the long-term unemployed group 'below' the employed classes – the challenge, as for other categories of people, is to theorise both the social and psychological factors which oppress them and those which encourage their resistance. For Campbell, the collective empowerment of people in the neighbourhood and the community are threatened predominantly by masculine values and practices:

> The criminal fraternity is, typically, exclusive, secretive, coercive, destructive. Its pay-off is that it yields to impoverished places access to basic material provisions and the commodities for cultural consumption that connect them to the world they live in. Their challenge, however, is not to the systems surrounding the neighbourhood that produce economic and political crisis, but to the community itself. The criminal fraternity is nothing if not about the means by which coteries of men constitute their dominance ... Crime and coercion are sustained by men. Solidarity and self-help are sustained by women. It is as stark as that (Campbell 1993: 319).

Drawing the threads together

Whilst theoretical perspectives deployed in the literature and practice of empowerment and protests in the human services rely on a diversity of Marxist, radical, feminist, anarchist and ecological perspectives, they share a concern with what we might call transformational politics, policies and practices. Lena Dominelli has argued with increasing force (Dominelli and McLeod 1989; Dominelli 1997) for an approach to anti-oppressive practice recognising diversity and not driven by a single theoretical approach. In any given situation, of course, it will be useful to know whether such a strategy is informed by idealism or pragmatism and necessity. Further, beyond and behind diversity and the fragmentation emphasised by postmodern perspectives lie persistent and pervasive divisions and inequalities, exemplified in the gendered, ageist, disablist and class-based nature of much of the literature in the fields of empowerment and protest. It happens in the practice, too. For example, Auckland notes that the campaign opposing the extension to the M11 motorway north of London would have been more successful if more attention had been paid to women's suggestions of alternative strategies of protest, and also, practically, to the need for blankets and food (Auckland 1997: 10). Again, Auckland comments that groups and communities may be empowered through protest, but such empowerment in reality is differentially distributed through a particular group or community (Auckland 1997: 11).

Participatory methodologies community action and social development

It is recognised in the personal social services in the UK that the choice of empowering research methodologies can, and should, make a significant contribution to the development of more participatory policies and practices (Croft and Beresford 1990a: 62). A research agenda which was increasingly accountable to people receiving services and their carers, of course, and which supported self-advocacy and user involvement, would be based on a code of ethics, guidelines and criteria for issuing contracts (Beresford 1992: 31). Beresford and Croft argued in 1984 that the reshaping of new Fabianism overlaid a politics of the status quo, despite its radical rhetoric (Beresford and Croft 1984: 106). The issue of citizen participation in localities, raised in a much-quoted analysis in the late 1960s (Arnstein 1969), had earlier been argued by Beresford to be a question not just of the way social services are organised, but to posit 'fundamental shifts in the distribution of power and resources in society' (Beresford 1982: 20). Croft and Beresford used an evaluation of existing research into patch-based social services initiatives as the basis for a critique of some research as the tool of government and professional interests in legitimating and perpetuating the status quo, rather than resonating with patch-based principles of services: being 'accessible, participatory, locally based, popularly controlled and accountable and popularly owned and constructed' (Croft and Beresford 1984: 23).

Approaches to social development

Much can be learned in social work from increasingly global experience of practice-based research in social development. Two main perspectives may be encountered, according to Marsden (1990: 8): sectoral (specialist) and holistic (generalist). The sectoral approach distinguishes different spheres of activity for diverse professional treatment, through health, housing, social services and so on. The sectoral approach is based on questionable assumptions, according to Marsden (1990: 8): that a distinction can be made between the public and private domains; that different criteria should be used in their evaluation and that different areas of human activity can be isolated for different treatment. Within the sectoral approach, there is a debate between residualists and substantivists about the amount of government intervention which should be maintained to underpin activity. The substantivists argue that more intervention plays a redistributive role and lessens inequalities.

According to the holistic approach, the planner, policy maker and the change agent are all viewed as part of the analysis (Marsden 1990: 8). Holistic evaluation may well take place above the level of direct action and thus will probably be perceived as less capable of achieving instrumental goals. In contrast, the sectoral approach to evaluation is likely to fail to appreciate the interconnectedness of phenomena and to achieve desired aims.

Marsden, Oakley and Pratt identify three main approaches (1994: 14–23): first, the managerialist. This involves 'control by enlightened leaders aimed at achieving targets, building organisational capacity and of extending and processing information and knowledge within the organisation' (p. 19). The second approach is the academic. This may involve the participants in critical analysis, but their role commonly is to assist the expert, 'outside' researcher to come to his or her conclusions, rather than to shape the direction of the evaluation and control its outcomes (p. 18). The advocates of approaches based on this perspective tend to argue that participative approaches lead to an emphasis on the experience, action and learning of the participants at the expense of neglect of the wider 'objective' appraisal of the project. The third approach is the participative. This 'goes beyond the mere involvement of beneficiaries in some externally conceived intervention' (p. 31). It starts from the viewpoint that much development effort has failed to improve people's living standards significantly, and to enable them to overcome barriers to the more equal distribution of resources. It rejects positivist, traditional and experimental approaches to research, as instruments of domination (p. 33). It involves the researcher and the other participants in collaborative action. Evaluation is not viewed as an instrument of investigation wielded by outsiders, but is used as an instrument of dialogue and learning and thereby is integral to co-operation and the project itself. The authors envisage four stages as involved in evaluation: preparation, execution, analysis and reflection (p. 5). The shift to including the beneficiaries of the project in the running of the evaluation is based partly on the expectation that this will generate more responsibility among people who are commonly excluded, for maintaining an initiative they regard as their own (p. 25). Some commentators advocate that people should be able to define and take responsibility for their own development on their own terms and be empowered to pursue it in their own chosen way. '"Participatory evaluation" becomes not only the means by which to create the dialogue necessary for such a process to develop but an integral part of the process itself' (p. 31). Great emphasis is placed on the language of the evaluation, focusing on the language used by the participants:

> They are seen to be the experts and their contribution to the evaluation, as those at the heart of the programme, is indispensable. They are thereby given priority in an attempt to learn about the processes involved in cultural and attitudinal change. (Marsden et al. 1994: 33)

Barriers to empowering evaluation

One barrier is the tendency to focus on the evaluation project, rather than on the development itself. The project should remain merely one means by which partnerships between organisations develop and solidarity is strengthened (Marsden et al. 1994: 11). Another major impediment, despite the rhetoric of empowerment, includes the chains which bind us to ways of thinking and acting, thereby inhibiting effective elaboration of successful methodologies (p. 12). A third problem is the tendency for approaches to evaluation to reflect managerial or academic rather than empowering goals (pp. 14–19).

Social development is viewed as global and not as solely an activity carried out only in the Third World. There is a need to negotiate different understandings, in evaluating social development projects (Marsden et al. 1994: 3) There is a need for projects to engage in capacity building, achieving self-reliance, empowerment and the ability to sustain them (p. 2), building partnerships with poor people to enrich networks and alliances (p. 10).

There would be much merit in latching discussions about empowerment within social work on to global debates about research into social development. There is not much conceptual distance between the more progressive discourse about empowerment in social work and notions of people-centred, transformational participation. Participatory methodologies offer the most conceptually sound, rigorous and practical ways of facilitating empowering approaches to theorising, practice and research in social work. Such approaches would be more likely than at present to accommodate challenges to existing systems and services by those on their receiving ends, or excluded from them.

Conclusions

In this chapter, I have argued that from the late 1980s, social work contributed increasingly to a discourse concerning the empowering of excluded and oppressed individuals and groups in society in the UK, but that this consciousness-raising activity was not sufficient of itself to produce collective challenges to discrimination. It lacked a political and social dimension; it was not complemented by cultural and organisational resources at local level, or by the requisite level of collective faith in direct action through mass protests, as a means of achieving political and social change. Interestingly, the overwhelming majority achieved by Labour in the General Election of 1 May 1997, and the ejection of the Conservatives from government after 18 years, indicates a high level of dissatisfaction with the status quo consistent with such an analysis. People desire change. What they need is the opportunity, the confidence and resources to bring it about. This is fine, as far as it goes, in relatively affluent Western countries. In poorer countries, this agenda needs extending to address two priorities: first the causes of poverty and second, the subordination of people within families, communities, organisations and societies. Empowerment presupposes shifts in resources and power. It should be linked not with acquiescence and apathy but with ideals and action. Citizens need not only the chance to participate but the right to refuse to take part on other people's terms, object, complain about shortcomings in services, blow the whistle on inferior practices, criticise things as they are, opt out of the status quo and take direct action to achieve social change.

References

Adams, R. (1991) *Protests by Pupils: Empowerment, Schooling and the State*. Basingstoke: Falmer.

Adams, R. (1994) *Prison Riots in Britain and the USA*. London: Macmillan.

Adams, R. (1996a) *The Personal Social Services: Clients, Consumers or Citizens?* London: Longman.

Adams, R. (1996b) *Social Work and Empowerment*. London: BASW/Macmillan.

Adams, R. (1997a) *The Abuses of Punishment*. London: Macmillan.

Adams, R. (ed.) (1997b) *Crisis in the Human Services: National and International Issues, Selected Conference Papers*. Hull: University of Lincolnshire and Humberside.

Adams R. (1998) *Quality Social Work*. London: Macmillan.

Adams, R., Dominelli, L. and Payne, M. (eds) (1998) *Social Work: Themes, Issues and Critical Debates*. London: Macmillan.

Aries, R. (1962) *Centuries of Childhood*. London: Jonathan Cape.

Arnstein, S. (1969) 'A Ladder of Citizen Participation', *Journal of the American Institute of Planners*, **35**(4): 216–20.

Auckland, Rachel (1997) 'Women and Protest'. In Barker and Tyldesley (1997): 1–12.

Bagguley, Paul (1991) *From Protest to Acquiescence? Political Movements of the Unemployed*. London: Macmillan.

Baistow, K. (1994) 'Liberation and Regulation? Some Paradoxes of Empowerment', *Critical Social Policy*, issue 42, **14**(3) (Winter, 1994–95): 34–46.

Barker, Colin (1997) 'Some Remarks on Collective Action and Transformation', *Conference Papers, Vol. 1, Third International Conference*. Manchester: Manchester Metropolitan University.

Barker, Colin and Tyldesley, Mike (1997) 'Alternative Futures and Popular Protest', *Conference Papers, Vol. 1, Third International Conference*. Manchester: Manchester Metropolitan University.

Barnes, M. and Wistow, G. (eds) (1992) *Researching User Involvement*. Leeds: The Nuffield Institute for Health Services Studies.

Beresford, P. (1982) 'Public Participation and the Redefinition of Social Policy'. In Jones and Stevenson (1982): 20–41.

Beresford, P. (1992) 'Researching Citizen Involvement: A Collaborative or Colonising Enterprise?'. In Barnes and Wistow (1992): 16–32.

Beresford, P. and Campbell, J. (1994) 'Disabled People, Service Users, User Involvement and Representation', *Disability and Society*, **9**(3): 315–25.

Beresford, P. and Croft, S. (1984) 'Welfare Pluralism: The New Face of Fabianism', *Critical Social Policy*, Issue 9, Spring: 19–39.

Beresford, P. and Croft, S. (1993) *Citizen Involvement: A Practical Guide for Change*. London: BASW/Macmillan.

Best, Steven and Kellner, Douglas (1991) *Postmodern Theory: Critical Interrogations*. London: Macmillan.

Brandon, David (1995) *Advocacy: Power to People with Disabilities*. Birmingham: Venture Press.

Braye, S. and Preston-Shoot, M. (1993) 'Empowerment and Partnership in Mental Health: Towards a different relationship', *Journal of Social Work Practice*, **7**(2): 115–28.

Burns, Danny (1992) *Poll Tax Rebellion*. Stirling and London: AK Press and Attack International.

Campbell, Beatrix (1993) *Goliath: Britain's Dangerous Places*. London: Methuen.

Campbell, Peter (1996) 'What We Want From Crisis Services'. In Read and Reynolds (1996): 180–3.

Carr, Marilyn, Chen, Martha and Jhabvala, Renana (1996a) 'Introduction'. In Carr, Chen and Jhabvala (1996b): 1–17.

Carr, Marilyn, Chen, Martha and Jhabvala, Renana (eds) (1996b) *Speaking Out: Women's Economic Empowerment in South Asia*. London: Intermediate Technology Publications.

Clarke, Michael and Stewart, John (1992) *Citizens and Local Democracy: Empowerment: A Theme for the 1990s*. Luton: Local Government Management Board.

Cooper, Andrew (1990) 'Neighbourhood and Network: A Model from Practice'. In Darvill and Smale (1990): 29–56.

Cox, Laurence (1997) 'Reflexivity, Social Transformation, and Counter Culture'. In Colin Barker and Mike Tyldesley (1997): 47–62.

Craig, G. and Mayo, M. (1995) *Community Empowerment: A Reader in Participation and Development*. London: Zed Books.

Croft, S. and Beresford, P. (1984) 'Patch and Participation: The Case for Citizen Research' Research Monograph, *Social Work Today*, 17 September: 18–24.

Croft, S. and Beresford, P. (1990a) 'Listening to the Voice of the Consumer: A New Model for Social Services Research Convergence', *Journal of the International Council for Adult Education, Canada*, xxiii (4): 62–70.

Croft, S. and Beresford, P. (1990b) 'Involving the Poor in Poverty Research', *Benefits Research, The Bulletin of the Social Fund Project*, University of Nottingham, Issue 5: 20–23.

Croft, S. and Beresford, P. (1992) 'The Politics of Participation', *Critical Social Policy*, Issue 35, Autumn: 20–44.

Croft, S. and Beresford, P. (1995) 'Whose Empowerment? Equalising the Competing Discourses in Community Care'. In Jack (1995): 59–73.

Dalla Costa, Mariarosa and James, Selma (1972) *The Power of Women and the Subversion of the Community*. Bristol: Falling Wall Press Ltd.

Dalrymple, Jane and Burke, Beverley (1995) *Anti-Oppressive Practice: Social Care and the Law*. Buckingham: Open University Press.

Darvill, Giles and Smale, Gerald (eds) (1990) *Partners in Empowerment: Networks of Innovation in Social Work*. London: National Institute for Social Work (NISW).

Department of Health (1991) *Care Management and Assessment: Practitioners' Guide*. London: HMSO.

Dominelli, L. (1997) *Sociology for Social Work*. London: Macmillan.

Dominelli, L. and McLeod, M. (1989) *Feminist Social Work*. London: Macmillan.

Donzelot, J. (1979) *The Policing of Families*. London: Hutchinson.

Durkheim, E. (1961) *The Elementary Forms of the Religious Life*. New York: Collier Books.

Durkheim, E. (1965) *Sociology and Philosophy*. London: Cohen and West.

Featherstone, Mike (1991) *Consumer Culture and Postmodernism*. London: Sage.

Field, F. (1989) *Losing Out: The Emergence of Britain's Underclass*. Oxford: Blackwell.

Fleming, J. (1997) 'Research in the Context of Human Services in Crisis'. In Adams (1997b): 27–33.

Freire, Paolo (1972) *Pedagogy of the Oppressed*. Harmondsworth: Penguin.

Ghazi, Polly and Jones, Judy (1997) *Getting a Life: The Downshifter's Guide to Happier Simpler Living*. London: Hodder and Stoughton.

Gibson, C. (1991) 'A Concept Analysis of Empowerment', *Journal of Advanced*

Nursing, **16**: 354–61.

Gramsci, Antonio (1971) *Selections from the Prison Notebooks.* London: Lawrence and Wishart.

Gurr, T.R. (1989a) 'The History of Protest, Rebellion and Reform in America: an overview'. In Gurr (1989b): 101–30.

Gurr, T. R. (ed.) (1989b) *Protest, Rebellion and Reform,* Vol. 2 of 'Violence in America'. Newbury Park, CA: Sage.

Hinton, James (1989) *Protests and Visions: Peace Politics in Twentieth Century Britain.* London: Hutchinson Radius.

Hoyes, L., Jeffers, S., Lart, R., Means, R. and Taylor, M. (1993) *User Empowerment and the Reform of Community Care: A Study of Early Implementation in Four Localities.* Bristol: School for Advanced Urban Studies (SAUS), University of Bristol.

Humphries, Beth (1996a) 'Contradictions in the Culture of Empowerment'. In Humphries (1996b): 1–16.

Humphries, Beth (ed.) (1996b) *Critical Perspectives on Empowerment.* Birmingham: Venture Press.

Jack, R. (ed.) (1995) *Empowerment in Community Care.* London: Chapman and Hall.

Jacobs, Sidney and Popple, Keith (eds) (1994) *Community Work in the 1990s.* Nottingham: Spokesman.

Jones, C. and Stevenson, J. (eds) (1982) *The Year Book of Social Policy.* London: Routledge.

Kieffer, C. (1984) 'Citizen Empowerment: A Developmental Perspective', *Prevention in Human Sciences,* 3: 9–36.

Labonte, R. (1994) 'Health Promotion and Empowerment: Reflections on professional practice', *Health Education Quarterly,* 21(2): 253–68.

Malterud, K. (1993) 'Strategies for Empowering Women's Voices in the Medical Culture', *Health Care for Women International,* 14: 365–73.

Marsden, David (1990) 'The Meaning of Social Development', In Marsden and David (1990).

Marsden, David and Oakley, Peter (eds) (1990) *Evaluating Social Development Projects.* Oxford: Oxfam.

Marsden, David, Oakley, Peter and Pratt, Brian (1994) *Measuring the Process: Guidelines for Evaluating Social Development.* Oxford: INTRAC Publications.

Mathiesen, T. (1974) *The Politics of Abolition.* Oxford: Martin Robertson.

Means, Robin and Smith, Randall (1994) *Community Care: Policy and Practice.* London: Macmillan.

Mullender, A. and Ward, D. (1991) *Self-directed Groupwork: Users Take Action for Empowerment.* London: Whiting and Birch.

Murray, Charles (1990) *The Emerging British Underclass.* London: IAC.

Murray, Charles (1994) *Underclass: The Crisis Deepens.* London: IAC.

Oka, Tomofumi (1994) 'Self-Help Groups in Japan: Trends and Traditions', *Prevention in Human Services,* 11(1): 69–95.

Parsloe, Phillida (ed.) (1997) *Pathways to Empowerment.* Birmingham: Venture Press.

Payne, Malcolm (1997) *Modern Social Work Theory.* London: Macmillan.

Phoenix, A. and Bhavnani, K. (eds) (1994) *Shifting Identities, Shifting Racism.* London: Sage.

Read, Jim and Reynolds, Jill (eds) (1996) *Speaking Our Minds: An Anthology.* London: Open University/Macmillan.

Rees, Stuart (1991) *Achieving Power: Practice and Policy in Social Welfare.* London: Allen and Unwin.

Rojek, C., Peacock, G. and Collins, S. (1988) *Social Work and Received Ideas*. London: Routledge.

Rose, S.M. and Black, B.L. (1985) *Advocacy and Empowerment: Mental Health Care in the Community*. London: Routledge and Kegan Paul.

Rowbotham, S., Segal, L. and Wainwright, H. (1979) *Beyond the Fragments: Feminism and the Making of Socialism*. London: Merlin Press.

Schon, Donald A. (1991) *The Reflective Practitioner: How Professionals Think in Action*. Aldershot: Avebury.

Scott, James C. (1985) *Weapons of the Weak: Everyday Forms of Peasant Resistance*. New Haven, CT: Yale University Press.

Scott, James C. (1990) *Domination and the Arts of Resistance: Hidden Transcripts*. New Haven, CT: Yale University Press.

Servian, Richard (1996) *Theorising Empowerment: Individual Power and Community Care*. Bristol: The Policy Press, University of Bristol.

Sines, David (1995) 'Empowering Consumers: The Caring Challenge', *British Journal of Nursing*, 4(8): 445–50.

Smale, G., Tuson, G., Biehal, N. and Marsh, P. (1993) *Empowerment, Assessment, Care Management and the Skilled Worker*. London: National Institute for Social Work Practice Development Exchange, HMSO.

Stokes, Bruce (1981) *Helping Ourselves: Local Solutions to Global Problems*. London: W.H. Norton and Co.

Tax, Sol (1976) 'Self-Help Groups: Thoughts on Public Policy', *Journal of Applied Behavioural Science*, 12, Part 3: 448–54.

Taylor, M., Hoyes, L., Lart, R. and Means, R. (1992) *User Empowerment in Community Care: Unravelling the Issues*. Bristol: School for Advanced Urban Studies (SAUS), University of Bristol.

Wallerstein, N. and Bernstein, E. (1994) 'Introduction to Community Empowerment: Participatory Education and Health', *Health Education Quarterly*, 21(2): 141–9.

Wallerstein, N. and Bernstein, E. (1988) 'Empowerment Education: Freire's Ideas Adapted to Health Education', *Health Education Quarterly*, 15(4): 379–94.

Ward, D. and Mullender, A. (1991) 'Empowerment and Oppression: An Indissoluble Pairing for Contemporary Social Work', *Critical Social Policy*, 32: 21–30.

Wertheimer, Alison (ed.) (1991) *A Chance to Speak Out: Consulting Service Users and Carers About Community Care*. London: King's Fund Centre.

Willis, P. (1978) *Learning to Labour: How Working Class Kids Get Working Class Jobs*. Farnborough: Saxon House.

Winn, Liz (ed.) (1992) *Power to the People: the Key to Responsive Services in Health and Social Care*. London: King's Fund Centre.

Wootton, B., Seal, V.G. and Chambers, R. (1959) *Social Science and Social Pathology*. London: Allen and Unwin.

Yuval, Davis, N. (1994) 'Women, Ethnicity and Empowerment', In Phoenix and Bhavnani (1994).

9 Towards a Theory of Emancipatory Practice

Neil Thompson

Abstract

Social work operates at the intersection of the personal and the social and, as such, has the potential for either reinforcing or challenging inequalities, the processes of discrimination that sustain them and the forms of oppression that result from them. In recent years considerable efforts have been invested in developing forms of practice that challenge, rather than reinforce, discrimination and oppression – in short, emancipatory practice. However, what has tended not to receive adequate attention in the overall scheme of things has been the development of an underpinning theory base. It is therefore my aim in this chapter to explore the basic building blocks of a theory of emancipatory practice, drawing specifically on existentialist thought.

Introduction

The move towards emancipatory practice has its roots in the radical social work movement of the 1960s and 1970s, with its focus on class-based oppression (Thompson 1997a). The theory base underpinning radical social work was predominantly one informed by marxism, whether explicitly or implicitly, although much of the theorising was of a very crude nature, far removed from the sophistication of Marx's dialectical materialism (Rojek et al. 1988). A concern with broader sociopolitical factors, a strong theme of the radical paradigm, has continued to feature in the theoretical literature but has not been 'theorised' in the sense of being developed as a systematic framework of analysis to make sense of social work within this microsocial context.

165

The development of anti-discriminatory and anti-oppressive practice has, of course, not been atheoretical, in so far as practice necessarily involves a set of guiding principles, concepts and so on (Thompson, 1995a). However, my argument here is basically that, in the effort to develop emancipatory forms of practice, the theoretical underpinnings, whilst not being neglected altogether, have not attracted the attention they deserve. Clearly, one chapter will not rectify the situation but will, it is to be hoped, set the scene for further theoretical development.

I shall begin by 'defining the territory' – that is, seeking to clarify what it is that the theory base should be attempting to explain. From this I shall move on to begin to construct a conceptual framework, drawing on a range of concepts and theoretical themes. This will draw heavily, but not exclusively, on existentialist thought. Next, I shall seek to relate the theory to practice in order to begin the process of 'testing' the theory, examining to what extent it 'holds water' in explaining a range of social and psychological phenomena which have a close bearing on social problems and the attempts of social workers to address those problems. This leads to a discussion of what remains to be done, a brief overview of what I see as the developments that need to be made in order to build on the theoretical foundations I am proposing here.

I should emphasise that the theory being presented here is not intended as a definitive statement or 'the last word' on a theory of emancipatory practice. For theory to avoid the slippery slope into dogmatism, it must remain alive, growing and developing and open to new ideas and possibilities. As Slack (1996: 113) comments: 'Successful theorizing is not measured by exact theoretical fit but by the ability to work with our always inadequate theories to help us move understanding "a little further on down the road".'

My contribution here, then, should be seen as one part of an important process rather than a misguided attempt to end such a process by coming up with 'the right answer'.

Defining the territory

At its most basic level, a theory is a set of related ideas that are used to explain or make sense of a particular phenomenon or set of phenomena. Before moving too far into developing a theory, it is therefore necessary to clarify what it is that we want the theory to explain. In order to do this we also need to be clear about what type of theory we are proposing to use.

Postmodernist thinkers have been very critical of 'grand theories' or 'metanarratives', attempts to develop one broad-ranging theory or perspective that encompass a wide and vast array of phenomena and issues (Hollinger 1994). However, I will not be taking on board these criticisms for two reasons: first, as Boyne and Rattansi (1990) point out, postmodernism itself can be seen as just such a metanarrative; and, second, this approach ignores the important distinction to be made between nomothetic and ideographic theories. The former refers to theories that try to provide a generalising framework, an overarching conceptual structure that can be applied to a wide range of phenomena, while the latter is more restricted in its scope and confines itself to explaining a relatively narrow set of phenomena, with little or no attempt to generalise or develop a wider theory base. Sibeon comments:

> there is a danger of an overreaction against grand generalizations. Nomothetic (or generalizing) forms of knowledge refer to categories of persons, places, events, etc.; ideographic (or particularizing) knowledge refers to a particular person, place or event. The social sciences deal mainly in nomothetic knowledge; this is acceptable, indeed necessary ... [S]ocial science generalizations are entirely appropriate, provided they are of more limited scope than the generalizations associated with grand theory. (1996: 3)

Sibeon then goes on to introduce a parallel distinction between sensitising theory and substantive theory:

> Substantive theories aim to provide us with new empirical information, whereas sensitizing theoretical frameworks are intended to furnish general orientations or perspectives; they are intended to equip us with ways of thinking about the world. (1996: 4)

The theoretical developments being proposed here would come under the heading of sensitising theory, an attempt to provide a set of concepts that help us make sense of the social world and provide a platform from which further (substantive) theory development and research can be achieved.

Of course, in one chapter it is not possible to identify, and comment upon, all the relevant aspects of emancipatory practice. I will therefore, of necessity, restrict myself to what I see as some of the more salient points. In particular, I shall concentrate on attempting to answer three of the key questions (or sets of questions) underpinning emancipatory practice. These questions are as follows:

● What concepts can help us understand the ways in which discrimination operates in society generally and within a social work context in particular?

- How do these concepts relate to each other? What framework links them together?
- What implications do the first two sets of questions have for social work practice?

Constructing a framework

Theories comprise a number of related concepts interwoven into a more or less coherent framework. The task in this part of the chapter, then, is to identify the relevant concepts, or a number of them at least, comment on their significance and consider how they relate to each other.

It is important to emphasise that the ideas I am presenting here are not chosen at random. They derive largely from existentialist philosophy, a theoretical perspective on which I have drawn in my previous writings, either implicitly or explicitly. In effect, this chapter could be seen as an account of an existentialist approach to emancipatory practice. However, the debt owed to existentialist thought should not be confused with a dogmatic or uncritical attachment to a particular approach. One of the strengths of existentialism is that it is not a closed system of thought, and is therefore capable of amendment, development and enhancement.

The key concepts to be used to illustrate the applicability of existentialist thought to emancipatory practice are those of ontology, ontological security, the dialectic of subjectivity and objectivity, authenticity, intentionality, meaning, contingency and power. These will be used to cast some light on the three sets of questions identified above in relation to inequality, discrimination and oppression.

Ontology

Ontology is the study of being. As such, it is concerned with the nature of human existence in terms of its scope, purpose, limitations, implications and so on. Ironically, such questions have often tended to be neglected, particularly those that relate to death and the finite nature of human existence (Thompson 1995b).

A key issue in relation to ontology is the need to recognise that human existence cannot be characterised as either personal, individualised and unique (the personal dimension) or part of a shared social reality (the social dimension). The academic boundaries between psychology and sociology often encourage such an either/or dichotomy, with relatively little dialogue between the two disciplines. However, what the insights of ontology show us is that such a dichotomy is a gross oversimplification of a very complex set of issues. From an ontological perspective, human existence is simultaneously personal and social. Indeed, to draw a distinction between the two sets of issues can be seen as an artificial and arbitrary act, one that distracts attention from the fact that all our thoughts, actions and utterances are both personal and social in their genesis and in their implications. That is, a person's existence occurs in both a personal and social sphere at one and the same time. What I say, think or do owes much to my personal biography (those aspects of my life that are unique to me) and to the social context in which such statements, thoughts or actions occur (those aspects of my life that I share with others).

At one level this may seem a straightforward and unremarkable matter, but a moment's reflection should confirm that this notion is actually quite different from common-sense conceptions of reality which so often reflect this arbitrary distinction between the personal/psychological and the sociological dimensions of our existence.

This ontological notion of human existence as simultaneously personal and social has a number of implications for social work in general and emancipatory practice in particular. For example, it helps us understand why many traditional approaches to social work paid relatively little attention to the social aspects of clients' lives (especially the macrosocial aspects related to social structure – see Wineman 1984), while more radical approaches have been criticised for emphasising the social aspects while, somewhere along the line, losing sight of the fact that social work deals with unique individuals with a specific, personal biography (Pearson 1975).

A focus on ontology alerts us to the fact that we should not concentrate on the individual at the expense of the social context in which he or she exists, nor should we concentrate too closely on that context and thereby dehumanise the individual(s) concerned by seeing a context but not the person in that context. It is necessary to recognise both the personal and social dimensions and the relationship between the two. To fail to do this is to fall foul of reductionism, an important concept to be discussed in more detail below.

This two-sided model of human existence is therefore an important aspect of our understanding and it is one to which we shall return later when considering the related concept of the dialectic of subjectivity and objectivity.

Ontological security

Ontological security refers to the individual's ability to maintain a coherent thread of meaning and a relatively stable sense of self over time and across a range of situations. It is a sense of being a person in one's own right and feeling comfortable with oneself and one's current circumstances. It is through ontological security that we maintain a sense of self or identity. This eschews the common-sense notion that selfhood is somehow given or fixed, an essence that cannot be changed in any substantive way (Thompson 1992a). Our sense of self can be threatened at any time, for example through changes in our personal or social circumstances. Indeed, a degree of short-lived ontological insecurity is a common experience as we encounter new and unfamiliar situations. However, for some people a relative absence of ontological security can be a sustained characteristic of their lives, perhaps leading to a high level of anxiety, considerable fear of change and a degree of paranoia – a fear that too much or too rapid change will 'swamp' them and undermine their feelings of confidence and security.

Ontological security can therefore feature in relation to discrimination and oppression in the form of a strong resistance to change and a tendency to regard social differences as a source of threat. In this way, differences are not seen as positive aspects of diversity and a rich variety of cultural or other perspectives, but rather as a challenge to one's sense of identity and ontological security. A lack of ontological security can therefore contribute to discrimination by reinforcing the view that social differences are a problem to be solved rather than a positive asset to celebrate.

The dialectic of subjectivity and objectivity

I have previously outlined the usefulness of the dialectic of subjectivity and objectivity as a concept that can cast light on social work with older people (Thompson 1998a). It can, however, also be applied more broadly to other client groups, and should not be restricted to work with elders:

> Social work involves understanding not only the subjective, personal dimension of experience but also the outer, objective dimension of the actions of others and the social structures in which they occur. Both dimensions need to be understood in terms of a dialectical interaction between them. This is a fundamental part of anti-discriminatory practice – recognizing the complex interactions between individuals and the broader sociopolitical forces which circumscribe them. (Thompson 1998a: 704)

It is not enough to concentrate on the individual's perspective on the world and his or her experience (the subjective dimension) without reference to those factors in the outside world that have a bearing on the individual (the objective dimension). The two elements, subjective and objective, constantly interact and influence each other. They also frequently come into conflict, for example when particular wishes or intentions are blocked by other people or by wider circumstances.

Social reality, then, is neither entirely subjective nor entirely objective. Rather, social reality, according to existentialism, exists at the intersection of the subjective and the objective. It is this dynamic process of interaction, this 'dance of experience', that constitutes our reality. In some respects it will be unique to the individual and his or her biography, but in others there will be a sharing of particular aspects, a shared encounter with the social world and the cultural and structural patterns that help to shape it:

> No human being is a subject alone, nor an object alone. It is even incorrect to say that a human being is 'both'. A human being is neither a subject nor an object but instead, in the language of Simone de Beauvoir and Merleau-Ponty, 'ambiguous'. This ambiguity is an expression of the human being as a meaningful, multifaceted way of being that may involve contradictory interpretations, or at least equivocal ones. Such ambiguity stands not as a dilemma to be resolved, as the case of an equivocal sentence, but as a way of living to be described. (Gordon 1997a: 72)

Addressing the subjective dimension without taking account of the objective elements of social location (class, race, gender and so on) is likely to result in forms of practice that run the risk of reinforcing or exacerbating existing inequalities. On the other hand, addressing the broader contextual factors without recognising the importance of the subjective dimension is likely to result in forms of practice that are dehumanising and therefore oppressive in their own right. What is needed, then, is a theory base which takes appropriate account of both the subjective and objective factors and the dynamic interplay between them.

Authenticity

A key concept in existentialism is that of 'bad faith'. This refers to the tendency to deny, in various ways, that we have control over our actions. It is an attempt to deny human freedom and be 'excused' from responsibility by placing the locus of control elsewhere, rather than accept our own part in particular situations – for example, by claiming that we were led into our actions by factors beyond our control (heredity, personality, upbringing and so on).

This is not to be confused with a culture of blame in which individuals are held entirely responsible for their circumstances without adequate consideration of the role of broader factors such as power structures, cultural expectations and powerful discourses. Rather, it is a recognition that, while a number of factors clearly constrain or influence our actions, they remain largely within our control – and so the possibility for changing problematic aspects of our behaviour lies with us, even though such change may take a period of time to effect, and may require the support of others.

Bad faith is based on 'essentialism', the tendency to present variable matters that are open to change as if they were fixed and immutable. For example, an essentialist perspective would see stereotypically masculine behaviour as 'natural' and not open to change, rather than as a set of learned behaviours that can be 'unlearned'. The opposite of bad faith is authenticity. This refers to the acceptance of responsibility for our own actions (both individually and collectively) and a commitment to avoiding bad faith for, as Birt (1997: 212) comments: 'The struggle for ... an authentic human existence which is the core of "our spiritual strivings", is a radical effort to transform the world, to transform ourselves, and to give birth to a new humanity.'

Intentionality

Another important element of existentialism is its future orientation. That is, while many other theoretical approaches seek to explain behaviour in terms of its antecedents or assumed prior external causes, existentialism emphasises the future dimension in terms of our intentions, plans or aspirations. This is not to deny the significance of the past and its influence upon us, but rather to act as a counterbalance to the tendency of so many other theories to focus on the past at the expense of the future. The future is not only, in some sense, partly the result of our present actions, it is also an influence on our current actions in the sense that the future dimension provides us with goals and aspirations that have a bearing on the choices we make and the decisions we enact.

Our actions are geared towards particular goals, even if we do not make such goals explicit. We act on the basis of our attempts to achieve a particular end, and so, in order to understand a person's actions, we need to be able to see these in the context of his or her intentions – to what end were the actions intended? To neglect this future dimension or to ignore the significance of intentionality as a feature of human existence is to run the risk of dehumanising people, denying a vital part of their life-world.

The neglect of intentionality is, of course, not simply an oversight on the part of the people concerned, it also reflects a powerful discourse in which oppressed people's wishes, intentions, aspirations and hopes are disregarded – they are not given a voice. Intentionality is therefore an important concept in the emancipatory vocabulary: what are people trying to achieve, individually and collectively? This is a question that must feature strongly in emancipatory forms of practice.

Meaning

Existentialism is a form of phenomenology, a branch of philosophy which emphasises the important role of meaning and interpretation. Human experience is not presented to us as a *fait accompli* – we have to make sense of it through a process of interpretation in which we attach meanings to particular events or actions. Indeed, phenomenology in general and existentialism in particular portray human existence as a process of meaning-making.

One of the important implications of this for emancipatory theory and practice is the importance of shared meanings through the symbolism involved in culture, ideology and discourse. Although meanings are personal and subjective to a certain extent, they also have their roots in culture and society. Indeed, culture could be seen as precisely a set of meanings, symbols and shared understandings.

Meaning is, in some ways, a form of mediation between the individual and the wider social world, between subjectivity and objectivity. It therefore reflects both the concerns of the individual and the wider sociopolitical factors which constrain and influence them. Meaning arises in part from the interaction between these two ontological dimensions. Because discrimination operates through the medium of language and discourse (Pugh 1996), we need to take very seriously the meanings attached to particular issues by the individuals and groups concerned. That is, we must be wary of imposing our own meanings on other people, thereby denying them a voice and contributing further to oppression – a point that applies to both practice and theory. Mama provides an example of this when she discusses the various ways in which dominant discourses and sets of meanings have played a central role in constructing black peoples as 'colonised' groups:

> It is worth pointing out that enslavement and colonisation did not only materially exploit and politically subordinate African resources and ways of life but at the same time transformed and subjected Africans to the imaginings and caprices of imperial culture and psychology ... So it was that the imperial powers were able to assert, maintain and reproduce white supremacy across the globe. White supremacy can thus be conceptualised as a set of discourses and practices that subjugated non-European people and cast them in the position of subjected Others, while it advanced the interests of European nations. (Mama 1995: 17)

Contingency

'Contingency' can be seen as the opposite of certainty. It is an important concept in existentialism in so far as it helps us understand that human existence is characterised by change and uncertainty, or, to use the technical term, 'flux'. Although much of social reality is highly predictable in terms of the recurring patterns that can be observed, we should not allow this to mislead us into thinking that contingency is not an important factor to consider. Indeed, a lack of attention paid to contingency as a feature of human ontology can lead to complacency and a failure to react effectively to existential challenges.

Contingency can be recognised as a major factor in relation to inequality, discrimination and oppression. This is because the key role of contingency illustrates that existence is characterised by change and fluidity. Because we are self-creating, meaning-making creatures, the basis of our reality is movement and change. Where stability occurs it is because it has been created in and through the actions of individuals and groups – it is not a 'natural' state threatened by change. Stability and continuity, then, are particular forms of contingency; they are the result of efforts to maintain particular patterns and practices. They are the end product of our actions, rather than a starting point for them.

This can be seen to be particularly relevant to patterns of inequality, as it is often assumed at a common-sense level that such patterns are relatively fixed and immutable, ingrained in the social fabric and/or the human psyche. To recognise, then, that social patterns are not 'written in tablets of stone' and are amenable to change as a result of individual and collective efforts is to open the door to the possibility for positive changes in promoting equality and challenging discrimination and oppression. This is not to say that such changes are likely to be simple to implement or short-term in their impact – clearly that would be a naïve oversimplification and a failure to recognise the powerful forces that work towards maintaining the status quo and the unequal power relations that are part and parcel of it. It does, however, give us an avenue to pursue in promoting change. It avoids the defeatism and cynicism that characterises some people's attitudes towards the possibility for change. Change may well have to be slow, difficult and at times painful, but the key concept of contingency helps us understand that change is possible. If, as Berger and Luckmann (1967) point out, reality is socially constructed, then it can be socially reconstructed to reflect a greater emphasis on equality and social justice.

Power

Power is a very complex concept and one that is often oversimplified in discussions relating to social work. While some forms of traditional social work have rightly been criticised for neglecting the power dimension (see Hugman 1991), more modern forms of practice geared towards empowerment have also not escaped criticism for oversimplifying complex issues (see Humphries 1996) and therefore falling into the trap of reductionism (see the discussion of reductionism below).

Power is not simply a matter of something that people either have or do not have. As Humphries (1996) observes, power is more usefully seen as something that is exercised rather than something that is possessed – it is not a fixed sum that some people have but which others do not. At base, power refers to our ability to achieve our ends, and this depends on a range of factors linked to both subjective elements (skills, knowledge, attitudes, confidence) and objective ones (our position in the social order in terms of class, race, gender and so on; position within an organisation). As Giddens comments:

> Action intrinsically involves the application of 'means' to achieve outcomes, brought about by the direct intervention of an actor in a course of events, 'intended action' being a sub-class of the actor's doing or refraining from doing; power represents the capacity of the agent to mobilize resources to constitute those 'means'. In this most general sense, 'power' refers to the transformative capacity of human action. (Giddens 1993: 116–7)

It is also worth noting the argument that power operates most effectively when we do not realise that it is being used, when it is ideologically 'camouflaged' within one or more discourses (Morrow 1994). It is not surprising, then, that the workings of power are often submerged and not recognised. Consequently, power is a dimension that is often missing from theoretical analyses.

The existentialist approach to power is one in which every action we take is seen to be imbued with power, in the sense that everything we do has a bearing on the people and structures around us. That is, we are constantly engaging with the social world through our interactions with other people and with the social structure more broadly conceived – and therefore constantly exercising power and being subjected to the power of others. Of course, the scope to exercise power is not distributed equally across the population – social structure plays a major role in giving people different starting points in their ability to exercise control over their lives and circumstances and to influence others around them. Indeed, a common misunderstanding of existentialism is that it is an individualistic philosophy that neglects the social and political dimensions of human existence. Even a cursory glance at works such as those by Sartre (1963 and 1982) will show that this is clearly not the case.

From an existentialist point of view, every step we take contains within it the potential for either taking greater control of our lives and supporting others in doing so (a process of empowerment based on authenticity) or we can seek to evade responsibility for ourselves and/or seek to take away a degree of control from other people through racism, sexism and so on (a process of disempowerment based on bad faith).

Linking the concepts

At one level it is not necessary to attempt to link the concepts together to form a coherent framework as this has already been largely achieved in the existing existentialist literature. However, my aim in this section is to show a pattern of linkages across the concepts specifically as they relate to inequality, discrimination and oppression. For this purpose I shall use PCS analysis as a linking thread, a framework that provides an overview of how the concepts interrelate. PCS analysis is explained in Thompson (1997a) and further developed in Thompson (1998b).

PCS refers to the personal, cultural and structural levels of analysis in relation to the operation of discrimination and oppression. Personal prejudice (P level) is part of the scenario, although we need to be wary of overemphasising this element to the detriment of the other two. The cultural level relates to the range of assumptions, stereotypes, images, symbols and shared meanings that play a crucial role in sustaining discriminatory social relations and their oppressive consequences. The structural level refers to the power relations intrinsic to the social structure and premised on social divisions such as class, race, gender, age, sexual identity and disability.

The various concepts discussed in this chapter can each be integrated into the PCS framework, as follows:

- Ontology. Human existence is simultaneously personal and social, and so all three levels, personal cultural and structural, affect us at the same time – they are integrated elements of our experience.
- Ontological security. This relates to the individual's ability to maintain a coherent sense of self (at the P level) in and through interactions with the cultural and structural dimensions of the social context.
- The dialectic of subjectivity and objectivity. The interplay between subjectivity (the P level) and objectivity (the C and S levels) is a feature of everyday life. The different levels interact constantly as a basic feature of human ontology.
- Authenticity. Many aspects of the C level (stereotypes, dominant discourses) reinforce bad faith and essentialism, and thereby bolster existing power relations and inequalities at the S level. Authenticity

therefore refers, in this context, to the ability, at the P level, to resist such pressures and not succumb to bad faith.

- Intentionality. Intentionality operates at the intersection of the personal and cultural levels. Plans, aspirations and so on are negotiated here, with cultural assumptions influencing which goals can or should be achieved. Dominant discourses give us very strong messages about what we should be striving for – the work ethic and family values, for example. Intentionality is also linked with the structural level in the sense that what can be achieved is largely shaped by wider structural factors – access to resources, for example.
- Meaning. Meaning is partly personal (biographical) and partly cultural (in the sense that our perceptions are largely structured by the cultural context in which we live or into which we have been socialised). Meanings are also linked to the structural level in the sense that our position in the social order will influence what meanings we attach to particular events or phenomena and will also influence what meanings are attached to us – how we are perceived by other people because of the colour of our skin, our age, our gender and so on.
- Contingency. The interactions between the P, C and S levels are part of a constant process of change. Contingency is therefore a feature of PCS analysis. Because each level can influence the others, there is no certainty as to what configuration will result. The possibilities for change are therefore ever present.
- Power. We can locate power at all three levels: P relates to the power of the individual in terms of knowledge, skills, charisma and so on – important factors in exercising personal power. C relates to the subtle power of language, imagery and discourses generally in shaping people's thoughts and actions. S relates to the power (or relative powerlessness) that arises from occupying a particular position within the social hierarchy.

Although my exposition here does not show all the possible linkages or theorise the relationship between them, it should none the less offer a useful starting point for developing a coherent conceptual framework to act as a basis for emancipatory practice.

Relating the theory to practice

One of the strong characteristics of Sartrean existentialism is its clear focus on the need for philosophy to address everyday life, to be a philosophy of 'lived experience' (*le vécu*). Sartre was keen to ensure that philosophy should be of value in wrestling with some of the problems of day-to-day reality, a basis for responding to existential challenges. It is therefore appropriate that we should explore the linkages between theory and practice, rather than simply address theoretical issues in the abstract. We should therefore ensure that we do not simply consider existentialism as an abstract philosophy but, rather, explore its links with actual practice, its significance as a guide to action in responding to complex and difficult situations. I shall go some way towards integrating theory and practice by revisiting the main concepts discussed and considering, albeit very briefly, their implications for social work practice:

- Ontology. Social divisions such as class, race and gender are a fundamental part of our existence, not abstract generalisations. It is therefore important that, in undertaking assessments and developing plans of action for intervention, we should take on board issues relating to the social context of the individual, family or group concerned – issues relating to the experience of oppression arising from one's social location or position within the social hierarchy.
- Ontological security. A lack of ontological security can make people anxious and defensive, and therefore resistant to change and prone to seeing social difference as a source of threat. One practice implication of this is that we should be wary of removing people's ontological security and thereby making them likely to be more defensive and resistant to change. Such changes need to be sensitively handled so that attempts to promote positive change do not become counter-productive.
- The dialectic of subjectivity and objectivity. Human existence has both personal, subjective elements (biography) and broader contextual elements, each interacting with the other and often in conflict. In order to understand social reality, we need to understand the interaction of the subjective and objective dimensions – to focus on one element at the expense of the other is to distort and oversimplify the complexities of human existence. We should therefore ensure that we avoid too narrow a perspective in our practice so that we do not fail to appreciate the complexities of the subjective life-world, the objective social context and the interactions between the two.
- Authenticity. Bad faith is a common barrier to change. For example, sex offenders frequently argue that they 'could not help themselves' (Thompson 1992a). Opportunities for undermining bad faith and promoting authenticity are therefore important goals to pursue in developing emancipatory practice.
- Intentionality. Human beings are 'in process'. That is, we are not fixed

entities that can be manipulated to suit the wishes of others without experiencing some degree of alienation, disaffection and thus oppression. We should therefore ensure that our practice at all times reflects intentionality as an important component of human ontology. That is, we should not lose sight of the fact that people have desires, wishes, aspirations and so on. For example, a medical model of depression can so easily lead us into forms of practice that neglect some of the factors that may be contributing to the depression – a loss of plans or aspirations brought about by a bereavement, for example.

● Meaning. As mentioned above, we are 'meaning-making creatures' in the sense that we seek to make sense of our experiences and integrate them with our existing understandings of the social world and our place within it. Consequently, from an emancipatory practice point of view, we need to be wary of the danger of imposing our own meanings on other people, thereby denying them a voice and dehumanising them. The development of the user involvement movement (Beresford and Croft 1993; S. Thompson 1997) has been, in large part, a reaction to the tendency to disregard the important role of meaning in people's lives.

● Contingency. An important point to arise from the concept of contingency is that positive change always remains a possibility. It acts as an antidote to the mood of pessimism, cynicism and defeatism displayed by many people in relation to inequality, discrimination and oppression. Change is a basic feature of human existence and so the extent to which such change is positive and emancipatory on the one hand, or negative and oppressive on the other, is partly dependent upon our actions, hence the notion that we are either part of the problem or part of the solution, with no neutral middle ground in between (Thompson 1992b). Contingency therefore teaches us that we cannot see emancipatory practice as 'not an issue for us', as that would be a further example of bad faith.

● Power. As we have seen, power is an ever-present dimension of human existence and social interactions. We therefore have to take account of the role of power in all aspects of practice. To neglect the central role of power is seriously to distort and oversimplify the reality of practice and runs the risk of reinforcing or exacerbating existing inequalities.

Clearly, my comments here are of an introductory nature and only begin to sketch out the links between theory and practice. There is, of course, a long way to go in developing these linkages further.

Developing the theory

It should be clear from the preceding discussions that, although existentialist thought can help us to develop our understanding of the complex theoretical issues underpinning emancipatory practice, it does not offer a comprehensive analysis of the whole range of phenomena that apply to this complex aspect of social work. It is evident, then, that much remains to be done to continue the development of existentialism as a theory base for emancipatory practice.

There are many more existentialist concepts that could be brought to bear here and their implications explored, for example the possible use of what is known as the 'progressive-regressive method' (Thompson 1998a). The task, then, is far from complete and will no doubt be one that we may wrestle with for some considerable time to come yet. We should recognise that theory development is a continuous process, rather than a time-limited task. As Stuart Hall puts it: 'I am not interested in Theory, I am interested in going on theorizing' (cited in Grossberg 1996: 150).

It would therefore be unrealistic for me to expound here in any great detail how the theory needs to develop. I shall therefore restrict myself to brief comments as to three pitfalls I feel the further development of the theory needs to avoid if it is not to lose its coherence and its value as a basis from which to develop high-quality emancipatory forms of practice. These are reductionism, essentialism and reification.

Reductionism

This refers to the tendency to oversimplify complex matters and to 'reduce' multifaceted phenomena to simple, one-dimensional matters. For example, the complex interweavings of P, C and S are often reduced to a simple matter of personal prejudice, as if the P level were the only dimension to consider. Inequality, discrimination and oppression are extremely complex, multilevel phenomena and so we have to resist the temptation of settling for simple, single-level analyses or solutions. We need to continue to wrestle with the theoretical complexities and not abandon these in favour of reductionism.

Essentialism

As we have seen, essentialism refers to the tendency to portray active, variable processes (such as selfhood) as fixed entities, open to little or no change. In social theory it often amounts to presenting socially constructed entities as if they had some sort of natural or pre-given basis, separate from their status as social constructions. For example, discrimination may be seen as 'part of human nature', rather than a complex psychosocial phenomenon that is historically and culturally variable. As Sibeon comments:

> Essentialism, then, presupposes on a priori grounds a unity or homogeneity of social phenomena. The phenomena in question might be, for example, the state, the law, or culture, or taxonomic collectivities such as 'women', 'men', 'white people', 'the middle class', etc. (Sibeon 1996: 34)

Instead of such matters being seen as historically rooted and thus prone to variation and change over time, they are treated as if they were relatively fixed 'essences'. Essentialism therefore distorts the basis of social reality by presenting contingent processes and social constructions as if they were fixed entities.

Reification

To 'reify' means literally to 'turn into a thing', and is therefore often used as a synonym for to 'dehumanise' or to 'depersonalise'. However, in the social sciences, it is often used in the narrower, more specific sense of to treat an object or entity that has no personal agency or decision-making capabilities as if it did. For example, terms like 'patriarchy', 'capitalism' and so on are treated by some writers and activists as if they were simple entities, rather than a convenient shorthand for a complex range of interconnected concepts and processes. Therefore, to argue that patriarchy is the 'cause' of sexist behaviour is to make the mistake of assigning agency to an abstract concept, to fall into the trap of reification. As Deetz puts it: 'In reification a social formation is abstracted from the ongoing conflictual site of its origin and treated as a concrete, relatively fixed entity. As such the reification, rather than life processes, becomes the reality' (1994: 175). Reification therefore involves oversimplifying a complex set of ontological issues by presenting abstract concepts as if they had the ability to act directly upon the world – as if they had agency.

All three of these processes, reductionism, essentialism and reification, have at least three things in common:

1　They involve oversimplifying very complex, multifaceted social and psychological phenomena.
2　They 'distort' reality, in the sense that they present an unrepresentative picture of the social world.
3　They stand in the way of further theory development by undermining attempts to develop a theoretical framework that is sufficiently

sophisticated to provide an adequate account of the range of phenomena that need to be addressed in the context of challenging discrimination and oppression.

Clearly, then, these are important pitfalls to avoid in taking further our understanding as part of the major challenge of developing a theory of emancipatory practice, and therefore matters that are worthy of serious attention in evaluating attempts to build an appropriate theory base to guide and inform practice.

Conclusion

While attempts to develop emancipatory policies and forms of practice continue, it is important to ensure that developments in the theory base are also pursued. Without this emphasis on theory development there is a danger that dogmatism will replace theory as a source of ideas to inform practice. There are already many examples of how misguided attempts to promote equality can fail or even be counterproductive (see Thompson, 1998b), and so it is important that we think through very carefully the theoretical basis of our efforts to challenge discrimination and oppression.

   The application of existentialist thought to issues of oppression is, of course, not new. Much of Sartre's work was concerned with oppression (Sartre 1948, 1982), as was that of de Beauvoir (1970, 1977) and, of course, the work of Frantz Fanon is primarily concerned with racial oppression (Fanon 1986, 1991). We should not be surprised, then, to realise that existentialist concepts have a lot to offer in seeking to understand, and respond to, various forms of oppression. Indeed, as Birt points out, oppression is an important ontological issue in its own right:

> In the context of a social existence free of oppression, alienation and immiseration, the striving for identity could become an exuberant expression of the joy of existence in a liberated life that is an open field of possibilities ... The various forms of oppression and domination obstruct the actualization of that freedom which constitutes the being of human reality, thereby blocking the ultimate source of energy for the creative formation of identity. Thus, *oppression may be seen as an existential violation, an ontological crime.* Is this not what is meant when we describe oppression and exploitation as dehumanizing? (Birt 1997: 206, emphasis added)

In effect, this passage can be seen to sum up the emancipatory project of social work – to challenge the dehumanisation inherent in the various forms of oppression that beset so many people who find themselves the subjects of social work interventions. Emancipatory practice is a rehumanising practice.

By way of concluding summary I shall now return to the three sets of questions posed at the beginning of the chapter and consider how the concepts I have discussed cast some light on these questions.

1   What concepts can help us understand the ways in which discrimination operates in society generally and within a social work context in particular?

The various concepts here all have a contribution to make to our understanding of how processes of discrimination operate to produce oppressive outcomes for particular groups of people. This is because these concepts are part of a philosophy concerned with ontology, the study of being, and are therefore useful in understanding how psychological and sociopolitical factors interact. Indeed, this focus on the interaction of subjective and objective factors is a key aspect of the theory in so far as it acts as a counterbalance to psychological reductionism and sociological determinism.

2   How do these concepts relate to each other? What framework links them together?

As we have seen, these concepts have not been selected at random. They all form part of existentialist philosophy, particularly Sartrean existentialism. What links them together is a concern to make sense of everyday life, to develop a theoretical framework which goes beyond abstract formulations and seeks to address the concrete issues of social reality. As oppression is a feature of human existence in the context of the contemporary social order, existentialism is particularly well-suited to making sense of the factors that contribute to it, both in society generally and in relation to social work practice.

3   What implications do the first two sets of questions have for social work practice?

I began earlier to spell out some of the implications for practice arising from the application of existentialist thought to emancipatory practice. Clearly, though, much remains to be done to identify and develop the implications for practice. It is to be hoped, though, that the development of theory and practice can go hand in hand so that practice does not come to rely on dogma and theory does not become an irrelevance to the demanding world of social work policy and practice.

References

Beauvoir, S. de (1970) *The Second Sex*, Harmondsworth: Penguin.

Beauvoir, S. de (1977) *Old Age*. Harmondsworth: Penguin.

Beresford, P. and Croft, S. (1993) *Citizen Involvement: A Practical Guide for Change*. London: Macmillan.

Berger, P. and Luckmann, T. (1967) *The Social Construction of Reality*. Harmondsworth: Penguin.

Birt, R. (1997) 'Existence, Identity and Liberation'. In Gordon (1997b).

Boyne, R. and Rattansi, A. (1990) *Postmodernism and Society*. London: Macmillan.

Deetz, S. (1994) 'The New Politics of the Workplace: Ideology and Other Unobtrusive Controls'. In Simons and Billig (1994).

Fanon, F. (1986) *Black Skin, White Masks*. London: Pluto.

Fanon, F. (1991) *The Wretched of the Earth*. New York: Grove Press.

Giddens, A. (1993) *New Rules of Sociological Method*. 2nd edn. Cambridge: Polity.

Gordon, L.R. (1997a) 'Existential Dynamics of Theorizing Black Invisibility'. In Gordon (1997b).

Gordon, L.R. (ed.) (1997b) *Existence in Black: An Anthology of Black Existential Philosophy*. London: Routledge.

Grossberg, L. (1996) 'On Postmodernism and Articulation: An Interview with Stuart Hall'. In Morley and Chen (1996).

Hugman, R. (1991) *Power in Caring Professions*. London: Macmillan.

Hollinger, R. (1994) *Postmodernism and the Social Sciences*. London: Sage.

Humphries, B. (ed.) (1996) *Critical Perspectives on Empowerment*. Birmingham: Venture Press.

Mama, A. (1995) *Beyond the Masks: Race, Gender and Subjectivity*. London: Routledge.

Morley, D. and Chen, K-H. (eds) (1996) *Stuart Hall: Critical Dialogues in Cultural Studies*. London: Routledge.

Morrow, R.A. (1994) *Critical Theory and Methodology*. London: Sage.

Pearson, G. (1975) *The Deviant Imagination*. London: Macmillan.

Pugh, R.G. (1996) *Effective Language in Health and Social Work*. London: Chapman & Hall.

Rojek, C., Peacock, G. and Collins, S. (1988) *Social Work and Received Ideas*. London: Routledge.

Sartre, J-P. (1948) *Anti-Semite and Jew*. New York: Schocken.

Sartre, J-P. (1963) *Search for a Method*. New York: Vintage.

Sartre, J-P. (1982) *Critique of Dialectical Reason*. London: Verso.

Sibeon, R. (1996) *Contemporary Sociology and Policy Analysis: The New Sociology of Public Policy*. Eastham: Tudor Business Press.

Simons, H.W. and Billig, M. (eds) (1994) *After Postmodernism: Reconstructing Ideology Critique*. London: Sage.

Slack, J.D. (1996) 'The Theory and Method of Articulation in Cultural Studies'. In Morley and Chen (1996).

Thompson, N. (1992a) *Child Abuse: The Existential Dimension*. Norwich: University of East Anglia Social Work Monographs.

Thompson, N. (1992b) *Existentialism and Social Work*. Aldershot: Avebury.

Thompson, N. (1995a) *Theory and Practice in Health and Social Welfare*. Buckingham: Open University Press.

Thompson, N. (1995b) 'The Ontology of Disaster', *Death Studies*, **19**(5).

Thompson, N. (1997a) *Anti-Discriminatory Practice*, 2nd edn. London: Macmillan.
Thompson, N. (1998a) 'The Ontology of Old Age', *British Journal of Social Work*, **28**(5): 695–707.
Thompson, N. (1998b) *Promoting Equality: Challenging Discrimination and Oppression in the Human Services*. London: Macmillan.
Thompson, S. (1997) *User Participation: Giving Older People a Voice*. Wrexham: Prospects Publications.
Wineman, S. (1984) *The Politics of Human Services*. Toronto: Black Rose Books.